Tristram and Coote's Probate Pr

Tristram and Coote's Probate Practice

First Supplement to Thirty-first edition

R D'Costa
Formerly District Probate Registrar, Oxford

P Teverson
Master of the Senior Courts, Chancery Division

T Synak
Formerly HMRC Inheritance Tax

Members of the LexisNexis Group worldwide

United Kingdom	RELX (UK) Limited, trading as LexisNexis, 1-3 Strand, London WC2N 5JR
Australia	Reed International Books Australia Pty Ltd trading as LexisNexis, Chatswood, New South Wales
Austria	LexisNexis Verlag ARD Orac GmbH & Co KG, Vienna
Benelux	LexisNexis Benelux, Amsterdam
Canada	LexisNexis Canada, Markham, Ontario
China	LexisNexis China, Beijing and Shanghai
France	LexisNexis SA, Paris
Germany	LexisNexis GmbH, Dusseldorf
Hong Kong	LexisNexis Hong Kong, Hong Kong
India	LexisNexis India, New Delhi
Italy	Giuffrè Editore, Milan
Japan	LexisNexis Japan, Tokyo
Malaysia	Malayan Law Journal Sdn Bhd, Kuala Lumpur
New Zealand	LexisNexis New Zealand Ltd, Wellington
Singapore	LexisNexis Singapore, Singapore
South Africa	LexisNexis, Durban
USA	LexisNexis, Dayton, Ohio

© RELX (UK) Limited 2017
Published by LexisNexis

All rights reserved. No part of this publication may be reproduced in any material form (including photocopying or storing it in any medium by electronic means and whether or not transiently or incidentally to some other use of this publication) without the written permission of the copyright owner except in accordance with the provisions of the Copyright, Designs and Patents Act 1988 or under the terms of a licence issued by the Copyright Licensing Agency Ltd, Saffron House, 6–10 Kirby Street, London EC1N 8TS. Applications for the copyright owner's written permission to reproduce any part of this publication should be addressed to the publisher.
Warning: The doing of an unauthorised act in relation to a copyright work may result in both a civil claim for damages and criminal prosecution.

Crown copyright material is reproduced with the permission of the Controller of HMSO and the Queen's Printer for Scotland. Parliamentary copyright material is reproduced with the permission of the Controller of Her Majesty's Stationery Office on behalf of Parliament. Any European material in this work which has been reproduced from EUR-lex, the official European Communities legislation website, is European Communities copyright.
A CIP Catalogue record for this book is available from the British Library.

ISBN for this volume: 9781474306836

Printed and bound in Great Britain by Hobbs the Printers Ltd, Totton, Hampshire

Visit LexisNexis at www.lexisnexis.co.uk

Preface

This Supplement updates practice, statutes and statutory instruments in the main work. In particular, in Appendix II the Non-Contentious Probate Rules 1987 incorporate the changes made by the Non-Contentious Probate (Amendment) Rules 2016 (SI 2016/972). The amendment rules allow personal applicants to make online applications for a grant of representation. This may be the sign of things to come but it does not yet apply to the practitioner-led applications. There has been much talk on the subject in recent years but no information is available at this time about the replacement of current probate rules. The Government published a consultation exercise on proposals to reform fees for grants of probate in February 2016. After consideration, the Government has decided to proceed with the proposals and implement the new fees in May 2017. This is of course subject to the necessary statutory instrument being in place. The proposed new fee structure is included in the body and Appendix III of this supplement.

The paragraphs in this supplement update and replace in their entirety those published in the main work.

The question of who has standing to challenge a will has now been the subject of review by the Court of Appeal in *Randall v Randall* [2016] EWCA Civ 494. By reference to the earliest editions of this work, it was explained that the rules of the old probate court were 'infinitely flexible to meet the justice of each case'. It was held that H who was a creditor of W as part of a divorce settlement had a sufficient interest to challenge the validity of a will made by W's mother in circumstances where if the will were declared invalid, H stood to receive an estimated £75,000 from W. The practical effect of this decision is that the probate court will have to consider on a case by case basis whether the claimant or defendant by counterclaim has a sufficient 'interest' to challenge a will. A distinction still needs to be drawn between 'a mere busybody' and someone who has 'a real interest in challenging the validity of the will'.

As envisaged in the preface to the 31st edition, the Finance Act (No2) 2015 did incorporate a provision for a portion of the main family home to be exempted if passing to direct descendants. This element of the legislation is effective in respect of deaths on or after 6 April 2017. Details are included in this supplement but, at the time of writing, the commencement date has not been reached and accordingly the actual practice involved relating to the completion of the IHT 400 series of forms has not been finalised. It is expected that the forms will be suitably updated prior to the commencement date.

Preface

The other significant development regarding the submission of the Inheritance Tax forms so far as practitioners are concerned is that the Document Exchange [DX] system is no longer used by HMRC Trusts and Estates, Inheritance Tax. This change was effective from 1 April 2016.

With regard to likely changes in 2017, as part of the HMRC move towards working digitally, all post received concerning IHT will be scanned and worked digitally. As part of this change, the addresses used will be amended in most cases, but details are not currently available. It is also expected that, following the completion of a trial, personal applicants will be eligible to use an online service where no Inheritance Tax is payable, but professional agents will continue to use normal processes during this phase of IHT Online.

It is proposed that legislation will enacted in 2017 to amend the 'deemed domicile' rules reducing the qualifying period from the current 17 years down to 15 years out of the last 20 years to be regarded as UK domiciled. It is also proposed that there will be legislation amending the relief for donations to political parties to include parties with representatives in devolved legislatures and parties that have acquired representatives through by-elections.

RD'C

PT

TS

February 2017

Contents

Preface		v
Table of abbreviations		ix
Table of statutes		xiii
Table of statutory instruments		xv
Table of cases		xvii

PART I THE COMMON FORM PROBATE PRACTICE

1	The probate jurisdiction of the Family Division	3
2	General procedure in registry	5
3	Wills and codicils	11
4	Probates	13
5	Letters of administration with the will annexed	17
6	Letters of administration	23
7	Minority or life interests and second administrators	31
8	HMRC accounts	33
11	Limited grants	43
12	Grant where deceased died domiciled out of England and Wales	49
13	Grants 'de bonis non' – Cessate grants – Double probate	51
14	Right of the court to select an administrator; 'Commorientes'	53
15	Renunciation and retraction	55
16	Amendment and notation of grants	57
17	Revocation and impounding of grants	59

18	Resealing	61
21	Searches and copies – Exemplifications – Duplicate grants	63
22	Affidavits, affirmations and statutory declarations	65
23	Caveats (objections)	67
24	Citations (notifications)	71
25	Applications to District Judge, Registrar or High Court Judge (Non-Contentious Business)	73

PART II CONTENTIOUS BUSINESS

26	Introduction	79
27	Claims	81
28	Parties to claims	85
29	Claim form	87
31	Testamentary documents	89
32	Statements of case generally	91
34	Defence and counterclaim	93
36	Disclosure	99
37	Costs and case management of probate claims	101
39	Trial	105
40	Costs	107
41	Associated actions	109

APPENDICES

I	Statutes	115
II	Rules, Orders and Regulations	141
III	Fees (Non-Contentious Business)	147
IV	Rates of Inheritance Tax and Capital Transfer Tax	161
VI	Forms	163
Index		191

List of abbreviations

AC (preceded by date)	Law Reports, Appeal Cases, House of Lords and Privy Council
Add	Addams' Ecclesiastical Reports
A & E, Ad & El	Adolphus and Ellis, QB reports
Adam	Adam's Justiciary Reports
All ER (preceded by date)	All England Law Reports
All ER Rep (preceded by date)	All England Law Reports Reprint
App Cas	Law Reports, Appeal Cases
B & Ad	Barnewall and Adolphus
Beav	Beavan's Rolls Court
Bos & Pu	Bosanquet and Puller
Bro CC	Brown's Chancery Reports
CA	Court of Appeal
CB	Common Bench Reports
Ch	Law Reports, Chancery Division (1890 onwards)
Ch D	Law Reports, Chancery Division (1875–1890)
Cox	Cox's Chancery Reports
CPD	Law Reports, Common Pleas Division
CPR	Civil Procedure Rules
Curt	Curteis's Ecclesiastical Reports

List of abbreviations

Deane Ecc R	Deane's Ecclesiastical Reports
Dea & Sw	Dean and Swabey's Ecclesiastical Reports
De GM & G	De Gex, MacNaughten and Gordon's Reports
Dick	Dickens's Reports
Dir Ag	Directions to Agents
E & B	Ellis and Blackburn's Reports
Eq Cas	Equity Cases
Fam	Family Division, Series of Law Reports
F & F	Foster and Finlayson's Reports
Gow	NP Gow's Nisi Prius Cases
Hag Cons	Haggard's Consistory Court Cases
Hag Ecc	Haggard's Ecclesiastical Reports
Hare	Hare's Chancery Reprots
HL	House of Lords
Ir Eq Rep	Irish Equity Reports
JP	Justice of the Peace Reports
JP Jo	Justice of the Peace and Local Government Review
Johns & H	Johnson and Hemming's Reports
Jur	Jurist Reports
KB (preceded by date)	Law Reports, King's Bench Division
Knapp	Knapp's Privy Council Cases
LGR	Local Government Reports
LJR	Law Journal Reports
LR Ir	Law Reports (Ireland)
LRP & D	Law Reports, Probate and Divorce
LT	Law Times Reports
LTJo	Law Times Newspaper
Lee	Lee's Ecclesiastical Reports
Lev	Levinz, KB
M & W	Meeson and Welsby's Reports
Moo	Moore's Privy Council Reports
NC	Notes of Cases
NC	Non-Contentious

List of abbreviations

NCPR	Non-Contentious Probate Rules 1987
NLJ	New Law Journal
P (preceded by date)	Law Reports, Probate, etc, Division
PC	Privy Council Cases
PCC	Prerogative Court of Chancery
PD	Law Reports, Probate Division
P & D	Law Reports, Probate and Matrimonial
P & M	Law Reports, Probate and Matrimonial
Phill	Phillimore's Ecclesiastical Reports
Phill Ch R	Phillip's Chancery Reports
Plowd	Plowden, KB
Prec C	Precedents in Chancery
P Wms	Peere Williams' Chancery Reports
QB	Queen's Bench Reports
QBD	Law Reports, Queen's Bench Division
R	The Reports
RR	Revised Reports
Rob	Robertson's Ecclesiastical Reports
RSC	Rules of the Supreme Court
Russ Ch Rep	Russell's Chancery Reports
SCF	Supreme Court Fees
Sim	Simon's Chancery Reports
Sol Jo	Solicitor's Journal
Spinks	Spinks' Ecclesiastical and Admiralty Reports
S & T	Swabey and Tristram's Reports
Sw & Tr	Swabey and Tristram's Reports
Sugd Pow	Sugden on Powers
TLR	Times Law Reports
Vern	Vernon's Chancery Reports
Ves	Vesey's Chancery Reports
Ves Sen	Vesey's Chancery Reports
WLR	Weekly Law Reports

List of abbreviations

WN (preceded by date)	Law Reports, Weekly Notes
WR	Weekly Reporter
WW & D	Willmore, Woolaston and Davisson, KB or QB
Y & CCC	Young and Collier's Chancery Reports

Table of Statutes

Paragraph references printed in **bold** type indicate where an Act is set out in part or in full.

A

Administration of Estates Act 1925
.... 5.99, 6.27
   Pt IV 6.75
   s 46A 6.67
      47(1)(i) 6.67
Adoption Act 1958
   s 16(1) 6.310
Adoption Act 1976
   s 39 .... 6.310
Adoption and Children Act 2002
   s 53 .... **A1.508**
      67 .... 6.310
   s 69(4)(c) 6.90
   Sch 6 .... **A1.537**

C

Children Act 1989
.... 1.49
   s 33 .... **A1.445**
      101 .... **A1.451**
   Sch 14
      para 4 .... 11.161
          6 .... 11.161
Courts and Legal Services Act 1990
   s 53 .... **A1.469**

F

Family Law Reform Act 1969
   s 4(1) 11.161
      14(4) 6.75
Family Law Act 1986
   s 56 .... 27.22
      58(4) 27.22
      60(1) 27.22
Finance Act 1894
   s 5(2) 8.138
Finance Act 1975
   s 19 .... 8.20
      20(2), (3) 8.20
      22(4) 8.138
   Sch 4
      para 16 .... 8.203
   Sch 6 .... 8.20
Finance Act 1989
   s 178(1) 8.202
Finance Act 1996
   s 158 .... 8.138
Finance Act 1998
   s 161 .... 8.138
Finance Act 2012
   s 109 .... 8.50
   Sch 33 .... 8.50
Finance Act 2016
   s 93 .... 8.50
      95 .... 8.229
      94 .... 8.44
      97 .... 8.44
   Sch 15 .... 8.138
Finance Act (No 2) 2015
   s 9 .... 8.50
      14 .... 8.172
      15 .... 8.203
Forfeiture Act 1982
   s 2 .... **A1.359**

H

Human Fertilisation and Embryology Act 2008 .... 1.49
Human Rights Act 1998
   Sch 1
      art 6 .... 7.19, 25.245

I

Inheritance (Provision for Family and Dependants) Act 1975
.... 11.376, 27.26, 27.41, 28.03, 41.41
   s 15(1) 16.50
Inheritance Tax Act 1984
   s 1, 2 .... 8.20
      3(1), (2) 8.20
      3A 8.20
      6 .... 8.20
      7 .... 8.50, **A1.727**
      18 .... 8.20
      65(4) 8.172
   Pt III (ss 43-93) 8.172
   s 102(1) 8.172
      144(2) 8.172
      147(4) 8.203
      234 .... 8.203
   Sch 1A 8.20
      6
         paras 2 .... 8.138
   Sch 7
      para 3(1) 8.20

Table of Statutes

Inheritance Tax Act 1984 – *cont.*
    para 5(1) 8.20
        (6) 8.20

L

Law of Property (Amendment) Act 1926
    s 3 .... **A1.138**
Legal Services Act 2007
    .... 4.49
Legitimacy Act 1926
    s 1(4) 6.199
    Sch 6.199

M

Marriage (Same Sex Couples) Act 2013
    s 9 .... **A1.699**
    Sch 3
      Pt 1 .... 3.40A
Merchant Shipping Acts 1970
    .... 4.160
Merchant Shipping Acts 1995
    .... 4.160
Mental Capacity Act 2005
    .... 11.44, 11.82, 17.52, 17.67
    s 19 .... 25.37

P

Powers of Attorney Act 1971
    s 3 .... 11.44
Presumption of Death Act 2013
    .... 27.41, 41.42
    s 1 .... 25.20, 25.50
      (3) 41.43, 41.44

Presumption of Death Act 2013 – *cont.*
    s 1(4) 41.43
      2(1)(a), (b) 41.44
      3 .... 41.45
        (1)–(4) 25.20
      11 .... 41.46
      15 .... 41.46
    Sch 1
      para 4 .... 41.47
Public Records Act 1958
    s 5(5) **A1.165**
      8 .... **A1.166**

S

Senior Courts Act 1981
    s 16 .... **A1.304**
      17 .... **A1.304**
      101 .... 2.01
      116 .... 27.10
        (1) 24.11
South Africa Act 1962
    s 2 .... 18.37
Stamp Duty Act 1891
    .... 5.253
Supreme Court Act 1981
    s 114(2) 5.205

W

Wills Act 1837 .... 5.99
    s 1 .... **A1.01**
      18B **3.43**
Wills Act 1963 .... 12.31
    s 3 .... 3.417
      33A 5.196

Other Jurisdictions

New Zealand

Public Trust Act 2001
    .... 18.81

Table of Statutory Instruments

Paragraph references printed in **bold** type indicate where an Act is set out in part or in full.

C

Civil Procedure Rules 1998, SI 1998/3231 .... 27.10
Pt 3
PD 3E
para 5 .... 41.41
Pt 8 .... 41.41
Pt 19
r 19.6, 19.7 .... 28.07
   19.8 .... 11.379
   19.8A 28.07
Pt 23 .... 11.365
Pt 29
r 29.2(3)(f) 25.245
   29.4 .... 37.07
PD 29
para 4.6 .... 37.07
Pt 39
r 39.2 .... 25.245
PD 39
para 2 .... 25.245
     3.2–3.9 .... 37.26
Pt 57
r 57.1, 57.2 .... 32.07
   57.6(1) 28.03
   57.7 .... 27.26
      (5) 40.37
         (a), (b) 27.26
   57.12, 57.13 .... 27.41
Section IV (r 57.14–57.16) 41.46
Section V (r 57.17–57.23) 27.41
PD 57A 27.41
para 2(2) 31.14
     4(1), (2) 28.07
     8.4 .... 11.367
PD 57B 25.50, 27.41
para 3.2 .... 41.46
Courts Guides
Chancery Guide
para 17.6 .... 37.07
     17.25 .... 37.07
     20.1 .... 37.21
     20.3 .... 37.21
     20.4 .... 37.22
     20.5 .... 37.23
     20.6 .... 37.24
     20.7 .... 37.20
     20.11 .... 39.06

Civil Procedure Rules 1998, SI 1998/3231 – cont.
para 21.20 .... 37.28, 39.08
     21.21 .... 37.28
     21.22 .... 37.28, 39.06
     21.23–21.26 .... 37.28
     21.29, 21.30 .... 39.08
     21.34–21.72 .... 37.26
     21.90, 21.91 .... 39.09
     21.93 .... 39.15
     21.94 .... 39.15
     29.45 .... 26.18
     29.53–29.55 .... 31.15
     29.56 .... 26.18

F

Family Procedure Rules 2010, SI 2010/2955
r 8.20 .... 27.10

N

Non-Contentious Probate Rules 1987 SI 1987/2024
r 2(1) 4.31, 25.182
   5 .... **A2.44**
   (1) 2.81
   5A 2.81, 2.94, **A2.44A**
   7 .... 25.182
   (1) 2.05, 2.16, 2.19,
      (a) 11.367
   (2), (3) 2.19
   20 .... 4.31, 13.96
   class (c) 5.111
   23 .... 1.49
   27(1) 2.81
   30 .... 18.51
   31(1) 11.44, 11.82
   38 .... 4.229
   39(5) 18.60
   43 .... 23.01
   44 .... 23.01
      (1) 23.29
      (5) 23.39
      (6) 23.15
      (8) 23.15
      (11) 23.15
      (13) 25.221
      (15) 23.29
   45(4) 23.17
   46(5) 24.19
   49 .... 23.42
   52(b) 25.182

Table of Statutory Instruments

Non-Contentious Probate Rules 1987 SI 1987/2024 – *cont.*
  r 53 .... 25.20B
    61(1) 11.292

L

Lasting Powers of Attorney, Enduring Powers of Attorney and Public Guardian Regulations 2007, SI 2007/1253
  r 2 .... **A2.145**
    6 .... **A2.148**
    7 .... **A2.149**
    9 .... **A2.151**
   10 .... **A2.152**
   11 .... **A2.153**
  Sch 1
    Pt 1 .... 11.44

Lasting Powers of Attorney, Enduring Powers of Attorney and Public Guardian Regulations 2007, SI 2007/1253 – *cont.*
  Sch 1 – *cont.*
    Pt 2 .... 11.44

N

Non-Contentious Probate Fees Order 2004, SI 2004/3120
  art 4 .... **A3.04**
  Sch A1 .... **A3.10**

T

Taxes and Duties (Interest Rate) (Amendment) Regulations 2009, SI 2009/2032 .... 8.202

Table of Cases

A

Adams, Re [1990] Ch 601, [1990] 2 All ER 97, [1990] 2 WLR 924, [1990] 2 FLR 519, [1990] Fam Law 403, 134 Sol Jo 518, (1989) Times, 12 December 34.87
Adepoju v Akinola [2016] EWHC 3160 (Ch) 27.22
Atkinson v Morris [1897] P 40, 66 LJP 17, 45 WR 293, 41 Sol Jo 110, 75 LT 440, 13 TLR 83, CA 34.87

B

Baudains v Richardson [1906] AC 169, 75 LJPC 57, 94 LT 290, 22 TLR 333, PC 34.48
Bibb v Thomas (1775) 2 Wm Bl 1043, 96 ER 613 .... 34.87
Boughey v Moreton (1758) 3 Hag Ecc 191, 2 Lee 532, 161 ER 429 .... 34.87
Bowie (or Ramsay) v Liverpool Royal Infirmary [1930] AC 588, 99 LJPC 134, [1930] All ER Rep 127, 143 LT 388, 46 TLR 465, HL 12.07
Breslin v Bromley & Lockwood [2015] EWHC 3760 (Ch), [2016] WTLR 219, [2015] 6 Costs LR 1115 .... 40.30
Broadway v Fernandes [2007] EWHC 684 (Ch), [2007] All ER (D) 485 (Mar) 34.87
Brunt v Brunt (1873) LR 3 P & D 37, 37 JP 312, 21 WR 392, 28 LT 368 .... 34.87
Burgess v Hawes [2013] EWCA Civ 74, [2013] All ER (D) 220 (Feb) 34.64

C

Chana v Chana [2001] WTLR 205 .... 34.87
Charles George Bingham, Re [2015] EWHC 226 (Ch) 41.44
Clarke v Scripps (1852) 2 Rob Eccl 563, 16 Jur 783, 163 ER 1414, 20 LTOS 83 .... 34.87
Cooney v Cooney (1950) 100 L Jo 705, Ct of Sess 12.07
Cowderoy v Cranfield [2011] EWHC 1616 (Ch), [2011] WTLR 1699, [2011] All ER (D) 191 (Jun) 34.48
Crispin v Dogliani (1860) 29 LJP 130, 2 Sw & Tr 17, 9 WR 19, 164 ER 897, 3 LT 179 .... 28.01

D

Dale v Murrell (March 1879, unreported) 40.30
Davies v Jones [1899] P 161, 68 LJP 69, 80 LT 631, P, D and Admlty 40.37
Dickson, Re [1984] LS Gaz R 3012, [1984] Lexis Citation 368, CA 34.87

E

Edkins v Hopkins and others [2016] EWHC 2542 (Ch) 34.48
Elliott v Simmonds [2016] EWHC 962 (Ch), [2016] WTLR 1375 .... 34.32, 40.37
Emerald Supplies Ltd v British Airways plc [2010] EWCA Civ 1284, [2011] Ch 345, [2011] 2 WLR 203, [2010] NLJR 1651, [2010] All ER (D) 200 (Nov) 28.07
Eyre v Eyre [1903] P 131, 72 LJP 45, 51 WR 701, 88 LT 567, 19 TLR 380, P, D and Admlty 34.87

Table of Cases

G

Ghafoor v Cliff [2006] EWHC 825 (Ch), [2006] 2 All ER 1079, [2006] 1 WLR 3020, [2006] All ER (D) 165 (Apr) 25.182

Giles v Warren (1872) LR 2 P & D 401, 36 JP 663, 41 LJP & M 59, 20 WR 827, 26 LT 780 .... 34.87

Gill v Gill [1909] P 157, 78 LJP 60, 53 Sol Jo 359, 100 LT 861, 25 TLR 400, P, D and Admlty 34.87

Green's Estate, Re, Ward v Bond (1962) 106 Sol Jo 1034, P, D and Admlty 34.87

Gullan's Goods, Re (1858) 27 LJP & M 15, 4 Jur NS 196, 1 Sw & Tr 23, 5 WR 307, 164 ER 612, 30 LTOS 326 .... 34.87

H

Harris v Berrall (1858) 1 Sw & Tr 153, 7 WR 19, 164 ER 671 .... 34.87

How's Goods, Re (1858) 27 LJP & M 37, 4 Jur NS 366, 1 Sw & Tr 53, 164 ER 626, 31 LTOS 26 .... 25.20B

Hudson (deceased); Nicholls v Hudson [2006] EWHC 3006 (Ch), 150 Sol Jo LB 1333, [2006] All ER (D) 60 (Oct) 34.87

Humblestone v Martin Tolhurst Partnership (a firm) [2004] EWHC 151 (Ch), 6 ITELR 900, (2004) Times, 27 February, [2004] All ER (D) 67 (Feb) 3.95

I

IRC v Bullock [1976] 3 All ER 353, [1976] 1 WLR 1178, [1976] STC 409, 51 TC 522, [1976] TR 179, 120 Sol Jo 591, L(TC) 2598 .... 12.07

J

Jackson's Goods, Re (1902) 47 Sol Jo 93, 87 LT 747, 19 TLR 74, P, D and Admlty 25.20B

Jolley, Re, Jolley v Jarvis [1964] P 262, [1964] 1 All ER 596, [1964] 2 WLR 556, 108 Sol Jo 115, CA 24.36

K

Kipping and Barlow v Ash (1845) 1 Rob Eccl 270, 9 Jur 542, 163 ER 1035, 4 Notes of Cases 177 .... 28.01

L

Lamothe v Lamothe [2006] EWHC 1387 (Ch), [2006] All ER (D) 153 (Jun) 34.87

Larke v Nugus (1979) 123 Sol Jo 337 .... 26.31

Leonard v Leonard [1902] P 243, 71 LJP 117, 46 Sol Jo 666, 87 LT 145, 18 TLR 747, P, D and Admlty 34.87

Long-Sutton's Estate, Re [1912] P 97, 81 LJP 28, 56 Sol Jo 293, 106 LT 643, P, D and Admlty 25.20B

M

Mackenzie's Estate, Re [1909] P 305, 79 LJP 4, 26 TLR 39, P, D and Admlty 34.87

Mark v Mark [2005] UKHL 42, [2006] 1 AC 98, [2005] 3 All ER 912, [2005] 3 WLR 111, [2005] 2 FCR 467, [2005] 2 FLR 1193, [2005] Fam Law 857, [2005] 28 LS Gaz R 32, (2005) Times, 5 July, [2005] All ER (D) 370 (Jun) 12.07

Marley v Rawlings [2014] UKSC 2, [2015] AC 129, [2014] 1 All ER 807, [2014] 2 WLR 213, 16 ITELR 642, [2015] 1 FCR 187, [2014] 2 FLR 555, [2014] Fam Law 466, 164 NLJ 7592, (2014) Times, 28 January, [2014] All ER (D) 132 (Jan) 3.95
Menzies v Pulbrook and Ker (1841) 2 Curt 845, 163 ER 605, 1 Notes of Cases 132 .... 27.10
Mills v Millward (1889) 15 PD 20, 59 LJP 23, 61 LT 651, P, D and Admlty 34.87

N

Nesbitt v Nicholson; Boyes, Re [2013] EWHC 4027 (Ch), [2014] All ER (D) 102 (Jan) 34.48

O

O'Brien v Seagrave [2007] EWHC 788 (Ch), [2007] 3 All ER 633, [2007] 1 WLR 2002, (2007) Times, 2 May, [2007] All ER (D) 56 (Apr) 27.22, 28.03, 32.07
O'Keefe, Re, Poingdestre v Sherman [1940] Ch 124, [1940] 1 All ER 216, 109 LJ Ch 86, 84 Sol Jo 44, 162 LT 62, 56 TLR 204 .... 12.31
Orton v Smith (1873) LR 3 P & D 23, 37 JP 503, 42 LJP & M 50, 28 LT 712 ...... 40.30

P

Patten v Poulton (1858) 22 JP 180, 27 LJP & M 41, 4 Jur NS 341, 1 Sw & Tr 55, 6 WR 458, 164 ER 626, 31 LTOS 40 .... 34.87
Perrins v Holland [2010] EWCA Civ 840, [2011] Ch 270, [2011] 2 All ER 174, [2011] 2 WLR 1086, 13 ITELR 405, [2010] NLJR 1076, 154 Sol Jo (no 29) 34, [2010] All ER (D) 210 (Jul) 34.17
Perry v Dixon (1899) 80 LT 297, P, D and Admlty 40.37
Poole v Everall [2016] EWHC 2126 (Ch), [2016] WTLR 1621, [2016] All ER (D) 80 (Aug) 34.64
Practice Direction (reading lists and time estimates) [2000] 1 All ER 640, (2000) Times, 1 February, [1999] All ER (D) 1512 .... 37.28
Practice Direction (Citation of Authorities (2012)) [2012] 2 All ER 255, [2012] 1 WLR 780, [2012] NLJR 504, [2012] Lexis Citation 21, [2012] All ER (D) 190 (Mar) 37.27
Practice Note (citation of cases: restrictions and rules) [2001] 2 All ER 510, [2001] 1 WLR 1001, SC 37.27
Practice Note; (Evidence of Mental Incapacity in Probate Matters) [1962] 2 All ER 613, P, D and Admlty 17.52

R

Randall v Randall [2016] EWCA Civ 494, [2016] 3 WLR 1217, 19 ITELR 273, [2016] Fam Law 969, 166 NLJ 7703, (2016) Times, 28 June, [2016] WTLR 1277, [2016] All ER (D) 25 (Jun) 27.10, 27.22, 28.01, 28.03, 28.06, 32.07
Ross, Re, Ross v Waterfield [1930] 1 Ch 377, 99 LJ Ch 67, [1929] All ER Rep 456, 142 LT 189, 46 TLR 61 .... 12.31

S

Singellos v Singellos [2010] EWHC 2353 (Ch), [2011] Ch 324, [2011] 2 WLR 1111, (2010) Times, 22 December, [2010] All ER (D) 130 (Sep) 34.17
Singh and McDonald v Vozniak [2016] EWHC 114 (Ch) 34.87
Solicitor, A, Re [1975] QB 475, [1974] 3 All ER 853, [1975] 2 WLR 105, 118 Sol Jo 737 .... 34.64

Table of Cases

Spencer v Anderson (Paternity Testing: Jurisdiction) [2016] EWHC 851 (Fam), [2016] 3 WLR 905, [2016] Fam Law 808, 151 BMLR 92, 166 NLJ 7697, [2016] All ER (D) 140 (Apr) 34.87
Spicer, Re, Spicer v Spicer [1899] P 38, 68 LJP 19, 47 WR 271, 79 LT 707, 15 TLR 40, P, D and Admlty 40.37
Sprigge v Sprigge (1868) LR 1 P & D 608, 33 JP 104, 38 LJP & M 4, 17 WR 80, 19 LT 462 .... 34.87
Sykes, Re, Drake v Sykes (1906) 22 TLR 741, P, D and Admlty; affd (1907) 23 TLR 747, CA 34.87

T

Taylor's Estate, Re, National and Provincial and Union Bank of England v Taylor (1919) 64 Sol Jo 148, P, D and Admlty 34.87
Treloar v Lean (1889) 14 PD 49, 58 LJP 39, 37 WR 560, 60 LT 512, P, D and Admlty 34.87

W

Watton v Crawford [2016] NICh 14 .... 26.31
Welch v Phillips (1836) 1 Moo PCC 299 .... 34.87
Wharton v Bancroft [2011] EWHC 3250 (Ch), [2011] WTLR 693, [2011] All ER (D) 84 (Dec) 34.48
Wilkinson v Kitzinger [2006] EWHC 2022 (Fam), [2007] 1 FCR 183, [2007] 1 FLR 295, [2006] 33 LS Gaz R 25, (2006) Times, 21 August, [2006] All ER (D) 479 (Jul) 3.43
Wilson v Bassil [1903] P 239, 72 LJP 89, 52 WR 271, 89 LT 586, [1900–3] All ER Rep Ext 1047, P, D and Admlty 40.30
Wilson's Estate, Re, Walker v Treasury Solicitor (1961) 105 Sol Jo 531, P, D and Admlty 34.87
Winstone's Goods, Re [1898] P 143, 67 LJP 76, 78 LT 535, P, D and Admlty 25.20B
Wintle v Nye [1959] 1 All ER 552, [1959] 1 WLR 284, 103 Sol Jo 220, HL 34.64
Wren v Wren [2006] EWHC 2243 (Ch), [2006] WTLR 531, 9 ITELR 223, [2006] 3 FCR 18, [2006] All ER (D) 30 (Sep) 34.87

Y

Yule's Estate, Re (1965) 109 Sol Jo 317, P, D and Admlty 34.87

Part I

THE COMMON FORM PROBATE PRACTICE
of the Family Division of the High Court of Justice

Chapter 1

THE PROBATE JURISDICTION OF THE FAMILY DIVISION

COMMON FORM BUSINESS

Rules

1.49 The current rules are the Non-Contentious Probate Rules 1987 (SI 1987/2024) (see **1.52** below), as amended by the Non-Contentious Probate (Amendment) Rules 1991, 1998, 1999, 2003, 2004 and 2016. The Rules were further amended with effect from 1 October 2007 by the Mental Capacity Act (Transitional and Consequential Provisions) Order 2007 (SI 2007/1898). The most recent are the Non-Contentious Probate (Amendment) Rules 2009 (SI 2009/1893) (effective from 1 September 2009) which reflect amendments to the Children Act 1989 consequential upon the Human Fertilisation and Embryology Act 2008. These rules govern the practice in the case of death on or after 1 January 1926. Where the deceased died before 1 January 1926 the right to a grant is, subject to the provisions of any enactment, to be determined by the principles and rules under which the court would have acted at the date of the death (see r 23 of the 1987 Rules).

1.50 In 2009 Sir Mark Potter, then President of the Family Division, invited the then Lord Justice Mumby (now President of the Family Division) to chair a working group to undertake the revision of the Non-Contentious Probate Rules 1987 and produce a set of draft rules and supporting practice directions, which set out fair and efficient procedures which are both simple and simply addressed. The working party produced a consultation paper following which draft rules were prepared. The working party has since reported to the President and the implementation of these revised rules is now awaited. In anticipation of these rules, this work includes references to some of the new practice changes which will emerge.

PROPERTY FOR WHICH GRANT REQUIRED

Vesting of property prior to issue of grant

1.70 When an estate has so vested and it is necessary to serve on the Public Trustee a notice to quit the notice should be served direct on the Public Trustee at the Office of the Official Trustee and Public Trustee, Victory House, 30–34

Kingsway, London WC2B 6EX *or* DX 0012 Chancery Lane. Tel: 020 3681 2600. Fax: 020 3681 2762. Email: enquiries@offsol.gov.gsi.uk.

SMALL SUMS: PAYMENT WITHOUT GRANT

Production of unproved wills to National Savings and Investments

1.93 In dealing with applications for payment under the provisions set out in the preceding paragraphs without the production of a grant of representation National Savings and Investments (NS&I) will normally accept, in lieu of the original will, a clear photocopy or other facsimile of the will, certified personally by a solicitor to be a true copy of the original. Typewritten copies are not accepted[1].

[1] Notice by Department for National Savings: *Law Society's Gazette*, 6 October 1976.

Chapter 2
GENERAL PROCEDURE IN REGISTRY

Note: In anticipation of the revision of the Non-Contentious Probate Rules the expression 'witness statement' where it is used in this work refers to the form of application or evidence required with reference to any rule in force at the time of the application.

AT THE PRINCIPAL REGISTRY

Situation of offices

2.01 Section 105 of the Senior Courts Act 1981[1] provides that application for a grant of probate or administration may be made at the Principal Registry of the Family Division. The Principal Registry is situated at First Avenue House, 42–49 High Holborn, London WC1V 6NP or DX 941 London/Chancery Lane. The Principal Registry's Probate Department's Public Enquiries telephone number is 020 7947 6939/6043/6801 and the fax number is 020 7947 6946. Email enquiries are to: londonpersonalapplicationsenquiries@hmcts.gsi.gov.uk

[1] See para **A1.324**.

Administration pending determination of a probate claim

2.05 Previously, a grant of administration pending determination of a probate claim (formerly administration pending suit) could only be made at the Principal Registry[1]. It may now be made to any district probate registry. As to application for an order for such a grant, see paras **38.01** ff.

[1] Direction, 1935; NCPR SI 1987/2024 r 7(1).

AT DISTRICT PROBATE REGISTRIES AND SUB-REGISTRIES

Situation of registries

2.09 The court and tribunal finder webpage lists district probate registries and sub-registries as situated at the following places[1]. However, in practice many of the offices are not open save by prior arrangement:

2.09 General procedure in registry

Registries	Sub-registries	Addresses, telephone numbers, fax number and document exchange number
Birmingham		The Priory Courts, 33 Bull Street, Birmingham B4 6DU
		Tel: 0121 681 3400/3401
		DX 701990 Birmingham 7
		Email: birminghamdprsolicitorsenquiries@hmcts.gsi.gov.uk
	Stoke on Trent	Combined Court Centre, Bethesda Street, Hanley, Stoke on Trent ST1 3BP (*address correspondence to Birmingham DPR*)
		Tel: 0121 681 3400
		Email: stokeontrentpsrenquiries@hmcts.gsi.gov.uk
		[alternatively *as for Birmingham DPR*]
		DX 703363 Hanley 3
Brighton		William Street, Brighton BN2 0RF
		Tel: 01273 573510
		Fax: 01273 625845
		DX 98073 Brighton 3
		Email: brightondprsolicitorsenquiries@hmcts.gsi.gov.uk
	Maidstone	[*details as for Brighton*]
Bristol		The Civil Justice Centre, 2 Redcliff Street
		Bristol BS1 6GR
		Tel 1: 0117 3664960
		Tel 2: 0117 3664961
		DX 94400 Bristol 5
		Email: bristoldprsolicitorsenquiries@hmcts.gsi.gov.uk
	Bodmin	Bodmin Magistrates Courts, Launceston Road, Bodmin PL31 2AL (*address correspondence to Bristol DPR*)
		Tel: 01208 261581
		DX 94400 Bristol 5
		Email: [*as for Bristol DPR*]
	Exeter	[*as for Bristol*]
		DX [*as for Bristol DPR*]
		Tel: [*as for Bristol*]
		Email: Exeterpsrenquiries@hmcts.gsi.gov.uk
Probate Registry of Wales [*Cardiff*]		Caradog House, 1–6 St Andrew's Place, Cardiff CF10 3BE
		Tel: 029 2047 4373
		Fax 029 2045 6411
		Email: cardiffdprsolicitorsenquiries@hmcts.gsi.gov.uk
		DX 743940 Cardiff 38
	Caernarfon [*Bangor*]	[*Address as for Probate Registry of Wales*]
		Tel: 01286 669 755
		Email: CaernarfonPSR@hmcts.gsi.gov.uk
		DX 744381 Caernarfon 6

At District Probate Registries and Sub-registries 2.09

Registries	Sub-registries	Addresses, telephone numbers, fax number and document exchange number
	Carmarthen	[*Address as for Probate Registry of Wales*] Tel: 01267 226781 Email: CarmarthenPSR@hmcts.gsi.gov.uk DX 99574 Carmarthen 2
Ipswich		Ground Floor, 8 Arcade Street, Ipswich IP1 1EJ Tel: 01473 284260 Fax: 01473 231 951 Email: IpswichDPRsolicitorsenquiries@hmcts.gsi.gov.uk DX 97733 Ipswich 3
	Norwich	Combined Court Building, The Law Courts, Bishopsgate, Norwich NR3 1UR (*address correspondence to Ipswich DPR*) Tel: 01603 728267 DX 97733 Ipswich 3 Email: NorwichPSRsolicitorsenquiries@hmcts.gsi.gov.uk
	Peterborough	[*Details as for Ipswich*]
Leeds		York House, York Place, Leeds LS1 2BA Tel: 0113 3896 133 Email: LeedsDPRsolicitorsenquiries@hmcts.gsi.gov.uk DX 26451 Leeds Park Square
	Lincoln	360 High Street, Lincoln LN5 7PS (*address correspondence to Leeds DPR*) Tel: 01522 523648 Email: LincolnPSRsolicitorsenquiries@hmcts.gsi.gov.uk DX 26451 Leeds Park Square
	Sheffield	PO Box 832 The Law Courts, 50 West Bar, Sheffield S3 8YR Tel: 0114 281 2596 Email: SheffieldPSRsolicitorsenquiries@hmcts.gsi.gov.uk DX 742916 Sheffield 6
Liverpool		Queen Elizabeth II Law Courts, Derby Square, Liverpool L2 1XA Tel: 0151 236 8264 Email: LiverpoolDPRsolicitorsenquiries@hmcts.gsi.gov.uk DX 14246 Liverpool 1
	Chester	[*Details as for Liverpool*] DX 702470 Chester 18
	Lancaster	[*Details as for Liverpool*]
Manchester		Ground Floor, Manchester Civil Justice Centre, 1 Bridge Street West, PO Box 4240, Manchester M60 9DJ Tel: 0161 240 5701/2

2.09 *General procedure in registry*

Registries	Sub-registries	Addresses, telephone numbers, fax number and document exchange number
		Email: ManchesterDPRsolicitorsenquiries@hmcts.gsi.gov.uk
		DX 724784 Manchester 44
	Nottingham	[*Details as for Birmingham*]
Newcastle upon Tyne		1 Waterloo Square, Newcastle upon Tyne NE1 4AL
		Tel: 0191 211 2170
		Email: NewcastleDPRsolicitorsenquiries@hmcts.gsi.gov.uk
		DX 61081 Newcastle upon Tyne 14
	Carlisle	[*Details as for Newcastle*]
	Middlesbrough	[*Details as for Newcastle*]
	York	[*Details as for Newcastle*]
Oxford		Combined Court Building, St Aldates, Oxford OX1 1TL
		Tel 1: 01865 793050
		Tel 2: 01865 793055
		Fax: 01865 793090
		Email: OxfordDPRsolicitorsenquiries@hmcts.gsi.gov.uk
		DX 96454 Oxford 4
	Gloucester	2nd Floor, Combined Court Building, Kimbrose Way, Gloucester GL1 2DG (*address correspondence to Oxford DPR*)
		Tel: 01452 834966 / 01865 793050
		Email: GloucesterPSRenquiries@hmcts.gsi.gov.uk
		DX 98663 Gloucester 5
	Leicester	Crown Court Building, 90 Wellington Street, Leicester LE1 6HG
		Tel: 0116 285 3380 / 01865 793050
		Email: LeicesterPSRenquiries@hmcts.gsi.gov.uk
		DX 17403 Leicester 3
Winchester		4th Floor, Cromwell House, Andover Road, Winchester SO23 7EW
		Tel: 01962 897029
		Email: WinchesterDPRsolicitorsenquiries@hmcts.gsi.gov.uk
		DX 96900 Winchester 2

The opening hours of district registries and those sub-registries which are open to the public are 9.30am until 4.00pm, Monday to Friday.

[1] The District Probate Registries Order 1982 (SI 1982/379) as amended (see paras **A2.30** ff).

Administration pending determination of a probate claim

2.16 A grant of administration pending determination of a probate claim (formerly administration pending suit) can be made only at the Principal Registry[1]. As to application for an order for such a grant, see paras **38.01** ff.

[1] Direction, 1935; NCPR SI 1987/2024 r 7(1). As to practice, see paras **11.364** ff.

Powers of district probate registrars

2.19 No grant may, however, be made by a district probate registrar in any case where there is contention until the contention is disposed of, or in any case where it appears to the district registrar that a grant ought not to be made without the directions of a High Court judge or a district judge of the Principal Registry[1]. Formerly, it was for this reason that an application for a grant pending determination of a probate claim could only be made to the Principal Registry. It is assumed that under delegated power the district probate registrar may now issue a grant in such an application. In any case where the district probate registrar seeks directions under the aforesaid provision, he is required to send a statement of the matter in question to the Principal Registry for directions[2]. Where directions are sought, a district judge of the Principal Registry may either confirm that the matter be referred to a High Court judge and give directions accordingly or he may direct the district probate registrar to proceed with the matter in accordance with such instructions as are deemed necessary, or direct him to take no further action in relation to the matter[3]. In practice this procedure is rarely used.

[1] Direction, 1935; NCPR SI 1987/2024 r 7(1).
[2] NCPR SI 1987/2024 r 7(2).
[3] NCPR SI 1987/2024 r 7(3).

Settling documents to lead grant

2.28 While it is not the practice to settle affidavits (*witness statements, when the Non-Contentious Probate Rules are revised*) of facts (eg affidavits to lead an order of the district judge, or affidavits as to due execution of wills) the probate manager or registrar may at his or her discretion peruse and comment on these complex draft affidavits.

PERSONAL APPLICATIONS

Personal application for grant

2.81 A personal application for a grant of probate or letters of administration (with will) or letters of administration may be made by the person entitled to the grant[1]. There is no financial limit on the value of the estate.

[1] NCPR SI 1987/2024 r 5(1).

Procedure

2.90A With effect from 1 November 2016, the Non-Contentious Probate Rules have been amended to allow a personal applicant to apply to any

2.90A *General procedure in registry*

probate registry to make an application for a grant online if invited to do so by that registry[1]. Under Rule 5A the personal applicant completes and sends the application online in accordance with instructions given by the registry. The new rule provides that the applicant shall produce original documents and information required in instructions given by the registry. In place of swearing an oath, the applicant verifies his application by a statement of truth in the online application. Any will is marked by the applicant's signature only. If the application is for probate, the applicant also confirms in the online form in accordance with instructions given by the registry that notice has been given to any executor to whom power is reserved in accordance with r 27(1). Where original documents are required in accordance with the registry's instructions, they must be sent separately to the registry. *This practice is in its infancy and may be subject to revision.*

[1] NCP(A)R SI 2016/973 r 5A. The revised rules are incorporated in Appendix II of this supplement; see para **A2.39**.

2.91 Save as stated in the preceding paragraph on receipt of the completed forms, notice of an appointment to attend at the chosen registry or office will be sent to the applicant. A second visit is sometimes necessary, and this will be arranged at the time of the first attendance or subsequently.

2.94 The revised probate rule 5A requires only that a personal application be completed in the form of a questionnaire in which the applicant verifies the answers in a statement of truth, as may be required by any instruction given by the registry. Unless otherwise directed, no attendance will be necessary.

Chapter 3
WILLS AND CODICILS

Note: In anticipation of the revision of the Non-Contentious Probate Rules the expression 'witness statement' where it is used in this work refers to the form of application or evidence required with reference to any rule in force at the time of the application.

REVOCATION OF WILLS

Revocation by subsequent marriage

Will made on or after 1 January 1983

3.40A With effect from 29 March 2014 marriage includes a reference to the marriage of a same sex couple[1].

[1] See Marriage (Same Sex Couples) Act 2013, Sch 3, Pt 1.

Revocation by subsequent formation of Civil Partnership

3.43 The effect of this Act is that it places a civil partnership on similar footing to a marriage. Section 71 and Sch 4 of this Act amend the Wills Act 1837 and other enactments so that they apply in relationship to a civil partnership as they apply to marriage. In *Wilkinson v Kitzinger* [2006] EWHC 2022 (Fam), [2007] 1 FCR 183, [2007] 1 FLR 295 the English court declined on grounds of public policy to recognise a form of marriage between two persons of the same sex which is valid and lawful in the jurisdiction in which it took place. Such relationship would qualify in the United Kingdom as a formation of a civil partnership. Schedule 4 amends the Wills Act 1837 to provide in s 18B:

'(1) Subject to subsections (2) to (6), a will is revoked by the formation of a civil partnership between the testator and another person.
(2) A disposition in a will in exercise of a power of appointment takes effect despite the formation of a subsequent civil partnership between the testator and another person unless the property so appointed would in default of the appointment pass to the testator's personal representatives.
(3) If it appears from a will –
  (a) that at the time it was made the testator was expecting to form a civil partnership with a particular person, and
  (b) that he intended that the will should not be revoked by the formation of the civil partnership,
  the will is not revoked by its formation.
(4) Subsections (5) and (6) apply if it appears from a will–

3.43 Wills and Codicils

    (a) that at the time it was made the testator was expecting to form a civil partnership with a particular person, and
    (b) that he intended that a disposition in the will should not be revoked by the formation of the civil partnership.
 (5) The disposition takes effect despite the formation of the civil partnership.
 (6) Any other disposition in the will also takes effect, unless it appears from the will that the testator intended the disposition to be revoked by the formation of the civil partnership.'

3.43A A form of marriage between two persons of the same sex which is lawful and valid in a jurisdiction in which it took place outside the United Kingdom before the Civil Partnership Act 2004 and the Marriage (Same Sex Couples) Act 2013 came into force is not recognised. However, where such a marriage was subsequently treated as a civil partnership in England and Wales, it is now recognised as a marriage.

EXECUTION OF WILLS—INTERNAL LAW OF ENGLAND AND WALES

Re-execution by acknowledgment

3.95 Practitioners who are instructed to draft a will but do not supervise its execution are under a duty to check that it is properly executed when it is returned to them for safekeeping[1].

[1] *Humblestone v Martin Tolhurst Partnership (a Firm)* [2004] EWHC 151 (Ch), (2004) Times, 27 February (it was found on examination after the death of the deceased that the will was not signed by him). See also *Marley v Rawlings* [2014] UKSC 2, [2015] AC 129, [2014] 1 All ER 807.

WILLS ACT 1963

Requirements of foreign law to be treated as formal

3.417 Where a law in force outside the United Kingdom applies in relation to a will, any requirement of that law whereby special formalities are to be observed by testators answering a particular description, or witnesses to the execution of a will are to possess certain qualifications is notwithstanding any rule of that law to the contrary, to be treated as a formal requirement only (s 3).

Chapter 4
PROBATES

Note: In anticipation of the revision of the Non-Contentious Probate Rules the expression 'witness statement' where it is used in this work refers to the form of application or evidence required with reference to any rule in force at the time of the application.

EXECUTORS

Corporation not a trust corporation

4.39 Where a corporation (not being a trust corporation) and an individual are appointed executors the individual's right to probate has priority under NCPR SI 1987/2024 r 20, and probate may be granted to the individual only, it being recited in the oath that the corporation is not a trust corporation as defined by NCPR SI 1987/2024 r 2(1). Alternatively, application for the grant of probate may be made by the individual alone, with power being reserved to the non-trust corporation: so the status of the corporation to extract a grant of double probate will be tested at the time when application is made for the subsequent grant[1].

[1] Registrar's Direction (1977) 6 December.

Alternative business structures

4.49 Nowadays the situation may arise where the appointment of an executor applies to a firm which is a corporate body comprised of share owner lawyers or probate practitioners (authorised persons) as well as other share owners or persons (non-authorised persons) who exercise control or have an interest in the body but are not lawyers or probate practitioners. Such a firm may provide a mixture of legal and other professional services (alternative business structure). It is licensable by the Solicitors Regulation Authority, an approved regulator under the Legal Services Act 2007. Unless the will expresses a contrary intention, the appointment of the firm as executor would appear to apply to all the shareholders. The question may arise as to who would constitute the executors where the appointment applies to a successor firm and the instituted executors were all share-owning probate practitioners or other legal practitioners.

4.90 *Probates*

HOW SOON A WILL CAN BE PROVED

Expedition of grant

4.90 For good reason, the issue of a grant may be expedited at the discretion of the district judge, registrar or probate manager.

REQUIREMENTS ON PROVING A WILL

The executor's oath (witness statement of application)

Description of documents to be proved

4.119 Where the original will is not available and the court has ordered a copy of the document to be proved in its stead, this document is referred to in the oath (*executor's witness statement*) as the will 'as contained in a copy (*or* draft) thereof', or 'as contained in the exhibit to the affidavit (*witness statement*) of ⎯⎯ sworn on the ⎯⎯ day of ⎯⎯ 19—', as the case may be, in accordance with the order of the court.

Certificates under Merchant Shipping Acts 1970 and 1995

4.160 The address of the Registry of Shipping and Seamen is Anchor Court, Keen Road, Ocean Way, Cardiff CF24 5JW (tel: 02920 448813). Evidence of death is provided by the Registrar General of Shipping and Seamen and death certificates are issued in the following instances:

(a)   known deaths or losses in United Kingdom ships;
(b)   known deaths or losses of citizens of the United Kingdom and Colonies in other ships which call at United Kingdom ports;
(c)   known deaths abroad of seamen employed in United Kingdom ships.

DEATH ON AND AFTER 6 APRIL 2004

4.209A *When reform of probate fees now contained in a draft Non-Contentious Probate Fees Order 2017 (scheduled to take effect in May 2017) are in place the court fees payable will be:*

Exceeding	Not exceeding	Court fee
£——	£50,000	(no fee)
£50,000	£300,000	£300
£300,000	£500,000	£1,000
£500,000	£1,000,000	£4,000
£1,000,000	£1,600,000	£8,000
£1,600,000	£2,000,000	£12,000
£2,000,000		£20,000

Notice to Treasury Solicitor

4.229 In any case in which it appears that the Crown is or may be beneficially interested in the estate of a deceased person, notice of the intended application for a grant must be given by the applicant to the Treasury Solicitor. The district judge or registrar may direct that no grant shall issue within 28 days after such notice has been given[1]. The notice should be sent to: The Treasury Solicitor (BVD), PO Box 70165, London WC1A 9HG *or* DX 123240 Kingsway (tel 020 7210 4700. Email: bvestates@governmentlegal.gov.uk).

[1] NCPR SI 1987/2024 r 38.

FEES

Fees on the grant

4.259A In 2016 the government issued a consultation paper setting out proposals for reforming fees payable on an application for a grant. The main proposals were to move from the current flat fee approach and introduce a banded structure where the fee increases in line with the value of the estate and to remove probate fees from the fees remission scheme. The senior judiciary, legal practitioners and representative groups, charities and members of the public responded to the consultation. At the time of publication of this supplement, the government announced it would proceed with all the proposals set out in the consultation. When the necessary statutory instrument takes effect, the threshold below which an application would not attract a fee will rise from £5,000 to £50,000 and above that increase according to the value of the estate up to a maximum of £20,000. See para **4.209A** and Appendix III, 'Fees' for further details of the fees increase.

Remission of probate fees

4.264A See para **4.259A**. The remission of fees scheme for probate applications will be removed when the proposed fee changes come into force.

Estate on which fees are assessed

4.267 The fees payable for the issue of a grant of probate or administration (or resealing of a grant, as to which, see Chapter 18) are assessed on the 'assessed value' being the value of the net real and personal estate (excluding settled land if any) before payment of inheritance tax passing under the grant as shown either in the HMRC Inheritance Tax account or Capital taxes affidavit, or, where an IHT 205 is delivered, in the oath (witness statement) to lead the grant[1]. This provision is not applicable in the case of those applications specified in Fee No 3 of the Non-Contentious Probate Fees Order 2004 (SI 2004/3120) as amended by the Non-Contentious Probate Fees (Amendment) Order 2011 (SI 2011/588), for which a fixed fee of £20 is provided.

[1] NC Probate Fees (Amendment) Order 2014 (SI 2014/876), Fee 1, as interpreted by para 2(b).

Chapter 5

LETTERS OF ADMINISTRATION WITH THE WILL ANNEXED

Note: *In anticipation of the revision of the Non-Contentious Probate Rules the expression 'witness statement' where it is used in this work refers to the form of application or evidence required with reference to any rule in force at the time of the application.*

ORDER OF PRIORITY

5.05A As to the effect of a disclaimer by a beneficiary under the will, see para 5.99.

PERSONS INTERESTED IN THE RESIDUARY ESTATE

Gift to charities

5.86 Under the Charities Act 2011, the trustees of any charity for religious, educational, literary, scientific or public charitable purposes may apply to the Charity Commissioners for a certificate of registration as a corporate body. If the certificate is granted the trustees become a corporate body able to hold and acquire property, and thereafter all gifts of property to the charity or the trustees or otherwise for the purposes thereof take effect as if made to the incorporated body for the like purposes. The Charities Act 2011 came into force on 14 March 2012; it is a consolidating Act and replaces previous Charities Acts (including the Charitable Trustees Incorporation Act 1872, which governed this matter formerly).

5.87 Where a gift of residue is made to charity generally, or for charitable purposes or objects without specifying particular institutions, the Attorney General, by royal prerogative, has the sole right to represent the beneficial interest of charity. The Treasury Solicitor acts on his behalf in charity matters. On application to him the Attorney General will make a direction nominating a particular charity or charities so that a residuary beneficiary may be constituted to take a grant of letters (with will annexed). Enquiry or application to the Attorney General should be addressed to: The Government Legal Department, One Kemble Street, London WC2B 4TS or DX 123242. Tel. 020 7210 4700. Email treasurysolicitor@governmentlegal.gov.uk

5.99 *Letters of administration with the will annexed*

Clearing off

Disclaimer

5.99 In respect of deaths on or after 1 February 2012 where a person disclaims an inheritance either under a will or under the law of intestacy the inheritance devolves as if that person has died immediately before the deceased. The Estate of Deceased Persons (Forfeiture Rule and Law of Succession) Act 2011 amends the Wills Act 1837 and Administration of Estates Act 1925 to this effect; see para **5.194** ff below. For an example of a disclaimer, see Form No 52B (**A6.57B**). On application for a grant of representation the oath (*witness statement of application*) should clear off the person disclaiming by citing the facts and the probate papers should include the original disclaimer. If the disclaimer is required for some other purpose an examined copy should be should also be filed and the reason for the return of the original should be set out in writing. For forms of oath (*or as adapted, witness statement of application*) for letters of administration (with will) see Nos 155 and 162 (**A6.160** and **A6.167**). These may be adapted to suit the particular circumstances of the application. See also para **8.166** as to the effect of a disclaimer with regard to inheritance tax.

TO WHOM GRANTED

Rule 20, Class (c)

Any other residuary legatee or devisee, including one for life, or a person entitled to share in undisposed-of estate

5.111 Subject to the preference of vested to contingent interests and of persons of full age to guardians of minors (see the following paragraphs) all persons in this class are equally entitled to a grant. Thus:

(a) a residuary legatee and a residuary devisee have an equal right to the grant, irrespective of the nature of the estate[1];
(b) if there is a residuary gift of personalty but not of the immoveable estate, persons entitled to share in the estate not disposed of have an equal title to that of the residuary legatee, and similarly in the converse case;
(c) if the residuary estate was given to two or more persons in specified shares (and not as joint tenants) and the share of one of them has lapsed by his pre-decease, the surviving residuary legatees have a title equal to that of the persons entitled to share in the undisposed-of estate. (As to lapse of gifts, see paras **5.164** ff).

[1] In the event of a dispute, however, if other considerations are equal the practice is to prefer the person having the predominating interest (see paras **14.25** and **14.26**).

Preference of persons of full age

5.130 Under NCPR SI 1987/2024 r 27(5), unless otherwise directed by a district judge or registrar, administration (with will) is to be granted to a person not under disability in preference to a guardian of a minor entitled in the same degree. When it is desired that a grant should be made to guardians

Residuary legatee or devisee

Death by murder or manslaughter

DEATHS AFTER 31 JANUARY 2012

5.196 The Estates of Deceased Persons (Forfeiture Rule and Law of Succession) Act 2011[1] gives effect to the Law Commission's recommendations. Where a testator dies on or after 1 February 2012, s 2 of the Act which deals with disclaimer or forfeiture of a gift under a will amends the Wills Act 1837 by inserting a new s 33A. This provides in part that where the forfeiture rule precludes a person from taking a devise or bequest made in a will that person is, unless a contrary intention is expressed in the will, to be treated as having died immediately before the testator. Accordingly such person should be cleared off in the oath (*witness statement of application*) to lead the grant of letters of administration (with will) by setting out the facts and the details of the conviction of murder or manslaughter and confirming that: the conviction remains in force, no appeal is pending nor in the case of manslaughter was an application made within three months from the date of conviction to modify the effect of the forfeiture rule. For form of oath see No 163 (**A6.168**) which may be adapted to suit the circumstances of the application. An official copy of the conviction certificate should be filed with the probate papers.

[1] See para **A1.685A**.

Persons entitled to share in undisposed-of estate

Where deceased left a surviving spouse or (after 5 December 2005) surviving civil partner

5.205 Where the net value of the estate not disposed of, arrived at as aforesaid, exceeds the appropriate statutory figure applicable for a death occurring after 1952, or the sum of £1,000 where the death occurred before 1953, a grant may be made to any person entitled to share in the residue[1] not disposed of. Where the deceased died after 1952 leaving a spouse or (from 5 December 2005) civil partner and issue, or before 1953 leaving a spouse, a life interest arises in these circumstances, and the grant must accordingly be made to not less than two individuals or to a trust corporation with or without an individual, unless the court thinks it expedient in all the circumstances to appoint a sole administrator[2]. (As to grants to trust corporations, see Chapter 9.)

[1] This is the wording of the rule, but in practice the normal order of priority would operate, and, for example, a grant would not be made to children of the deceased without clearing off the surviving spouse or civil partner.

5.205 *Letters of administration with the will annexed*

² Supreme Court Act 1981, s 114(2) (see para **A1.333**).

No surviving spouse or civil partner

5.209 Where the residuary estate is wholly or partly not disposed of, or has lapsed, and the deceased died leaving no spouse or civil partner, the order of priority of right to a grant is that applicable in cases of total intestacy (see para **6.40** Table B), and is not affected by the amount of the estate not disposed of. The grant may be made to any person entitled to share in the estate not disposed of, or, if every such person has since died or is otherwise cleared off, to the personal representative of any such person who has since died. (Form of oath (*or as adapted, witness statement of application*), No 154 (**A6.159**)).

Disposition of residue not ascertainable

5.215 Where the residuary estate is not wholly disposed of by the will, a grant may be made to any person entitled to share in the residue not disposed of, or, if every such person has since died or is otherwise cleared off, to the personal representative of any such person who has died.

Notice to Treasury Solicitor

5.217 Where the residuary estate is wholly or partly undisposed of and the deceased died without kin entitled to share in the estate not disposed of, or without known kin entitled to share, notice of the application for the grant must be given to the Treasury Solicitor in accordance with NCPR SI 1987/2024 r 38, and an acknowledgment of such notice filed with the papers to lead the grant. Under the same rule the district judge or registrar may direct that no grant shall issue within 28 days after the notice has been given. Notice of the application should be sent to: The Government Legal Department (BVD), PO Box 70165, London WC1A 9HG *or* DX 123240 Kingsway. Tel 020 7210 4700. Email bvestates@governmentlegal.gov.uk

Virtual disposition of residue

5.219 This provision does not derogate from the right of a person entitled to the estate not disposed of to obtain a grant if he applies for it, but it frequently facilitates the issue of a grant to a legatee or devisee who has the sole, or a substantial, interest under the terms of the will where the deceased left kin who, although having little or no interest in the estate, would otherwise have to be cleared off.

5.222 If it is clear from the papers that there are kin who would be entitled to share in any estate not disposed of, the Crown need not be regarded as interested. Unless this is clear, however, the applicant should either provide evidence that there are such kin, or give notice to the Treasury Solicitor (see para **5.211** for address) in accordance with NCPR SI 1987/2024 r 38 (even though the whole of the ascertained estate is disposed of). Where such notice is to be given, the district judge or registrar may direct that no grant shall issue within 28 days after notice has been given in order to give the Treasury Solicitor the opportunity of opposing the making of the grant if he wishes.

5.223 If any person who would be entitled to, or to share in, any estate not disposed of is a minor it is necessary (unless the court thinks it expedient in all the circumstances to appoint a sole administrator) for the grant to be made to not less than two individuals or to a trust corporation with or without an individual, even though the whole of the known estate has been disposed of.

5.224 In the event of a dispute between a legatee and a person entitled to the estate not disposed of, the matter is one for decision upon issue of a summons under NCPR SI 1987/2024 r 27(6) (see paras **14.08** ff).

Rule 20, Class (e)

Estate not wholly disposed of by the will

5.228 Where the residuary estate is partly or wholly undisposed of, all persons taking any part of the residue disposed of by the will, and in addition, all persons entitled to share in the undisposed-of estate, or the personal representatives of any that have died, must be similarly cleared off before the grant can be made to a legatee, devisee or creditor.

Estate not disposed of vested in spouse who has since died

5.230 Where the whole of the estate not disposed of has vested in the surviving spouse of the deceased, who has since died intestate, a child of the deceased who is also the child of the spouse should constitute himself personal representative of the surviving spouse by taking a leading grant in that estate, and then apply in that capacity for a grant in the estate of the first to die.

Rule 20, Class (f)

Persons having no interest under the will

5.235 It should be noted that the NCPR SI 1987/2024 r 20, unlike the previous rules, do not include provision for a grant to be made to a member of the nearest class of kin of the deceased having no interest under the will (except where that class is entitled to the estate undisposed of by the will, in respect of which see paras **5.110** ff).

Miscellaneous grants of administration (with will)

Grant to assignee

5.253 The Finance Act 2003 introduced Stamp Duty Land Tax which came into effect on 1 December 2003. The effect of this tax does away with the requirement of the Stamp Duty Act 1891 to original deeds unless they relate to the transfer of shares and securities. The Stamp Taxes enquiry line (tel. 0300 200 3510) will provide assistance about particular deeds or transactions.

Chapter 6

LETTERS OF ADMINISTRATION

Note: In anticipation of the revision of the Non-Contentious Probate Rules, the expression 'witness statement' where it is used in this work refers to the form of application or evidence required with reference to any rule in force at the time of the application.

IN WHAT CIRCUMSTANCES GRANTED

Representative grants

6.15 The papers in respect of both applications may be lodged at the registry simultaneously, a note that this has been done being made in the oaths (*witness statement of application*). If the applications are in order the grants will be made successively, usually on the same day.

Application by attorney administrator for representative grant

6.16 An attorney administrator may obtain a grant in another estate to which he is entitled as personal representative of the deceased without any further authority from the donor of the power being necessary[1]. If it is known that a further grant will be required, the power of attorney may, if so desired, be so worded as to authorise the attorney to obtain both grants (see para **11.76** and Form No 190 (**A6.195**) for a precedent for such a power of attorney).

[1] Registrar's Direction (1974) 11 October.

TO WHOM GRANTED

Assignment of life interest or reversion

6.27 In a consultation paper entitled the Forfeiture Rule and the Law of Succession [2003] EWLC 172(1) (30 September 2003) and subsequent Report No 295 the Law Commission in reviewing the problems associated with disclaimers recommended a reform of the law so that where a person has disclaimed an interest whether under a will or intestacy the property is distributed as if that person had died immediately before the deceased. The Estate of Deceased Persons (Forfeiture Rule and the Law of Succession) Act 2011[1] gives effect to the Law Commission's recommendation. The Act amends the Administration of Estates Act 1925 so that where the deceased dies on or

6.27 Letters of administration

after 1 February 2012 intestate and the person who would be entitled to the residuary estate disclaims it, that person is treated as having died immediately before the intestate. Accordingly, issue of the person disclaiming acquire title to the estate to which the disclaimer would otherwise be entitled. For an example of a disclaimer on intestacy, see Form No 52A (**A6.57A**). Form of oath, No 115 (**A6.120**).

[1] See para **A1.685A** ff.

Marriage same sex couples

6.31A The Marriage of Same Sex Couples (Conversion of Civil Partnership) Regulations 2014 (SI 2014/3181) sets out the procedure for converting a civil partnership into a same sex couple's marriage.

DISTRIBUTION OF AN INTESTATE'S ESTATE WHERE THE DEATH HAS OCCURRED ON OR AFTER 1 JANUARY 1926

Statutory trusts for issue

6.67 If the intestate dies leaving issue, then, subject to the rights of the husband or wife or civil partner of the intestate (if any), the residuary estate is to be held in trust, in equal shares if more than one, for all or any of the legitimate or illegitimate children of the intestate, living at the death of the intestate, who attain the age of 18 years or marry under that age, and for all or any of the issue of such children who predeceased the intestate (ie lawful issue where the intestate died before 4 April 1988 or lawful or illegitimate issue where he died on or after that date) who are living at the death of the intestate and who attain the age of 18 years or marry under that age, such issue to take through all degrees, according to their stocks, in equal shares if more than one, the share which their parent would have taken if living at the death of the intestate, and so that no issue shall take whose parent is living at the death of the intestate and so capable of taking[1]. However this is subject to s 46A of the Administration of Estates Act 1925 as amended by the Estates of Deceased Persons (Forfeiture Rule and Law of Succession) 2011[2]. The effect of this is that in respect of the intestate who dies on or after 1 February 2012 a person who is entitled to the residuary estate but disclaims it or is a person who would be entitled if he was not excluded by the forfeiture rule (unlawful killing of the intestate) is to be treated as having died immediately before the deceased so that his issue takes in his place. See oath forms Nos 52A, 95 and 115 (**A6.57A, A6.100** and **A6.120**). In cases of this type the applications papers should include an official copy of the conviction certificate or deed of disclaimer as is appropriate. Further if any issue fail to attain an absolutely vested interest because such issue has died without having reached the age of 18 years, without having married or forming a civil partnership and left a child, such issue is to be treated as having died immediately before the intestate. See oath form No 123 (**A6.128**).

[1] Administration of Estates Act 1925, s 47(1)(i), as amended by Family Law Reform Act 1969, s 3(2) (para **A1.192**) and Family Law Reform Act 1987, s 18; para **A1.418** and see fn 2 below.
[2] See paras **A1.114** ff.

Right to the grant **6.286**

Parents of illegitimate child

6.75 It is, however, provided by s 14(4) of the Family Law Reform Act 1969 that for the purposes of s 14(2), and of Pt IV of the Act of 1925, an illegitimate child is to be presumed not to have been survived by his father unless the contrary is shown. A statement in the oath by the child's father confirming that he is the father is a sufficient contrary indicator for the purposes of an application for a grant of administration.

6.79 As to an application for letters of administration of the estate of an illegitimate person, see paras **6.300** ff.

Failure of statutory trusts

6.90 In its report entitled 'Intestacy and Family Provision Claims on Intestacy' (Law Com No 331) dated 17 November 2011, the Law Commission recommended that if immediately before adoption a child has any contingent interest in the estate of his or her deceased parent, other than an interest in remainder, that interest shall not be affected by the adoption. This recommendation was given effect in respect of death on or after 1 October 2014 by the Adoption and Children Act 2002, s 69(4)(c), as amended by the Inheritance and Trustees' Powers Act 2014, s 4(2). Accordingly, a child being a minor preserves the interest he has in his deceased parent's estate prior to his adoption.

RIGHT TO THE GRANT

Legitimated persons

Legitimation on marriage of parents

6.199 The parents of a legitimated person are under a duty to furnish to the Registrar-General within a specified time information with a view to obtaining the re-registration of birth[1].

[1] Legitimacy Act 1926, s 1(4) and Sch which provisions are since repealed and re-enacted by the Legitimacy Act 1976, s 9; see also fn 1 to para **6.235**.

Adopted persons

Requirements on obtaining grant

6.285 Other degrees of relationship should be described in similar terms. All persons may be described (if so entitled) as being 'entitled to (share in) the estate'. Forms of oath (*witness statement of application*), Nos 99 and 100 (**A6.104** and **A6.105**).

6.286 Where it is necessary to clear off a person who, because of his adoption, has no interest in an estate in which he would otherwise have participated, the Forms of oath (*witness statement of application*) Nos 97 (**A6.102**) or 98 (**A6.103**) may be used. It is not necessary to exhibit or produce the adoption order, and the adopted person should be referred to throughout the documents

6.286 *Letters of administration*

by the name under which he was known prior to the adoption[1].

[1] Registrar's Circular, 2 March 1966.

Grant to parents

Adoptive parents

6.310 In the case of death on or after 1 January 1950, and after the making of an adoption order, s 16(1) of the Adoption Act 1958, or s 39 of the Adoption Act 1976, or s 67 of the Adoption and Children Act 2002 (as the case may be, depending upon the date of death) has the effect of placing an adoptive parent or, in the case of a joint adoption, both the adoptive parents, in the position of lawful parents for the purpose of succession on intestacy to the real and personal estate of the adopted person; accordingly, the adoptive parent has the same priority of right under NCPR SI 1987/2024 r 22 to a grant of administration of the estate of an adopted child who dies intestate on or after 1 January 1950 as if he had been a child of the adoptive parent born in lawful wedlock. See paras **6.282–6.285**, as to the practice in obtaining a grant where the entitlement arises by virtue of an adoption. Form of oath, No 100 (**A6.105**).

REQUIREMENTS ON OBTAINING ADMINISTRATION

Description of applicant

Death on or after 5 December 2005

6.391 Otherwise than as described in para **3.390** persons applying for administration, where the death occurred after 5 April 1988, are to be described as follows[1]:

A husband	'the lawful husband'
A wife	'the lawful widow and relict (*or* (if she has remarried) the lawful relict)'. (Where the net estate, after allowing the permissible deductions, does not exceed £250,000 (or £450,000 if the deceased left no issue)[2] the husband or relict should be further described as 'the only person *now* entitled to the estate'. It is only where it can be sworn that there are no kin within the degrees mentioned in the tables in para **6.40** (no issue nor parent nor brother nor sister of the whole blood nor issue of a brother or sister of the whole blood), that the spouse can be described as 'the only person entitled to the estate'.
Issue of marriage	'the son (or daughter), and only person entitled to the estate'; or

Requirements on obtaining administration 6.391

Note: A child or other issue who has acquired an alternative gender under the Gender Recognition Act 2004 at the death of the deceased is described as a child or issue in the acquired gender	'the son (or daughter), and only person entitled to the estate'; or 'the son (or daughter), and one of the persons entitled to share in the estate'; 'the lawful adopted son *or* daughter' or 'the lawful legitimated son *or* daughter', as the case may be[3]. 'the grandson (or granddaughter), and only person entitled to the estate'; or
	'the grandson (or granddaughter), and one of the persons entitled to share in the estate'[4]. (In the case of grandchildren or more remote issue, the oath (*witness statement of application*) should establish that the applicant has a beneficial interest, ie it should show either that the deceased died without child, or that the applicant is 'the [*or* lawful adopted *or* lawful legitimated] son (or daughter) of A. B., the [lawful] [*or* natural *or* lawful adopted *or* lawful legitimated] son (or daughter) of the said intestate, who died in the lifetime of the said intestate.')
A father	'the father (or mother), and only person entitled to the estate'; or
or	'the father (or mother), and one of the persons entitled to share in the estate.'
a mother	
	Note: a parent who has acquired an alternative gender under the Gender Recognition Act 2004 retains the original status as father or mother of the intestate.
A brother	'the brother (or sister) of the whole blood, and only person entitled to the estate'; or
or	
a sister	'the brother (or sister) of the whole blood, and one of the persons entitled to share in the estate'. *If there be no brother or sister of the whole blood, nor any issue of such brother or sister*, then the half blood is described as 'the brother (or sister) of the half blood, and' etc.
	Note: a sibling who has acquired an alternative gender under the Gender Recognition Act 2004 at the death of death of the deceased is described as a sibling of the acquired gender.
Issue of a brother or sister	'the nephew, or great-nephew (or niece), of the whole blood, and only person entitled to the estate'; or
	'the nephew, or great-nephew (or niece), of the whole blood, and one of the persons entitled to share in the estate'.

6.391 *Letters of administration*

	(The oath (*witness statement of application*) must also establish that the applicant has a beneficial interest, in a similar manner to that given under 'Issue of marriage', above.)
	If there be no brother or sister of the whole blood, or any issue of such brother or sister, then the half blood, if entitled to take a beneficial interest in the estate, is described as 'the nephew, or great-nephew (or niece), of the half blood, and' etc.
	Note: *a person in this class who has acquired an alternative gender under the Gender Recognition Act 2004 at the death of death of the deceased is described as of the acquired gender.*
A grandparent	'the grandfather (or grandmother), and only person entitled to the estate'; or
	'the grandfather (or grandmother), and one of the persons entitled to share in the estate'
	Note: *A person in this class who has acquired an alternative gender under the Gender Recognition Act 2004 at the date of death of the deceased is described as of the acquired gender.*
An uncle or an aunt	'the uncle (or aunt) of the whole blood, and only person entitled to the estate'; or
	'the uncle (or aunt) of the whole blood, and one of the persons entitled to share in the estate'
	If there be no uncle or aunt (being brother or sister of the whole blood of a parent), or any issue of such uncle or aunt, such person shall be described as 'the uncle (or aunt) of the half blood, and', etc.
	Note: *a person in this class who has acquired an alternative gender under the Gender Recognition Act 2004 at the death of death of the deceased is described as of the acquired gender.*
Issue of an uncle or aunt	'the cousin german of the whole blood, and only person entitled to the estate'; or
	'the cousin german of the whole blood, and one of the persons entitled to share in the estate'.
	(The oath (*witness statement of application*) must also establish that the applicant has a beneficial interest: see above.)
	If there be no uncle or aunt (being brother or sister of the whole blood of a parent), or any issue of such uncle or aunt, such person shall be described as 'the lawful cousin german of the half blood, and' etc.

---

[1] Following President's Direction (1925) (Non-Contentious Probate).

[2] The values are applicable when the intestate died on or after 1 February 2009. For the relevant amounts for earlier dates of death, see para **6.42**.

3   As to a grant in the case of illegitimacy, adoption or legitimation, see paras **6.191** ff, **6.247** ff and **6.197** ff, respectively.
4   As to the practice under which, on the renunciation of the surviving spouse, the issue or other kin may apply as persons 'who may have a beneficial interest in the estate in the event of an accretion thereto', see para **6.112**.

Chapter 7

MINORITY OR LIFE INTERESTS AND SECOND ADMINISTRATORS

Note: In anticipation of the revision of the Non-Contentious Probate Rules, the expression 'witness statement' where it is used in this work refers to the form of application or evidence required with reference to any rule in force at the time of the application.

APPLICATION FOR ORDER JOINING CO-ADMINISTRATOR

7.19 The Human Rights Act 1998 (HRA 1998) came into force on 2 October 2000. Hearings in chambers are subject to the overriding considerations of the HRA 1998. In particular art 6 in Sch 1 to the Act allows everyone the right to a public hearing. This places on the district judge or registrar a duty to allow public access to any hearing or to a transcript of a judgement in chambers. CPR 39.2 and PD 39.1/39A.1 set out the matters which the court must have regard to in deciding whether to hold a public or private hearing. A hearing may be in private if it involves uncontentious matters arising in the administration of trusts or in the administration of a deceased person's estate (CPR 39.2(3)(g)).

ONLY ONE CHILD ETC OF FULL AGE

7.28 Where the deceased has left no spouse or civil partner, but several children, of whom only one is of full age, an application without notice under NCPR SI 1987/2024 r 25(2), supported by affidavit (*witness statement*), should be made to the district judge or registrar for the appointment of the proposed second administrator for the purpose of joining with the child of full age in taking the grant. The consent of the proposed co-administrator may be either exhibited to the affidavit (*witness statement*) or submitted separately with the affidavit (*witness statement*). A person entitled to a grant in his own right may not and will not be appointed on behalf of the minor to enable him to nominate a co-administrator[1].

[1] Registrar's Direction (1955) 7 November.

Chapter 8

HMRC ACCOUNTS

NECESSITY FOR ACCOUNT

8.03 The Inheritance Tax Account Form IHT400 and all completed appropriate supplementary pages should be sent to the HMRC Trusts and Estates, Inheritance Tax, Ferrers House, PO Box 38, Castle Meadow Road, Nottingham, NG2 1BB. From 1 April 2016 that office ceased to use the Document Exchange [DX] system. This office was formerly known as the HMRC Inheritance Tax, IR Capital Taxes Office or the Capital Taxes Office and may be shown as such on some forms or accounts. The previous Form IHT200 will no longer be accepted by HMRC Inheritance Tax, Trusts and Estates.

Personal applications

8.05 Form PA1 should be sent with the other papers necessary to apply for a Grant to the Probate Registry. Form IHT422 should be sent to HMRC Trusts and Estates, Inheritance Tax to obtain a reference and an IHT payslip at least two weeks prior to the submission of Form IHT400. Alternatively, it is possible to apply for a reference number online using the Inheritance Tax website. However, with effect from 6 April 2017, it is expected that the online procedure for obtaining a reference number will be withdrawn due to the proposed release of Inheritance Tax online in 2017. A reference number will be provided by post together with a pre-referenced payslip. Form IHT400, all the supplementary pages including Form IHT421 and any documents requested should then be sent to HMRC Trusts and Estates, Inheritance Tax, ideally at the same time as the form PA1 is sent to the Probate Registry. If the applicant has calculated the tax, the appropriate payment should also be sent in a separate envelope with the reference number and payslip obtained under the IHT422 procedure. If, however, the applicant wishes HMRC Trusts and Estates, Inheritance Tax to calculate the tax, a calculation will then be sent to the applicant. It is only necessary to apply for an Inheritance Tax reference if the estate is liable to Inheritance Tax. Where tax is payable and is being paid by cheque or money order, which should be crossed and made payable to 'HMRC' or 'Her Majesty's Revenue and Customs', the cheque or money order and the payslip should be sent in a separate envelope to HMRC Banking, St Mungo's Road, Cumbernauld, Glasgow, G70 5WY or by DX to HM Revenue & Customs, DX 550100, Cumbernauld 2. If payment is to be made by way of the Direct Payment Scheme, Form IHT423 should be sent to the bank or building society at the same time as the submission of the Form IHT400. See para **8.205** for details of the appropriate methods of payments

8.05 HMRC accounts

and relevant addresses. Once payment is received and all is in order, HMRC Trusts and Estates, Inheritance Tax will complete its part of the Form IHT421 and send it direct to the Probate Registry. The Probate Registry will normally issue the Grant within 10 days of the interview. The Form IHT400 will be retained by HMRC Trusts and Estates, Inheritance Tax. Form IHT400 Calculation or form IHT430 Reduced Rate of Inheritance Tax should also be submitted if the simple Inheritance Tax calculation on page 11 of the account cannot be used.

INHERITANCE TAX AND CAPITAL TRANSFER TAX

Scope of the tax

8.20 The efficacy of the tax depends upon a tree of concepts at the root of which is the—undefined—'disposition'. A liability for tax becomes a possibility if a disposition is a 'transfer of value': that is to say it is made by a person and, as a result, the estate of that person is less than it otherwise would have been[1]. The amount by which the value of the estate is so decreased is known as the 'value transferred'[2]. Most dispositions are transfers of value but some are specifically provided not to be. Moreover no account is taken of 'excluded property'[3]. If a transfer of value is made by an individual (as distinct from a person) and is not an 'exempt transfer'[4] or a potentially exempt transfer[5] then it is a 'chargeable transfer' and tax is chargeable[6] upon the value transferred[7]. The 'exempt transfer' needs no elaboration here; but a 'potentially exempt transfer' would become a chargeable transfer upon the death of the transferor within seven years thereafter.

[1] See fn 1 to para **8.16** as to the meaning of 'estate'.
[2] IHTA 1984, s 3(1) [FA 1975, s 20(2)].
[3] IHTA 1984, s 3(2) [FA 1975, s 20(3)]; IHTA 1984, s 6 [FA 1975, s 24(2) and Sch 7, paras 3(1), 5(1) and 6)].
[4] IHTA 1984, ss 18 ff [FA 1975, Sch 6].
[5] IHTA 1984, s 3A in relation to events on and after 18 March 1986.
[6] IHTA 1984, s 2 [FA 1975, s 20].
[7] IHTA 1984, s 1 [FA 1975, s 19] (see para **A1.723**).

Pension death benefits

8.44 On the death of an individual under the age of 75, a transfer of a lump sum payment of the remaining or eligible pension pot will be (income) tax-free if paid out within two years. The transfer of any remaining annuity or drawdown income will also be (income) tax-free if taken as an annuity or income drawdown (if designated within two years). If the individual is aged 75 or over as at the date of death, any lump sum payment will attract income tax at the rate of 45% during the year 2015/16 and, it is currently proposed, at the beneficiary's rate of income tax in following years. Following the transfer, any future drawdown or annuity income by the beneficiary will be taxed at the beneficiary's rate of income tax. Under the provisions of the Finance Act 2016, s 94, where a member or dependant's pension drawdown fund, or a money purchase arrangement under a corresponding scheme, has not been used up prior to death, a deemed distribution will not have been made. This legislation

Inheritance tax and capital transfer tax **8.50**

has effect in respect of deaths on or after 6 April 2011. Where the drawdown relates to a flex-access fund for the member, dependant or nominee, the effective date becomes 6 April 2015.

Rates of tax

8.50 Tax is chargeable if the total for rate exceeds the contemporary threshold, presently £325,000. The total for rate is found by aggregating the value transferred by the instant transfer with the cumulative total of the values transferred by any chargeable transfers made by the transferor within the previous seven years[1]. This does not involve a series of fixed seven-year periods but a moving seven-year cumulation period from which successive transfers fall away as time passes. The rate of tax chargeable can be summarised as follows:

(a) For deaths on and after 15 March 1988 the rate of tax on values in excess of the contemporary threshold is 40% but there is a taper relief in the form of a percentage reduction in the tax payable in respect of any chargeable transfer which occurred more than three years but less than seven years before the date of death[2]. If the transfer was a chargeable transfer immediately (as distinct from being a potentially exempt transfer) then any tax paid at that time is allowed as a credit against the tax payable in connection with the death. (A chargeable transfer made before 18 March 1986, however, is chargeable at the death rate only if made within three years before the transferor's death.)

(b) For deaths before 15 March 1988 but on or after 18 March 1986 the position is at (a) save that in place of the flat rate of 40% there was a progressively banded table of rates[3].

(c) For deaths before 18 March 1986 but on or after 10 March 1981 the cumulation period was ten years. There were two rate tables and tax in respect of the deceased's estate and any chargeable transfers made within three years before the death were charged according to the first table[4]. All other lifetime chargeable transfers were chargeable according to the second table. Any tax paid under the second table was allowed as a credit pro tanto against tax payable by reason of the transferor's death within three years after the transfer.

(d) For deaths before 10 March 1981 but on or after 13 March 1975 the position was as at (c) save that instead of a moving cumulation period of ten years there was a fixed period which commenced on 27 March 1974.

(e) Under the provisions of s 10 and Sch 4 to the Finance Act 2008, the transfer of any unused nil rate band of the estate of a spouse or civil partner who died before the deceased (the deceased must have died on or after 9 October 2007) may be made subject to the completion of the claim Form IHT402. The deceased's nil rate band is increased by the percentage of the nil rate band that was unused when his or her spouse or civil partner died. More detailed instructions are incorporated in the notes section on Form IHT402.

(f) Section 109 and Sch 33 of the FA 2012 provides with effect from 6 April 2012 a reduction in the rate of Inheritance Tax charged on a component part of the estate if at least 10% of that component part

8.50 *HMRC accounts*

passes to a charitable body. The rate of tax becomes 36% instead of 40% for the component part of the estate, subject to apportionment calculations. This new legislation provides a new Sch 1A to IHTA 1984. Form IHT430 must be completed and sent to HMRC Trusts and Estates, Inheritance Tax within two years following the date of death.

(g) Section 9, Finance Act (No 2) 2015 and s 93 and Sch 15 of the Finance Act 2016 provide, with effect from 6 April 2017, a potential addition to the nil-rate band in respect of the deceased's residence, subject to certain criteria. This legislation allows an additional figure of up to £100,000 from 6 April 2017, rising annually to £175,000 for the year 2020/21 and then to increase in line with the Consumer Prices Index for the year 2021/22. To qualify for this extra nil-rate addition, the property must be left to a child (including step-child, adopted child or foster child) of the deceased and/or their lineal descendants and must be a residential property. The relief is tapered for estates exceeding £2,000,000 and there are provisions in respect of downsizing of property prior to the date of death.

[1] IHTA 1984, s 7 as amended by the FA 1986, s 101(1) and Sch 19, para 2 [FA 1975, s 37 as amended by the FA 1981, s 93(1)].
[2] IHTA 1984, s 7 as amended by the FA 1986, Sch 19, para 2.
[3] See Appendix IV, para **A4.01**.
[4] See Appendix IV, para **A4.01**.

PRACTICE

Exemptions from tax

8.138 Where property, which forms part of the estate passing under the grant of probate or administration, is exempt from tax, its value should be included in the Inheritance Tax account, in order that the true value for the purpose of the grant may be shown, and detailed in the spaces provided in the account on pages 9 and 10 as property on which tax is either not payable at all or is not at present payable. In addition to the exemptions in respect of transfers between spouses or civil partners (from 5 December 2005)[1], to charities[2] and political parties, and gifts for national purposes, considered in para **8.49**, in connection with lifetime transfers, this applies, inter alia, to the following types of property, which are variously 'exempt', 'conditionally exempt', or 'excluded' from being included for the purpose of ascertaining the tax payable on the rest of the estate—in certain cases with the reservations stated:

(a) Heritage property. Objects of national, scientific, historic or artistic interest, land of scenic, historic or scientific interest; and historic buildings with their adjoining land and associated contents. A claim for conditional exemption must be made using Schedule IHT420 and accepted by the Commissioners of HMRC[3]. In addition, transfers to approved maintenance fund settlements for certain heritage property are exempt transfers[4]. Under the provisions of the Finance Act 2016, s 97, the estate duty conditional exemption afforded by the FA 1930, s 40 and the Finance Act (Northern Ireland) 1931, s 2, is cancelled if the objects under this section are lost or destroyed.

(b) Gifts of property of any kind to national heritage bodies such as national or local art galleries or museums, local authorities, government departments and universities. Under the provisions of the Finance Act 2016, s 96, the approval function for such bodies reverts to the Treasury, having previously transferred to the Commissioners of Inland Revenue under the FA 1985, s 95.

Gifts for public benefit to bodies not run for profit where the Treasury approves exemption. Such gifts are limited to objects and land as at item (a). In addition, a reasonable maintenance fund may be included[5].

(c) Property situate in the UK by UK law but treated as situate elsewhere by virtue of a double taxation convention or agreement where the deceased was domiciled outside the UK.

(d) Certain British Government securities which are excluded property where the deceased was domiciled and ordinarily resident abroad[6].

Under s 161 of the Finance Act 1998 which is effective for transfers on or after 6 April 1998, the excluded Government securities were expanded to include any gilt-edged security issued before 6 April 1998. Such securities are treated as if they were securities issued with the post-1996 Act conditions. The one exception to this exclusion relates to $3^{1}/_{2}$% War Loan 1952 or after.

Under s 154 of the Finance Act 1996, with effect from 29 April 1996, provided the deceased was ordinarily resident outside the UK, the Treasury was empowered to issue securities which were excluded from the charge to Inheritance Tax. The Domicile qualification previously required for such exclusion was negated for such securities. The securities issued within this qualification are 8% Treasury Stock 2000, Floating Rate Treasury Stock 2001, 7% Treasury Stock 2001, 7% Treasury Stock 2002, $6^{1}/_{2}$% Treasury Stock 2003, $7^{1}/_{4}$% Treasury Stock 2007, 8% Treasury Stock 2015, 8% Treasury Stock 2021 and 6% Treasury Stock 2028.

Details of the Government securities which were regarded as excluded property for earlier transfers are detailed below.

(e) Property of which the deceased was life tenant is exempt from tax if it would have been exempt from estate duty under the Finance Act 1894, s 5(2), duty having been paid thereon in connection with the death of the deceased's spouse, such death having occurred before 13 November 1974. Any apportionment of income received after his or her death to which the estate may be entitled is treated as covered by the exemption[7].

(f) Reversionary interests which have not been acquired by the deceased or by a person previously entitled to it for a consideration in money or money's worth are excluded property.

[1] The restricted exemption to spouses or civil partners was increased to the equivalent of the nil-rate band threshold (currently £325,000) for deaths on or after 6 April 2013 and is to rise in line with future changes to the threshold.

[2] For which form IHT408 is required in respect of household or personal goods.

[3] Undertakings are required, inter alia, as to maintenance and retention of the objects in the UK. Reasonable access for the public must also be provided in all cases: IHTA 1984, s 30 [FA 1976, s 76 replacing, in relation to deaths on and after 7 April 1976, FA 1975, s 31]. Tax will be chargeable when sold (unless the sale is by private treaty to a national heritage body or similar public body) or on failure to observe the terms of the undertaking imposed as a condition of relief. Claims for exemption or enquiries relating thereto are dealt with by HMRC Trusts and Estates, Inheritance Tax. Any claim for exemption is investigated after the issue of the grant, and inspection of the objects by Officers of the National Collections is usually necessary. The

8.138 *HMRC accounts*

objects should therefore not be dispersed before inspection has taken place, without adequate notice to HMRC Trusts and Estates, Inheritance Tax. If any objects were exempted on the ground of national, etc, interest in connection with a previous death, further inspection of those objects may be waived, but the name and date of death of the former owner and, if known, the HMRC Trusts and Estates, Inheritance Tax reference to his or her estate should be mentioned.

4   IHTA 1984, s 27 (see also Sch 4) [FA 1982, s 95 replacing, in relation to deaths on and after 9 March 1982, the FA 1976, s 84 which applied to deaths on and after 3 May 1976 as amended with effect from 1 August 1980 by the FA 1980, s 88. (See also the FA 1982, s 93 and 94 and Sch 16 replacing, in relation to deaths on and after 9 March 1982, the FA 1976, s 84, amended as aforesaid.)]

5   IHTA 1984, ss 25 and 26 [FA 1975, Sch 6, paras 12 and 13]. There is no limit in value, but, as regards gifts for public benefit, undertakings are required, inter alia, as to maintenance, use or disposal and as to reasonable access for the public.

6   Viz $3^{1}/_{2}$% War Loan; 13% Treasury Stock 1990; 8% Treasury Convertible Stock 1990; $8^{1}/_{4}$% Treasury Loan 1987–90; 11% Exchequer Loan 1990; 10% Treasury Convertible Stock 1991; $5^{3}/_{4}$% Funding Loan 1987–91; 2% Index Linked Treasury Stock 1992; 8% Treasury Loan 1992; $10^{1}/_{2}$% Treasury Convertible Loan Stock 1992; $12^{3}/_{4}$% Treasury Loan 1992; 10% Treasury Loan 1993; 6% Funding Loan 1993; $12^{1}/_{2}$% Treasury Loan 1993; $13^{3}/_{4}$% Treasury Loan 1993; 9% Treasury Loan 1994; 10% Treasury Loan 1994; $14^{1}/_{2}$% Treasury Loan 1994; $12^{3}/_{4}$% Treasury Loan 1995; 9% Treasury Loan 1992–96; $13^{1}/_{4}$% Exchequer Loan 1996; $15^{1}/_{4}$% Treasury Loan 1996; $8^{3}/_{4}$% Treasury Loan 1997; $13^{1}/_{4}$% Treasury Loan 1997; 7% Treasury Convertible Loan 1997; $6^{3}/_{4}$% Treasury Loan 1995-98; $4^{5}/_{8}$% Index-linked Treasury Stock 1998; $7^{1}/_{4}$% Treasury Stock 1998; $15^{1}/_{2}$% Treasury Loan 1998; 6% Treasury Stock 1999; $9^{1}/_{2}$% Treasury Loan 1999; $8^{1}/_{2}$% Treasury Loan 2000; 9% Conversion Stock 2000; $9^{1}/_{2}$% Conversion Loan 2001; 8% Treasury Stock 2003; $9^{3}/_{4}$% Conversion Loan 2003; 8% Treasury Loan 2002–06; $4^{3}/_{8}$% Index-linked Treasury Stock 2004; $6^{3}/_{4}$% Treasury Stock 2004; $8^{1}/_{2}$% Treasury Stock 2005; $7^{1}/_{2}$% Treasury Stock 2006; $7^{3}/_{4}$% Treasury Stock 2006; $8^{1}/_{2}$% Treasury Loan 2007; 9% Treasury Loan 2008; $6^{1}/_{4}$% Treasury Stock 2010; 9% Conversion Loan 2011; $5^{1}/_{2}$% Treasury Stock 2008–12; 9% Treasury Stock 2012; 8% Treasury Stock 2013; $7^{3}/_{4}$% Treasury Loan 2012–15; $8^{3}/_{4}$% Treasury Stock 2017; $2^{1}/_{2}$% Index-Linked Treasury Stock 2024; $4^{1}/_{8}$% Index-linked Treasury Stock 2030.

7   IHTA 1984, Sch 6, para 2 [FA 1975, s 22(4)].

RELIEFS

Variations: changes in the distribution of the estate on death

8.172 *Settlements with no beneficial interest in possession*[1]—s 144. The legislation provides not only for taxation in connection with transfers between individuals and transfers on death but also in connection with transfers by trustees of settlements[2]. Provisions are made for a chargeable event to occur in relation to a settlement with no beneficial interest in possession when, inter alia, funds are dealt with by the trustees so that an individual becomes entitled to those funds absolutely or takes a qualifying interest in possession[3] in them. The scheme of relief in this case postulates that the funds have been settled under the deceased's will on trusts under which no beneficial interest in possession subsists; and it secures relief from the charge to tax under those provisions[4] provided that the event concerned occurs within two years after the death of the testator. Also, it provides that tax is to be charged in connection with the death as though the testator's will had provided for the property so dealt with to be held as it was after the event concerned[4]. Under the provisions of s 14 of the FA (No2) 2015, section 144 is amended in respect of deaths on or after 10 December 2014, so that where property is settled by will and an appointment is made before an interest in possession subsists in the property,

Assessment, payment and delivery **8.202**

the provisions of s 65(4) are ignored.

1   Ie, broadly, discretionary trusts.
2   IHTA 1984, Pt III.
3   IHTA 1984, s 102(1).
4   IHTA 1984, s 144(2).

ASSESSMENT, PAYMENT AND DELIVERY

Assessment

8.202 Interest on tax on property not entitled to the 'instalment option' is payable from the end of the sixth month after the date of death to the date of payment. The rates of interest for all outstanding tax and effective periods are tabled below. The adjustments after 1989 until 12 August 2009 were made in accordance with the Finance Act 1989, s 178(1). The Taxes and Duties (Interest Rate) (Amendment) Regulations 2009 (SI 2009/2032), took effect on 12 August 2009 and contained provisions that replaced the single rate of interest of Inheritance Tax, Capital Transfer Tax and Estate Duty with one rate for charging interest on unpaid tax and another, lower, rate for the repayment interest supplement that is added to repayments. The interest rates so calculated are linked to the Bank of England base rate and will move with base rate changes announced by the Bank's Monetary Policy Committee (MPC).

Interest rate	*Effective dates*	*Authority*
6%	Up to 31 December 1979	FA 1974, Sch 4, para 19
9%	1 January 1980 to 30 November 1982	SI 1979/1688
6%	1 December 1982 to 30 April 1985	SI 1982/1585 and Inheritance Tax Act 1984, s 233
9%	1 May 1985 to 15 December 1986	SI 1985/560
8%	16 December 1986 to 5 June 1987	SI 1986/1944
6%	6 June 1987 to 5 August 1988	SI 1987/887
8%	6 August 1988 to 5 October 1988	SI 1988/1280
9%	6 October 1988 to 5 July 1989	SI 1988/1623
11%	6 July 1989 to 5 March 1991	Board's Order June 1989
10%	6 March 1991 to 5 May 1991	Board's Order 18 February 1989
9%	6 May 1991 to 5 July 1991	Board's Order April 1991
8%	6 July 1991 to 5 November 1992	Board's Order 21 June 1991
6%	6 November 1992 to 5 December 1992	Board's Order 22 October 1992
5%	6 December 1992 to 5 January 1994	Board's Order 20 November 1992
4%	6 January 1994 to 5 October 1994	Board's Order 15 December 1993
5%	6 October 1994 to 5 March 1999	Board's Order 20 September 1994
4%	6 March 1999 to 5 February 2000	Board's Order 18 February 1999
5%	6 February 2000 to 5 May 2001	Board's Order 20 January 2000
4%	6 May 2001 to 5 November 2001	Board's Order 23 April 2001
3%	6 November 2001 to 5 August 2003	Board's Order 19 October 2001
2%	6 August 2003 to 5 December 2003	Board's Order 21 July 2003
3%	6 December 2003 to 5 September 2004	Board's Order 17 November 2003

8.202 HMRC accounts

Interest rate	Effective dates	Authority
4%	6 September 2004 to 5 September 2005	Board's Order 10 August 2004
3%	6 September 2005 to 5 September 2006	Board's Order 5 September 2005
4%	6 September 2006 to 5 August 2007	Revenue and Customs (Interest Rates) Order 2006, dated 22 August 2006
5%	6 August 2007 to 5 January 2008	Revenue and Customs (Interest Rates) Order 2007, dated 20 July 2007
4%	6 January 2008 until 5 November 2008	Revenue and Customs (Interest Rates) Order 2007, dated 7 December 2007
3%	6 November 2008 until 5 January 2009	Revenue and Customs (Interest Rates) Order (No 2) 2008, dated 21 October 2008
2%	6 January 2009 until 26 January 2009	Revenue and Customs (Interest Rates) Order (No 3) 2008, dated 16 December 2008
1%	27 January 2009 until 23 March 2009	Revenue and Customs (Interest Rates) Order 2009, dated 12 January 2009
0%	24 March 2009 until 28 September 2009	Revenue and Customs (Interest Rates) Order (No 2) 2009, dated 10 March 2009
3% for late payments; 0.5% for overpayments	29 September 2009 onwards	HMRC announcement dated 29 July 2009. Recalculation of interest rates following September Monetary Policy meeting of Bank of England.
2.75% for late payments: 0.5% for overpayments	23 August 2016 onwards	HMRC guidance announcement dated 15 August 2016.

8.203 Interest on the tax on real property and other property entitled to the 'instalment option' is charged in the same way, except that in the case of business assets and unquoted shares in companies (excluding certain investment and dealing companies) and, in the case of deaths after 9 March 1981, property afforded agricultural relief, interest is only charged on each instalment as from the date it falls due (as regards chargeable transfers made before 10 March 1981 a limit of £250,000 is imposed on the value by reference to which tax may be paid by interest free instalments)[1]. Land and buildings held as business assets are entitled to this interest relief. The FA (No2) 2015, s 15, further defines the extent and start dates of interest charged, particularly regarding instalment option property and where tax becomes payable under the provisions of the IHTA 1984, s 147(4).

[1] IHTA 1984, s 234 [FA 1975, Sch 4, para 16 as amended by FA 1981, ss 95 and 96].

Payment of tax

8.205 Where tax is payable, the assessed Inheritance Tax account IHT400 and the Form IHT421 should first be sent to the HMRC Trusts and Estates, Inheritance Tax, Ferrers House, PO Box 38, Castle Meadow Road, Nottingham, NG2 1BB for the Form IHT421 to be authorised and impressed by that office once payment has been made. A receipt will not be issued by HMRC Trusts and Estates, Inheritance Tax as part of their normal practice. See also paras **8.02** and **8.17** above.

8.207 Where tax is payable and is being paid by cheque or money order, which should be crossed and made payable to 'HMRC' or 'Her Majesty's Revenue and Customs', the cheque or money order and the payslip should be sent in a separate envelope to HMRC Banking, St Mungo's Road, Cumbernauld, Glasgow, G70 5WY. With effect from 23 July 2016, the payslip sort code should be 25-61-21 and refer to Barclays Bank. Payslips using sort code 62-40-03 and referring to NatWest are no longer valid, and will be rejected in bank clearing and remain in the suspense account of the bank they are paid into. The cheque should be made payable to 'HM Revenue and Customs only' followed by the Inheritance Tax reference and should be crossed 'Account payee'. The full name of the deceased and the date of death should be written on the back of the cheque. The Inheritance Tax reference number may be obtained by contacting HMRC Trusts and Estates, Inheritance Tax, either by telephone to the Inheritance Tax helpline on 0300 123 1072, or by completing the Form IHT422 which is a supplementary form to the Inheritance Tax account. The Form IHT422 should be submitted to the HMRC Trusts and Estates, Inheritance Tax office at least two weeks before the expected submission of the Form IHT400. Alternatively, it is possible to apply for a reference number online using the HMRC website. However, with effect from 6 April 2017, it is proposed that the online procedure for obtaining a reference number will be withdrawn due to the proposed release of Inheritance Tax online in 2017. A reference number will be provided by post together with a pre-referenced payslip. It is only necessary to apply for an Inheritance Tax reference if the estate is liable to Inheritance Tax.

8.210 It is also possible for Inheritance Tax to be discharged using the deceased's Government Stock. In the first instance, write to the registrars for British Government Stock and let them know that it is desired for funds to be transferred from British Government Stock to pay Inheritance Tax on the deceased's estate and let them know how much it is desired to transfer. The registrars are: British Government Stocks (Gilts), Computershare Investor Services plc, The Pavilions, Bridgwater Road, Bristol, BS99 6ZW. Telephone number 0370 703 0143. E-mail: gilts@computershare.co.uk. Computershare may require the stock reference number to help them find a particular investment. This number appears on the stock certificate and correspondence from the Bank of England. They aim to deal with requests within five days.

CORRECTIVE ACCOUNTS

Pre-owned assets

8.229 Under the provisions of the Finance Act 2016, s 95, a relief is now available for payments to victims of persecution during World War II in respect of deaths on or after 1 January 2015 where a payment has been received by an appropriate person or their personal representatives. The relief takes the form of a reduction in the tax which would have been charged on the qualifying

8.229 HMRC accounts

payment or the equivalent of the relevant percentage of the qualifying payment, the relevant percentage being the rate of tax over the nil-rate threshold.

Chapter 11
LIMITED GRANTS

Note: In anticipation of the revision of the Non-Contentious Probate Rules, the expression 'witness statement' where it is used in this work refers to the form of application or evidence required with reference to any rule in force at the time of the application.

INTRODUCTORY NOTES

Settling oaths (witness statements)

11.07 Where the application is complex, the oath (*witness statement of application*) may be submitted in draft, for settling to the probate department of the Principal Registry or to the district probate registry at which the application for the grant is to be made. The nature of the complexity must be clearly set out.

GRANTS TO ATTORNEYS AND CONSULAR OFFICERS

Form of power of attorney

11.44 The Lasting Powers of Attorney, Enduring Powers of Attorney and Public Guardian Regulations 2007 prescribe forms of lasting powers of attorney (Sch 1, Parts 1 and 2). References to the forms mentioned in the Regulations include a Welsh version of the forms. A donor may execute an instrument intended to create a property and affairs lasting power of attorney or/and an instrument intended to create a personal welfare lasting power of attorney. Of these, only a lasting power of attorney in respect of property and (financial) affairs may be used for the purpose of obtaining a grant for the use and benefit of the donor. The donor of a lasting power of attorney may appoint more than one donee. A lasting power of attorney is not created and therefore unusable until the Public Guardian registers it irrespective of whether the donor lacks capacity within the meaning of the Mental Capacity Act 2005 or not. An application made under NCPR SI 1987/2024 r 31(1) that relies upon a registered lasting power of attorney should include a statement in the oath (*witness statement of application*) that the donor does not lack capacity within the meaning of the Act to manage his property and affairs and that the registered lasting power of attorney has not been revoked nor has the donee disclaimed his appointment. However, the practice now is that if this statement is not included, the probate registry will assume that the donor has capacity

11.44 *Limited grants*

within the meaning of the Act. The registered lasting power of attorney stamped by the Office of the Public Guardian together with a copy should be submitted with the application. The registry returns the original stamped power after inspection. Equally acceptable is an office copy of the registered lasting power or a copy certified on each page pursuant to s 3 of the Powers of Attorney Act 1971.

Power filed in the registry

11.79 A probate practitioner lodging a *general* or an *enduring* or *lasting* power of attorney, which is required for other purposes, may lodge with it a copy, and request that the original be returned with the grant. The original power must be duly stamped if it was executed before 19 March 1985 (see para **11.46**). The examined copy is filed with the oath (*witness statement of application*), and the original returned with the grant. A power of attorney limited only for the purpose of obtaining a grant is not returnable[1].

[1] Registrar's Direction (1952) 14 March.

Oath (witness statement of application) of attorney

11.82 The oath (*witness statement of application*) should contain all the particulars which would be necessary in the case of a direct grant to the donor of the power. Additionally an attorney acting under an enduring power must confirm that the power is not registered with the Public Guardian and that the donor remains mentally capable. See paras **11.265** ff below for practice where the power is registered. An attorney acting under a registered lasting power of attorney should confirm that the donor does not lack mental capacity within the meaning of the Mental Capacity Act 2005, but if this is omitted the probate registrar will assume this to be the case. The appropriate limitation must be included. A grant to an attorney is expressed to be for the use and benefit of the donor and the usual limitation required by r 31(1) is 'until further representation be granted' but, under that rule, the district judge or registrar may direct some other form of limitation. The usual form of limitation in a grant allows a further grant to issue not only to the donor of the original power of attorney, or another attorney appointed by him, but to any other person with an equal title to a grant. The district judge or registrar would not normally allow a further grant to issue to anyone other than the original donor, or an attorney appointed by him in substitution for the original attorney, without good reason being given and without the original attorney or donor being given an opportunity to be heard on the matter. Some other possible forms of limitation are dealt with in the following paragraphs. See forms of oath, Nos 116–118, 165 and 172 (**A6.121–A6.123, A6.170** and **A6.177**).

GRANTS FOR USE OF MINORS

Grant to parents (including adoptive parents)

11.161 Where the father of a minor was not married to the mother at the time of the child's birth, but has parental responsibility in accordance with paras 4 or 6 of Sch 14 to the Children Act 1989 either (a) by virtue of an order under s 4(1) of the Family Law Reform Act 1987; or (b) by virtue of an order giving him custody or care and control of the child, in force immediately before the commencement of Pts I and II of the Children Act 1989, the oath must state that he is the father of the minor and a parent having parental responsibility by virtue of such an order which was in force immediately before the commencement of the Children Act 1989. A copy of the order must be produced in each instance[1]. The passage of time has now made this requirement redundant.

[1] Practice Direction, 26 September 1991 ([1991] 4 All ER 562, [1991] 1 WLR 1069).

Oath (witness statement of application) and supporting evidence

11.171 For form of oath see Form Nos 122–128 (**A6.127–A6.133**).

Nomination of co-administrator

11.239 It should be noted that a person apart from a spouse or civil partner entitled to a grant *in his or her own right* will not be appointed on behalf of a minor to enable him or her to nominate a co-administrator (see para **7.28**).

GRANTS FOR USE OF PERSONS UNDER DISABILITY

Notice to Court of Protection

11.262 The notice should be addressed to: The Court of Protection, PO Box 70185, First Avenue House, 42–49 High Holborn, London WC1A 9JA *or* DX 160013 Kingsway 7. The email address is: courtofprotectionenquiries@hmcts.gsi.gov.uk and the website is https://courttribunalfinder.service.gov.uk/courts/court-of-protection. The telephone number is: 0300 456 4600.

Sole executor or residuary legatee or devisee in trust lacks capacity to manage his affairs: grant to residuary legatee

11.284 As to the position where there are two or more executors, one of whom lacks capacity to manage his affairs, see 'Other persons having equal right', paras **11.251–11.254**.

Grant to persons appointed by district judge or registrar

11.292 Application for the order of the district judge or registrar is made by lodging an affidavit (*witness statement*) of the facts at the probate department of the Principal Registry, or if the application for the grant is to be made at a district probate registry, at that registry. Unless it is submitted separately the affidavit (*witness statement*) should exhibit a medical certificate of the person who lacks capacity as detailed in para **11.266** above. The applicant should also confirm that notice has been given to the Court of Protection. The district

11.292 *Limited grants*

judge or registrar may direct that the application be made on notice or summons (*application notice*) if it becomes apparent that it is being, or likely to be, opposed[1].

[1] NCPR SI 1987/2024 r 61(1).

GRANTS LIMITED AS TO PROPERTY

Grant to part of estate only

Fee for grant to trust property only

11.315 The Non-Contentious Probate Fees Order 2004 makes no provision for a fee on an application for a grant to trust property. Consequently, being a nil estate for the purpose of the grant, no fee is payable on making such application.

ADMINISTRATION PENDING DETERMINATION OF PROBATE CLAIM

Order required

11.365 Application for the appointment of an administrator pending determination of a probate claim is made by application notice in the probate claim (CPR Pt 23). For practice, see para **38.01**.

Issue of grant

11.367 If an order is made appointing an administrator pending determination of the claim, the solicitor or probate practitioner should prepare and lodge at the Principal Registry of the Family Division[1] the papers to lead the grant, ie the administrator's oath (*witness statement of application*) (Form No 135 (**A6.140**)), an HMRC Inheritance Tax account summary (if required, see Chapter 8), and an office copy of the order of the Chancery Division appointing the administrator. No reference need be made in the oath to any will of the deceased or grant that has already been issued. The grant is this case is always one of administration. The grant pending determination of a probate claim will be silent as to will or intestacy and will be limited pending determination of the claim.

[1] CPR PD 57.8.4. The practice direction directs that the application for the grant be made to the Principal Registry as the grant cannot be made by a district probate registrar because of the unresolved contention arising from the probate claim—NCPR SI 1987/2024 r 7(1)(a). In practice, the application for the grant is now referred to a district probate registrar, it is assumed under the delegated power of the Senior District Judge.

Practice

11.371 An office copy of the judgment or order in the probate claim must be obtained and lodged with the papers, and the oath (*witness statement*) must include particulars of the judgment (see also paras **4.180** and **4.181**), and of any previous grant pending determination of the probate claim.

MISCELLANEOUS

Grant limited to a claim

11.376 Difficulties can also arise in those cases where a dependant of a deceased person wishes to bring a claim under the Inheritance (Provision for Family and Dependants) Act 1975 for financial provision from the deceased's estate, but is prevented from bringing proceedings until a grant has issued and a personal representative has been constituted, and there is no person either entitled or (if entitled) willing to apply for a grant. The Official Solicitor may be approached to consider making application for a grant to himself for the purpose of being a party to the proposed proceedings against the deceased's estate[1]. As to claims under the Inheritance (Provision for Family and Dependants) Act 1975, and the position where the claimant is also the constituted personal representative, see Chapter 41.

[1] Secretary's Circular, 11 November 1976.

Proceedings against a deceased's estate

11.379 An alternative method of bringing proceedings against the estate of a deceased person where a cause of action has survived but no personal representative has been constituted is provided by rules of court made under the Civil Procedure Rules 1998: see CPR 19.8.

Chapter 12

GRANT WHERE DECEASED DIED DOMICILED OUT OF ENGLAND AND WALES

Note: In anticipation of the revision of the Non-Contentious Probate Rules the expression 'witness statement' where it is used in this work refers to the form of application or evidence required with reference to any rule in force at the time of the application.

DOMICILE

Domicile of choice

12.07 Residence in a country is not, of itself alone, sufficient to create a domicile of choice without evidence of volition to change domicile[1]. A domicile of choice is not acquired merely by accepting and holding a post of employment in a country[2]. A person whose residence in England is illegal is not barred thereby from acquiring a domicile of choice here[3].

[1] *IRC v Bullock* [1976] 3 All ER 353, [1976] 1 WLR 1178, CA.
[2] *Bowie (or Ramsay) v Liverpool Royal Infirmary* [1930] AC 588; *Cooney v Cooney* (1950) 100 L Jo 705.
[3] *Mark v Mark* [2005] UKHL 42, [2006] 1 AC 98, [2005] 3 All ER 912.

GRANTS WHERE DECEASED DIED DOMICILED OUT OF ENGLAND AND WALES

Reference to law of nationality

12.31 When the law of the country in which a person dies domiciled (he being a national of some other country) provides that the law applicable to the validity of his will and the devolution of his estate is that of his nationality, it is sometimes necessary to ascertain with which part of the 'empire' of which the deceased was a national he was directly associated. For this purpose it may be necessary to ascertain his domicile of origin[1]. As regards persons dying on or after 1 January 1964, reference should be made to the Wills Act 1963 as to nationality and to confirmation of which of several systems of law in force in a territory or state is applicable where the formal validity of a will is to be

12.31 *Grant where deceased died domiciled out of England and Wales*

decided. As to the Wills Act 1963, see paras **3.400** ff.

1   *Re O'Keefe, Poingdestre v Sherman* [1940] Ch 124, [1940] 1 All ER 216; *Re Ross, Ross v Waterfield* [1930] 1 Ch 377.

Chapter 13

GRANTS 'DE BONIS NON' – CESSATE GRANTS – DOUBLE PROBATE

Note: In anticipation of the revision of the Non-Contentious Probate Rules the expression 'witness statement' where it is used in this work refers to the form of application or evidence required with reference to any rule in force at the time of the application.

PARTICULAR CASES

Administration, with draft or copy of will annexed, 'de bonis non'

13.47 Where a will has been proved in a draft, copy or reconstruction, on the death of the sole or last surviving grantee who leaves part of the estate unadministered, the following practice applies. Provided that a chain of representation does not arise, letters of administration with the draft, copy or reconstructed will may be granted on the same terms as the original grant, it being confirmed that the original will has not been found. But if the original will has been found, the application is for a cessate grant (see paras **13.85** ff).

PRACTICE IN GRANTS 'DE BONIS NON'

Oath

13.64 Where the grant is required for making title only, it may be sworn that the grantee died 'without having completed the administration of the estate'. This situation may occur for example when the spouse or civil partner has appropriated the property to which he or she was entitled under the will or intestacy but did not assent to title of the property. The oath should confirm this fact.

CESSATE GRANTS

Grant for use of executor who lacks capacity to manage his affairs

13.96 If the incapable executor should die without recovering his capacity, administration (with the will annexed) de bonis non may be granted to the person next entitled in order of priority under NCPR SI 1987/2024 r 20. In

13.96 *Grants 'de bonis non' – Cessate grants – Double probate*

this event, careful consideration should be given to interpretation of the appointment clause in the will. Depending on the particular circumstances of the case, a substituted appointment of executor may take effect.

Chapter 14

RIGHT OF THE COURT TO SELECT AN ADMINISTRATOR; 'COMMORIENTES'

Note: In anticipation of the revision of the Non-Contentious Probate Rules the expression 'witness statement' where it is used in this work refers to the form of application or evidence required with reference to any rule in force at the time of the application.

COMMORIENTES

Deaths in disasters

14.54 Circulars have been issued from time to time by the Principal Registry in connection with the loss of ships or aircraft or other disasters, listing the names of passengers and members of the crew or other persons involved in respect of whom the Senior District Judge is satisfied, from evidence produced to him, that there is uncertainty as to which of them survived the others. Where such a circular has been issued no further evidence relating to commorientes is normally necessary on application for a grant in the estate of a person whose name is listed. Any request for information whether such a circular has been issued in any particular case should be addressed to the Senior Operations Manager, Probate, Rm WG 09, Royal Courts of Justice, Strand, London WC2A 2LL.

Chapter 15
RENUNCIATION AND RETRACTION

Note: In anticipation of the revision of the Non-Contentious Probate Rules the expression 'witness statement' where it is used in this work refers to the form of application or evidence required with reference to any rule in force at the time of the application.

RETRACTION

Practice

15.75 Form of retraction, Form 197 (**A6.202**).

Form of retraction by members of a partnership, Form 198 (**A6.203**).

Chapter 16

AMENDMENT AND NOTATION OF GRANTS

Note: In anticipation of the revision of the Non-Contentious Probate Rules the expression 'witness statement' where it is used in this work refers to the form of application or evidence required with reference to any rule in force at the time of the application.

AMENDMENT OF GRANT

Error as to deceased

16.04 Amendment of a grant may be allowed where the error was in the Christian name, address, or date of death of the deceased. Where an amendment is desired in the name of the deceased, or in the date of death, the certificate of birth or death must be produced.

Errors as to grantee

16.11 An executor may have omitted a first or medial name of his own, which has been omitted in his appointment in the will, or he may have used the surname stated in the will, without the right to do so. If he can give a sufficient and reasonable explanation, the necessary amendment will be made.

16.14 The district judges and registrars have allowed the insertion of a limitation for the use and benefit of named minors until one of them attains 18 years etc and also a note as to reservation of power to make a grant to another executor.

ORDERS FOR PROVISION OUT OF ESTATE OF DECEASED

Inheritance (Provision for Family and Dependants) Act 1975

16.50 A copy of every final order made under the relevant provisions of these Acts[1] is to be sent to the Principal Registry of the Family Division for entry and filing, and a memorandum of the order must be endorsed on, or permanently annexed to, the probate or letters of administration under which the estate is

16.50 *Amendment and notation of grants*

being administered.

[1] Other than an order made under s 15(1) of the Act, but including an order dismissing an application or a final order embodying a consent order or terms of compromise (Registrar's Direction (Divorce), 21 March 1962; *Practice Direction* (Chancery Division: Endorsement of Orders on Grants of Representation): [1978] 3 All ER 1032, [1979] 1 WLR 1); now CPR PD 57B(18.1)–(18.3).

Chapter 17
REVOCATION AND IMPOUNDING OF GRANTS

Note: In anticipation of the revision of the Non-Contentious Probate Rules the expression 'witness statement' where it is used in this work refers to the form of application or evidence required with reference to any rule in force at the time of the application.

BY WHOM REVOCATION IS OBTAINED

Other documents required

17.52 If one of the grantees lacks capacity to manage his property and affairs within the meaning of the Mental Capacity Act 2005, evidence of his lack of mental capacity is required. The district judge or registrar will normally accept a certificate or affidavit by the Responsible Medical Officer in the form set out in para **11.266**, or a certificate by the patient's doctor. If the Responsible Medical Officer or doctor is unable to give such a certificate, the matter should be referred to the district judge or registrar for his directions[1].

[1] *Practice Note* [1962] 2 All ER 613, [1962] 1 WLR 738; Registrar's Direction (1969) 31 January.

Combined application for revocation of probate and new grant

17.57 Where a grant of probate has issued to two or more executors, one of whom subsequently lacks mental capacity to manage his affairs, and it is proposed to revoke it and obtain a new grant of probate to the remaining original grantee or grantees, one sufficient affidavit may be used both to lead the order for revocation and to serve as the oath (*witness statement*) on which the new grant issues. The will may be referred to as that already proved, and need not be re-marked nor need a copy be annexed. No further HMRC Inheritance Tax account need be lodged.

17.67 *Revocation and impounding of grants*

IMPOUNDING GRANTS

When grant impounded

17.67 Where a sole, or sole surviving, grantee subsequently lacks mental capacity within the meaning of the Mental Capacity Act 2005, and a new grant is made, the former practice of impounding the old grant has been abandoned[1].

[1] *Registrar's Direction* (1985) 9 July.

Chapter 18

RESEALING

Note: *In anticipation of the revision of the Non-Contentious Probate Rules the expression 'witness statement' where it is used in this work refers to the form of application or evidence required with reference to any rule in force at the time of the application.*

COLONIAL GRANTS RESEALED IN ENGLAND AND WALES[1]

[1] The term 'colonial' is used for convenience in this chapter, but the Colonial Probates Acts also authorise the resealing of grants issued by a number of former colonies, protectorates, etc which have attained independence within the Commonwealth, by South Africa while it was a Republic outside the Commonwealth and more recently by Hong Kong which is now a Special Administrative Area of the People's Republic of China (see paras **18.35–18.39**).

18.27 By s 1 of the Colonial Probates Act 1892[1] it is provided that:

'Her Majesty the Queen may, on being satisfied that the legislature of any British possession has made adequate provision for the recognition in that possession of probates and letters of administration granted by the courts of the United Kingdom, direct by Order in Council that this Act shall, subject to any exceptions and modifications specified in the Order, apply to that possession, and thereupon, while the Order is in force, this Act shall apply accordingly.'

[1] For full text of the Act, see para **A1.45**. The term 'British possession' under s 1 of the Act means, by virtue of Sch 1 to the Interpretation Act 1978, 'any part of H.M. Dominions outside the United Kingdom', and is thereby not restricted to British dependent territories.

Changes in status of former colonies etc

18.37 In the case of South Africa, s 2 of, and the Second Schedule to, the South Africa Act 1962 specifically authorised the continued resealing of grants issued in South Africa notwithstanding that it became a Republic outside the Commonwealth. South Africa rejoined the Commonwealth in 1994.

Grantee not qualified under rule 30

18.51 Application for such leave should be made through the probate manager in the Probate Department of the Principal Registry or a district registry.

18.60 *Resealing*

Copy will to be lodged

18.60 Grants issued in certain countries, notably South Africa, are described as letters of administration or letters of executorship whether the deceased died testate or intestate, and no copy of the will is annexed to the grant. When preparing applications to reseal grants made in such countries it should be ascertained whether or not the deceased left a will, so that the copies of the will required by NCPR SI 1987/2024 r 39(5) can be lodged. The use of the expression 'executor testamentary' to describe the grantee is an indication that the deceased died testate and appointed an executor: on the other hand, the term 'executor dative' used as in the case of South African grants may apply both to cases of testacy and intestacy where the grantee is other than an executor named in the will.

New Zealand. Public Trustee

18.81 The effect of certain provisions in the New Zealand statute the Public Trust Act 2001 is as follows:

(a) the Public Trust of New Zealand may in various circumstances obtain from the New Zealand court either a grant or an order to administer, which, while in force, has the full effect of a grant;

(b) if the estate in New Zealand is within certain limits (estate out of New Zealand is irrelevant for this purpose), the Public Trust of New Zealand may file an election to administer. This, while in force, has the full effect of a grant.

18.83 In the case of elections, the document produced should be an official copy showing that the election itself has been filed in the New Zealand court; and the Public Trust should certify that the election is still in force, and undertake that in the event of further estate in New Zealand beyond the statutory limitation being discovered he will not act further in the administration of the estate in England and Wales without obtaining further representation there[1].

[1] Registrar's Direction (1958) 24 March.

18.84 A general power of attorney has been filed in the Principal Registry by the Public Trust of New Zealand appointing as his attorney the Public Trustee of England and Wales for the purposes of applying for resealing under the Colonial Probates Acts.

Chapter 21

SEARCHES AND COPIES – EXEMPLIFICATIONS – DUPLICATE GRANTS

SEARCHES AND COPIES

Wills proved since 11 January 1858

Public online searches

21.09 Facilities are now in place to search and order probate records online at www.probatesearch.service.gov.uk.

In order to search for and order a copy of a grant and any will, the site requires the surname and year of death of the deceased. A successful search displays the name of the deceased, the date of the grant, the probate number, the date of death, the record available to order, the grant and will if any, and the probate registry which issued the grant. The fee is £10 payable by credit or debit card following which the site informs the applicant when the probate record will be available to download and print (about ten days). In this context, the probate record is the grant and any testamentary papers that were proved.

Standing search for grant of representation

21.14 Postal applications should be addressed to the Probate Department, Principal Registry of the Family Division, 42–49 High Holborn, London WC1V 6NP *or* DX 941 London/Chancery Lane or to any district probate registry (see para **2.60** for addresses). Remittances for fees may be by credit or debit card in the Principal Registry but otherwise should be by crossed cheque or postal order payable to 'HMCS' or 'HM Court Service' or by cash.

Copies of wills, grants and other documents

21.17 As from 31 January 2000 the majority of probate records are kept at the Probate Records Centre in Birmingham which is privately managed. The records remain under the control and possession of the Family Division of the High Court. There is no public access to the Centre for the purpose of obtaining copies of or inspecting probate records. Record copies of all grants and wills are scanned and held as computer data at the Centre and the most

21.17 *Searches and copies – Exemplifications – Duplicate grants*

registries have online access to the Centre for the purpose of retrieving copies by facsimile transmission (see para **21.07**). The general public now have online access to record copies of all grants and wills (see para **21.09**). When any notation is made to an original grant as a result of amendment, revocation or other notice of this is sent to Birmingham District Registry which is assigned the responsibility for replacing or noting the record copy.

Chapter 22
AFFIDAVITS, AFFIRMATIONS AND STATUTORY DECLARATIONS

RULES

22.08 As to the description of the deponent, see under *Executor's oath*, paras **4.114–4.115**. The requirement that a female deponent's occupation or status should be given[1] is no longer rigidly enforced.

[1] Secretary's Circular, 12 May 1967.

Chapter 23

CAVEATS (OBJECTIONS)

Note: In anticipation of the revision of the Non-Contentious Probate Rules the expression 'witness statement' where it is used in this work refers to the form of application or evidence required with reference to any rule in force at the time of the application.

NATURE

Definition

23.01 A caveat is a notice in writing by a person wishing to show cause against the sealing of a grant, that no grant is to be sealed in the estate of the deceased named without notice to that person (NCPR SI 1987/2024 r 44). *Note*—If the person does not wish to prevent a grant issuing but requires to know when a grant issues, so that he may pursue a claim against the estate or for any other reason, instead of entering a caveat he should enter a standing search under r 43—see paras **21.11–21.14**.

ENTRY OF CAVEAT (OBJECTION)

Date and duration

23.15 The life of a caveat is also extended beyond the normal period of six months by the issue of a summons for directions pursuant to r 44(6) (see paras **23.67** ff) until that summons is disposed of or the district judge or registrar gives a direction, on the summons, for the caveat to cease to have effect (r 44(8)). Before this happens the caveat may be withdrawn under r 44(11), but in the event of a caveat being withdrawn before such a summons has been finally disposed of, no grant will be sealed without reference to a district judge or registrar[1]. This allows for the resolution of any issues which a party has raised following the entry of the caveat and which may have a bearing on the administration of the estate.

[1] Registrar's Circular, 12 June 1967.

Commencement of probate claim

23.17 The commencement of a probate claim operates to prevent the sealing of any grant (other than a grant of administration pending determination of

23.17 *Caveats (objections)*

the probate claim) until application for a grant is made by the person shown to be entitled thereto by the decision of the court in such claim. This is subject to the proviso that a district judge may direct that a grant issue on an application made by summons. On the application for a grant after the conclusion of a probate claim, any caveat (*objection*) entered by the claimant in the claim, and any caveat (*objection*) in respect of which notice of the claim has been given, ceases to have effect (r 45(4)).

Form of caveat

23.22 Care should be taken to include in the entry all alternative or alias names for the deceased to ensure that a grant does not issue in any of these names.

Extension of caveat

23.29 The proviso to NCPR SI 1987/2024 r 44(1) (which provides that a caveat (*objection*) is not effective to prevent the sealing of a grant on the day of entry) is not expressly attached to an application for the extension of a caveat (*objection*) with the result that a successful application for extension made, or received in the registry, on the date upon which the caveat is due to expire will operate to prevent the sealing of a grant. In all other respects, the procedures relating to the entry of a caveat (*objection*) apply to applications for extension[1].

[1] Registrar's Circular, 15 September 1976.

Restriction on entry of further caveat

23.33 Where leave of a district judge of the Principal Registry for the entry of a further caveat is granted, the further caveat is effective for six months from the date of its entry and not (as in the case of an application for extension of an existing caveat) from the date of expiry of the first caveat[1].

[1] Registrar's Direction (1958) 28 January.

Search for caveat

23.36 An application may also be made by post or email to the Principal Registry or any district registry asking for a search to be made and it will be answered by a letter or email stating whether or not there is an effective caveat (*objection*), and, if there is one, a copy of it will be posted to the applicant[1].

[1] Secretary's Circular, 11 August 1988.

WARNING OF CAVEATS – CURRENT PRACTICE

Caveats warned at the nominated registry—currently Leeds District Probate Registry

23.39 Caveats can be warned only at the nominated registry (NCPR SI 1987/2024 r 44(5)). 'Nominated registry' is defined by r 44(15). It is the registry nominated by the Senior District Judge for the purpose of r 44, and in the absence of such nomination it is the Leeds District Probate Registry – see para **23.41**.

23.42 The person warning the caveat must set out in the warning his interest in the estate including the date of any will or codicil under which he claims title to a grant (eg executor or residuary legatee, etc), or, in the case of intestacy, his interest in the estate of the deceased, and must also give an address within the jurisdiction, which is his address for service (NCPR SI 1987/2024 r 49).

APPEARANCE TO WARNING

How entered

23.60 To enter his appearance, a caveator may either attend in person or by his probate practitioner at the Leeds District Probate Registry and complete a form of memorandum of appearance, which may be obtained at the registry, or he may send at his own risk the completed form of appearance by post to that registry. Form of appearance, No 39 (**A6.44**).

Chapter 24

CITATIONS (NOTIFICATIONS)

Note: In anticipation of the revision of the Non-Contentious Probate Rules, the expression 'witness statement' where it is used in this work refers to the form of application or evidence required with reference to any rule in force at the time of the application.

OBJECT OF CITATIONS

Kinds of citations

(A) To accept or refuse a grant

24.04 The citation, therefore, answers two purposes:

(a) it compels those who are primarily entitled to take a grant to decide whether they will do so or not; and
(b) where such parties refuse either to take a grant or to renounce, it provides an alternative grantee.

24.11 *Alternative to citation (or notification).* Where it is sought to pass over persons entitled who cannot be traced, in favour of a lower title, and a citation served by advertisement would normally be required, a district judge or registrar may make an order, if he thinks fit, under s 116(1) of the Senior Courts Act 1981 after, in appropriate cases, requiring the publication of a suitable advertisement for the person who would normally be cited. This course may be adopted where costs associated with the citation procedure would deplete a small estate.

24.19 *Will must be filed.* Before any citation (*notification*) can issue every will referred to in it must whenever possible be lodged in the Principal Registry or a district probate registry[1]. This confirms the existence of the will and allows the probate registrar to establish that the will, the subject of the citation, is or appears to be valid and that in due course it may be proved.

[1] NCPR SI 1987/2024 r 46(5).

(C) To propound a will

24.36 *Will already proved in common form.* If a will has been proved in common form, procedure by citation to propound is inappropriate. A person disputing such a will and wishing to compel the grantee to prove it in solemn form should take steps to have the grant called in, and himself commence

24.36 *Citations (notifications)*

proceedings for revocation: the Non-Contentious Probate Rules have no application in such circumstances[1]. The proceedings are begun by a probate claim in the Chancery Division.

[1] *Re Jolley, Jolley v Jarvis* [1964] P 262, [1964] 1 All ER 596.

Chapter 25

APPLICATIONS TO DISTRICT JUDGE, REGISTRAR OR HIGH COURT JUDGE (NON-CONTENTIOUS BUSINESS)

Note: In anticipation of the revision of the Non-Contentious Probate Rules, the expression 'witness statement' where it is used in this work refers to the form of application or evidence required with reference to any rule in force at the time of the application.

APPLICATIONS WITHOUT NOTICE

Leave to swear death

25.20 The Presumption of Death Act 2013 came into force on 1 October 2014. Under s 3(1) of the Act, but subject to sub-ss (3) and (4) (which deal with appeals against a declaration), a declaration of presumed death is conclusive of the presumed death and the date and time of death, and under s 3(2) the declaration is effective against all persons for the purpose of the acquisition of an interest in any property and the ending of the marriage or civil partnership to which the missing person was a party. Section 1 of the Act lays down the following qualifications and conditions:

- the person who is missing is thought to have died or has not been known to be alive for a period of at least seven years;
- any person may apply to the High Court for a declaration that the missing person is presumed to be dead;
- the person was domiciled in England and Wales on the day on which he or she was last known to be alive or the person was habitually resident in England and Wales throughout the period of one year ending with that day; or
- on an application by a spouse or civil partner, the applicant is domiciled in England and Wales on the date of the application or has been habitually resident in England and Wales throughout the period of one year ending with that day;
- the court must refuse the application by someone other than the missing person's spouse, civil partner, parent, child or sibling and if the court considers that the applicant does not have a sufficient interest in the determination of the application.

73

25.20A *Applications to district judge, registrar or High Court judge*

25.20A An application for a declaration of presumed death of a person under the Presumption of Death Act 2013 may be made either to the Family Division or the Chancery Division. The Civil Procedure Rules apply to the proceedings in this regard save that in the Family Division the Family Procedure Rules apply to the drawing up and service of orders.

25.20B While limited in nature, an application may be made under NCPR SI 1987/2024 r 53 to a district judge or probate registrar for leave to swear to the death of a person. Where the applicant for a grant cannot swear in his oath to the death of the deceased, and there is no direct evidence of his being dead[1], but only evidence from which his death may be presumed to have taken place, application must be made for an order giving him leave to swear to the death[2]. Such a presumption may arise: (1) from the disappearance of the presumed deceased at or after a given time, and from the circumstances attending such disappearance, or from his not having been heard of for a prolonged period by those with whom he might reasonably have been expected to communicate[3]; or (2) from his having been on board a ship, which, from its non-arrival in port within a reasonable time, from the absence of tidings of any of those on board, and from other circumstances, is supposed to have been lost at sea; and similarly in the case of a missing or totally destroyed aeroplane.

[1] But where death can be sworn to have occurred between two dates, and the fact is not in doubt, the grant can be made in the registry without order (*Re Long-Sutton's Estate* [1912] P 97). In this case the oath should state that the deceased 'was last seen alive [or last known to be alive] on the   day of   19   and that his dead body was found on the day of   19   '.

[2] It must be always remembered in these cases that the court does not presume the death of the deceased; it merely gives the applicant leave to swear the death (*Re Jackson's Goods* (1902) 87 LT 747).

[3] The fact that the family or friends of a man whose habit was to communicate with them received no communication from or news of him for seven years leads to the presumption of his death at some time during the seven years, but not at the beginning or at the end of the seven years (*Re How's Goods* (1858) 1 Sw & Tr 53, 31 LTOS 26), provided that there is no assignable cause for the cessation of his communications. The mere fact, however, that he has not been heard of for seven years, where it was not his practice to communicate, does not lead to such an inference, but it may, coupled with other circumstances, induce the court to act on the presumption of his death.
Where application was made for an order on the ground that a man had not been heard of for nearly seven years, there being also a Chancery suit, it was ordered that the letters of administration were not to be given out (*except for the purposes of the suit*) till the end of the seven years (*Re Winstone's Goods* [1898] P 143).

Decree under Matrimonial Causes Act

25.37 A decree of presumption of death and dissolution of marriage made before 1 October 2014 by virtue of s 19 of the Matrimonial Causes Act 1973[1] does not remove the necessity of applying for an order for leave to swear to the death of the missing former spouse. Section 19 of the MCA 1973 was repealed by the Presumption of Death Act 2013, s 16(3), Sch 2, para 1. See paras **25.20** ff.

[1] 27 Halsbury's Statutes (4th edn) 720.

Person found to be living after order giving leave to swear death

25.50 A claim for a declaration of presumed death under the Presumption of Death Act 2013, s 1 is issued in the High Court in either the Family Division or the Chancery Division in accordance with CPR Pt 57 and PD 57B.

Grant 'ad colligenda bona' (collection grant)

25.182 The application must be supported by an affidavit (*witness statement*) setting out the grounds of the application, and provided that it is not opposed should be made without notice at the registry at which the application for the grant is to be made[1]. A district probate registrar may, if he considers it necessary, obtain the directions of a district judge of the Principal Registry on any application made to him[2].

[1] NCPR SI 1987/2024 rr 2(1), 52(b); see also *Ghafoor v Cliff* [2006] EWHC 825 (Ch), [2006] 2 All ER 1079, [2006] 1 WLR 320.
[2] NCPR SI 1987/2024 r 7.

APPLICATIONS BY SUMMONS (APPLICATION NOTICE)

Discontinuance of proceedings arising from caveat

25.221 When an appearance has been entered to the warning of a caveat, no grant can issue until the decision of the court in the proceedings (by probate claim) arising from the appearance to warning. But if, prior to the commencement of a probate claim the caveator abandons his opposition to the issue of a grant, application may be made by summons to a district judge of the Principal Registry for an order for discontinuance of the caveat and for the issue of a grant notwithstanding the caveat, warning and appearance (NCPR SI 1987/2024 r 44(13)). If the parties come to terms an application for discontinuance of the caveat is made by consent under the same rule to a district judge in the Principal Registry or to the registrar of the district probate registry to which the application for the grant has been, or is to be, made. It should be noted that an order by consent of a district judge or registrar may not include the pronouncing for or against the validity of a will as these are properly matters for Chancery. Form of summons, No 203 (**A6.208**).

25.223 As to the right of a caveator who has not appeared to a warning to withdraw his caveat and practice, see paras **23.48–23.51**. As to caveats generally, see Chapter 23.

PRACTICE AS TO SUMMONSES (APPLICATION NOTICES)

When heard

25.245 The Human Rights Act 1998 (HRA 1998) came into force on 20 October 2000. It gives effect to rights and freedoms guaranteed under the European Convention on Human Rights. In this regard the matter of hearings in chambers is subject to the overriding considerations of the Act. In particular HRA 1998, Sch 1, art 6 allows everyone the right to a public hearing. This places on the district judge or registrar a duty to allow public access to any

25.245 *Applications to district judge, registrar or High Court judge*

hearing or to transcript of judgment in chambers. CPR 39.2 and PD 39.2 set out the matters which the court must have regard to when deciding whether to hold a public hearing. CPR 29.2(3)(f) provides that a hearing, or any part of it, may be private if it involves non-contentious matters arising in the administration of trusts or in the administration of a deceased person's estate.

Orders

25.252 Orders are drawn up in the registry, and normally bear the date of the day on which they are made. Sealed copies of orders are sent by post to the applicant and respondent.

Part II

CONTENTIOUS BUSINESS

Chapter 26
INTRODUCTION

JURISDICTION OF THE COURT

High Court

26.18 Procedure and case management in the Chancery Division are set out in the Chancery Guide (February 2016). The Guide is regularly updated on the court website: www.gov.uk/courts-tribunals/chancery-division-of-the-high-court. The process of implementation of the Chancery Modernisation Review Report published in December 2013 has led to a significant number of recent changes to Chancery practice and it is essential to refer to the online version. Probate procedure is summarised between paras 29.45 and 29.56 of the Chancery Guide.

THE PRACTICE: HIGH COURT AND COUNTY COURT

Pre-action steps

(1) Larke v Nugus

26.31 The Law Society Practice Note '*Disputed Wills*' (6 October 2011) sets out what is good practice on receipt of a request for information by a solicitor and the consequences of the failure to provide full information. It refers to the issue of privilege and to where there is a possibility of negligence. See www.lawsociety.org.uk/support-services/advice/practice-notes/disputed-wills.

A refusal by an executor to provide a full response to a reasonable request for information contained in a *Larke v Nugus* letter or to provide disclosure of the central documents is likely to have serious costs consequences and may result in his being deprived of part of his costs[1].

[1] *Watton v Crawford* [2016] NICh 14 in which a previous will and medical notes and records were not disclosed in response to a request for information.

Chapter 27
CLAIMS

(1) CLAIMS FOR PRONOUNCING FOR OR AGAINST A WILL IN SOLEMN FORM

When proof in solemn form may be required

27.10 The above persons may put an executor, or other person interested under a will, to proof in solemn form either before or after probate has been taken in common form, but the following two, by reason of their particular status, can only do so before, and not after, probate in common form has issued, namely:

(4) *A creditor*. A creditor to whom administration has been granted[1].

(5) *An appointee of the court*. Any other person in possession of a grant of administration, as appointee of the court, eg, by order under the Senior Courts Act 1981, s 116, but not having a beneficial interest in the estate.

This should not be regarded as an exhaustive list of the circumstances in which persons have been found to be entitled to require proof of a will in solemn form. Paragraph 28.01(ff) is expressed very broadly. It states that the rules of the probate court as to standing have always been flexible. This is in line with the new procedural code introduced by the Civil Procedure Rules 1998 with their overriding objective of enabling the court to deal with cases justly and at proportionate expense[2].

[1] *Menzies v Pulbrook and Kerr* (1841) 2 Curt 845 at 851. The decision in *Menzies v Pulbrook and Kerr* was stated still to be good law by the Court of Appeal in *Randall v Randall* [2016] EWCA Civ 494, [2016] 3 WLR 1217 but it was held to be wrong to assimilate the position of a creditor of a beneficiary of an estate with that of a creditor of an estate. The interests of the two types of creditor were held to be fundamentally different. The interest of the creditor of a beneficiary is to ensure that the beneficiary receives what is due to him or her under the will or on an intestacy. The interest of a creditor of an estate is to ensure that there is due administration of the estate: see the judgment of the Master of the Rolls at [22].

[2] *Randall v Randall* [2016] EWCA Civ 494, [2016] 3 WLR 1217 at [28] per the Master of the Rolls and at [36] per McCombe LJ.

(2) INTEREST ACTIONS

27.22 The decision in an interest action may involve an issue of pedigree or of legitimacy, but a prayer for a declaration of legitimacy may not be included in the claim form. Applications for declarations as to legitimacy or legitimation

27.22 *Claims*

are now made under s 56 of the Family Law Act 1986 (as substituted by s 22 of the Family Law Reform Act 1987) and any such declaration may be made only under that section (Family Law Act 1986, s 58(4)). Any application for a declaration under s 56 of the Act of 1986 must be made in the form prescribed by rules of court (Family Law Act 1986, s 60(1)) and the Family Procedure Rules 2010 r 8.20 sets out what should normally be contained in an application for such a declaration. The proceedings should be brought in the Family Court. An interest action may arise from a dispute as to whether a person claiming to be a beneficiary and entitled to administer the estate was married to the deceased or whether the marriage was valid[1].

[1] For a recent example see: *Adepoju v Akinola* [2016] EWHC 3160 (Ch). The issue was tried within the framework of a probate claim.

(3) CLAIMS FOR REVOCATION OF GRANTS

Claims for revocation when a will has been proved

27.26 A claim under the Inheritance (Provision for Family and Dependants) Act 1975 was held to give the claimant an interest in the estate within the meaning of CPR 57.7 sufficient to bring a claim for revocation of a grant in circumstances where it was conceded that the claim under the 1975 Act would be more valuable under intestacy than if a previous will admitted to probate in common form were upheld[1]. A claim by a former husband to challenge the validity of a will made by his wife following divorce was held to give sufficient standing in circumstances where if the will was invalid the husband stood to be entitled to an additional £75,000 as part of a divorce settlement[2]. In both cases there was in practice held to be no other route by which the will in question would be brought before the court to be proved in solemn form or for the grant to be revoked.

[1] *O'Brien v Seagrave* [2007] EWHC 788 (Ch), [2007] 3 All ER 633, [2007] 1 WLR 2002. The broad construction of the meaning of 'interest' adopted by Judge Mackie QC was adopted and applied by the Court of Appeal in *Randall v Randall* [2016] EWCA Civ 494, [2016] 3 WLR 1217.
[2] *Randall v Randall* [2016] EWCA Civ 494, [2016] 3 WLR 1217.

Claims for revocation of letters of administration

27.29 No copy of the grant may issue, without leave, after the claim form has been issued until the claim has been concluded. For a form of order, see: CP13A (**A6.223A**): Chapter 28.

ASSOCIATED CLAIMS

27.41 The following claims or applications are not, strictly, contentious probate claims, but they have sufficient connection to the subject matter of a contentious probate claim to warrant mention in this book. They are:

(1) a claim for the rectification of a will;
(2) a claim or application for the substitution and removal of a personal representative;

(3) a claim under the Inheritance (Provision for Family and Dependants) Act 1975[1]; and
(4) an application for a declaration under the Presumption of Death Act 2013.

The first two such proceedings (claims for rectification of a will and claims or applications for the substitution and removal of a personal representative) are contained in CPR Pt 57 as 57.12 Section II and as 57.13 Section III and the corresponding sections in Practice Direction 57A. Claims under the 1975 Act are governed by the rules in CPR 57 Part IV and the corresponding section in Practice Direction 57A.

CPR 57 Section V and Practice Direction 57B concern proceedings under the Presumption of Death Act 2013. The 2013 Act assists the problems of families trying to resolve the affairs of missing persons: see Chapter 25 at paras **25.49–25.50** and see also paras **41.42** ff.

[1] See Chapter 41.

Chapter 28

PARTIES TO CLAIMS

WHO MAY BE A PARTY

28.01 The foundation of title to be a party to a probate claim is *interest*—so that whenever it can be shown that it is competent to the court to make a decree in a claim for probate or administration, or for the revocation of probate or of administration, which may affect the interest, or possible interest, of any person, such person has a right to be a party to such a suit[1].

Such was the rule in the Prerogative Court of Canterbury as to the foundation of title to be a party to a cause in that court.

[1] *Kipping and Barlow v Ash* (1845) 1 Rob Eccl 270; *Crispin v Doglioni* (1860) 2 Sw & Tr 17. This passage was quoted in *Randall v Randall* [2016] EWCA Civ 494, [2016] 3 WLR 1217 in support of adopting a flexible approach to issues of standing and interest entitling a person to bring a probate claim.

28.02 In a claim for the revocation of a grant every person who is or claims to be entitled to administer the estate under that grant must be made a party to the claim[1].

[1] CPR 57.6(1). This is by way of exception to the normal rule that executors are not necessary parties to a probate claim.

28.03 The question whether a person has a sufficient *interest* to be permitted to bring a probate claim is a procedural issue and not a matter of substantive law. The nature of an interest adequate to found a probate claim is a matter of practice and procedure. It is decided on a pragmatic basis from case to case. There is no rigidity about the test[1]. A claim under the Inheritance (Provision for Family and Dependants) Act 1975 was on particular facts a sufficient interest for the purposes of bringing a probate action. The claimant's motivation for challenging the will was that her Inheritance Act claim would be more likely to succeed on intestacy than under the will[2]. A divorced husband was allowed to proceed with a probate revocation claim to challenge the validity of a will made by his deceased ex-wife in circumstances where if the will was held to be invalid he would stand to receive an additional sum under their divorce settlement[3].

[1] *Randall v Randall* [2016] EWCA Civ 494, [2016] 3 WLR 1217 at [27] per the Master of the Rolls and at [32] per McCombe LJ.
[2] *O'Brien v Seagrave* [2007] EWHC 788 (Ch), [2007] 3 All ER 633, [2007] 1 WLR 2002, approved in *Randall v Randall* [2016] EWCA Civ 494, [2016] 3 WLR 1217. In *O'Brien*, a claimant with a prospective claim under the 1975 was held to have standing to challenge a will where the only surviving relation by blood or marriage was an elderly brother who did not wish to be a party to any proceedings. In *Randall*, the CA held there to be a distinction between

28.03 *Parties to claims*

the position of a creditor of a beneficiary of an estate with that of a creditor of an estate. The interests of the two types of creditor were said to be 'fundamentally different'. The interest of the creditor of a beneficiary is to ensure that the beneficiary receives what is due to that beneficiary under the will or on intestacy. The interest of a creditor is limited to ensuring that there is due administration of the estate; at [22] per the Master of the Rolls.

[3] *Randall v Randall* [2016] EWCA Civ 494, [2016] 3 WLR 1217.

PARTIES GENERALLY

Defendants

28.07 In certain cases it may be appropriate to apply for a representation order under CPR 19.6 (representation of parties with same interest) or CPR 19.7 (representation of interested parties who cannot be ascertained etc). These are matters to which the master or district judge will give consideration at a case management conference[1]: see CPR Pt 57 PD57A, para 4(1) and (2). For a recent review of the scope of CPR 19.6 in a non-probate context see: *Emerald Supplies Ltd v British Airways plc* [2010] EWCA Civ 1284, [2011] Ch 345, [2011] 2 WLR 203. If, for example, in a probate claim, there are very large numbers of persons who would be interested under intestacy were a will to be held invalid, including a significant number resident out of the jurisdiction, the appointment of a representative beneficiary may be easier than having to give individual notices under CPR 19.8A.

[1] See para 37.08.

Chapter 29
CLAIM FORM

STATEMENTS OF INTEREST

Forms of statement

29.11 See Forms CP14 ff (**A6.224** ff).

Chapter 31
TESTAMENTARY DOCUMENTS

INSPECTION OF TESTAMENTARY DOCUMENTS

Loan of testamentary documents for examination

31.12 If a party wishes his expert to examine a testamentary document, his solicitor should attend the master at the time for oral applications without notice to give a written undertaking (as to safekeeping and return) against loan of the testamentary document for a specified time. For a form of order, see CP4A (**A6.214A**): CH27 Handing out Testamentary Documents for examination.

Verification of testamentary documents

31.14 When the court orders trial on written evidence it is normally necessary for an attesting witness to sign a witness statement or swear an affidavit of due execution of the will or codicil sought to be admitted to probate, but the will or codicil is lodged at court and cannot be handed out of court for use as an exhibit to the witness statement or affidavit. Either the attesting witness can attend at the court and sign or swear his evidence before an officer of the court or, if he is unable to do so, his solicitor may request from the court a photocopy of the will or codicil. This will be certified as authentic by the court and may be exhibited to the witness statement or affidavit of due execution in lieu of the original. The witness statement or affidavit must state that the exhibited document is an authenticated copy of the document signed in the witness' presence[1].

[1] Chancery Guide paras 29.53 and 29.54; see para **26.18**.

Transmission of scripts in cases tried outside London

31.15 When a probate claim in the Royal Court of Justice is listed for trial at a Chancery District Registry the solicitor for the party responsible for preparing the court bundle must write to the Masters' Appointments (Ground Floor, Rolls Building), Chancery Chambers, Royal Courts of Justice, 7 Rolls Building, Fetter Lane, London EC4A 1NL and request that the testamentary documents be forwarded to the appropriate Chancery District Registry[1].

[1] Chancery Guide para 29.55; see para **26.18**; and see CPR Pt 57 PD(A) para 2.2.

Chapter 32
STATEMENTS OF CASE GENERALLY

PRACTICE AS TO STATEMENTS OF CASE

Statements of interest and denial of interest

32.07 The claim form must contain a statement of the nature of the interest of the claimant and of each defendant in the estate[1]. If a party disputes another party's interest in the estate he must state this in his statement of case and set out his reasons[2]. *The nature of an interest adequate to found a right to bring or defend probate proceedings falls to be determined on a case by case basis. The issue is one of practice and procedure rather than substantive law. A creditor of an estate does not have a sufficient interest in an estate to bring a probate claim. A creditor of a beneficiary on the other hand may do so depending on the circumstances*[3].

[1] CPR 57.7(1).
[2] CPR 57.7(2).
[3] In *O'Brien v Seagrave* [2007] EWHC 788 (Ch), [2007] 1 WLR 2002, [2007] 3 All ER 633 and in *Randall v Randall* [2016] EWCA Civ 494, [2016] 3 WLR 1217 sufficient interests to bring a probate claim were shown. In *Randall* the claimant was classified as being a creditor of a beneficiary. There will of course be cases in which on looking at all the circumstances it will be apparent that a person has no interest in bringing a claim. For that reason the parties are required to lodge testamentary documents at the outset of their involvement in a probate claim.

Chapter 34

DEFENCE AND COUNTERCLAIM

(1) WANT OF DUE EXECUTION

Notice under CPR 57.7(5)

34.13 Where it is proposed merely to put the executors to proof and only to cross-examine their witnesses, the notice as to such cross-examination must be given in the defence[1]. A notice under CPR 57.7(5) will not provide costs protection to a defendant who did not have reasonable grounds for opposing a will. This follows from the wording of CPR 57(5)(b)[2]. Once a defendant is in a position to make a proper assessment as to whether there were reasonable grounds to oppose a will, he is at risk for costs incurred from that date[3]. The notice will no longer provide costs protection.

[1] CPR 57.7(5)(a).
[2] CPR 57(5)(b) provides that if a defendant gives such a notice, the court will not make an order for costs against him 'unless it considers that there was no reasonable ground for opposing the will.'
[3] *Elliott v Simmonds* [2016] EWHC 962 (Ch), [2016] WTLR 1375 at [14] and [17].

The nature of the inquiry by the court

34.32 A will which is drawn up in accordance with instructions given by a testator at a time when he had full testamentary capacity but executed at a time when he no longer had such capacity will be upheld provided the testator knew that the document he was signing conformed with the instructions he had given and approved it by executing it in those terms[1]. The rule in *Parker v Felgate* 8 PD 171 does not displace the requirement for full testamentary capacity; it merely displaces the ordinary requirement that the testator should have had such capacity at the time he executed the will[2]. The rule has been held to apply in the case of inter-vivos dispositions[3].

For precedent of defence, see Form CP33 (**A6.243**).

[1] *Perrins v Holland* [2011] Ch 270, [2011] 2 WLR 1086 approving *Parker v Felgate* (1883) 8 PD 171.
[2] Per Moore-Bick LJ at [54] in *Perrins v Holland*.
[3] *Singellos v Singellos* [2010] EWHC 2353 (Ch), [2011] Ch 324; *Re Smith (decd)* [2014] EWHC 3926 (Ch), [2015] 4 All ER 329.

34.48 *Defence and counterclaim*

Summary of reported cases

What is not undue influence

34.48 Appeals to affection, ties of kindred, gratitude for past services, or pity for future destitution are legitimate; but not pressure if so exerted as to overpower the volition without convincing the judgment (*Hall v Hall* (1868) LR 1 P & D 481). Even immoral considerations do not amount to undue influence unless the testator is in such a condition that if he could speak his wishes to the last, he would say, 'This is not my wish, but I must do it' (*Baudains v Richardson* [1906] AC 169 at 184). See also *Cowderoy v Cranfield* [2011] EWHC 1616 (Ch), [2011] WTLR 1699, *Wharton v Bancroft* [2011] EWHC 3250 (Ch), [2012] WTLR 693 and *Nesbitt v Nicholson* [2013] EWHC 4027 (Ch) in which undue influence claims failed. A plea of undue influence failed in *Edkins v Hopkins* [2016] EWHC 2542 (Ch). The main beneficiary had had a significant level of control over the testator, his business and personal financial affairs, but that level of control was given by the testator and not taken by the main beneficiary. The main beneficiary had encouraged the testator to change his will but the testator had acted out of his own judgment.

(5) **WANT OF KNOWLEDGE AND APPROVAL**

Summary of reported cases

Burden of proof

34.64 Suspicious circumstances may arise where the testator is mentally or physically frail or where beneficiaries have been part of the process of drawing up the will. In such cases the judge must consider whether the suspicion has been dispelled (*Hawes v Burgess* [2013] EWCA Civ 74 at [12] per Mummery LJ). It may be obvious that the burden has not been dispelled (*Poole v Everall* [2016] EWHC 2126 (Ch), [2016] WTLR 1621 where a person on whom the testator depended had received the great bulk of the estate through a will drafted by him).

It is not the law that in no circumstances can a solicitor or other person who has prepared a will for a testator take a benefit under it; but that fact creates a suspicion that must be removed by the person propounding the will. In all cases the court must be vigilant and jealous. The degree of suspicion will vary with the circumstances of the case. It may be slight and easily dispelled; it may, on the other hand, be so grave that it can hardly be removed (*Wintle v Nye* [1959] 1 All ER 552, [1959] 1 WLR 284, HL). A solicitor beneficiary under a will has a personal obligation to see that the testator was separately advised before he could benefit (*Re a Solicitor* [1975] QB 475, [1974] 3 All ER 853).

(7) REVOCATION

Summary of reported cases

III. By burning, tearing, or otherwise destroying (Wills Act 1837, s 20[1])

[1] See para **A1.20**.

34.87 *(i) Generally:*

(a) *Intention to revoke.* The intention to revoke must accompany the act (*Bibb v Thomas* (1775) 2 Wm Bl 1043; *Clarke v Scripps* (1852) 2 Rob Eccl 563 at 567; *Giles v Warren* (1872) LR 2 P & D 401). Therefore a person of unsound mind cannot revoke his will by destruction (*Brunt v Brunt* (1873) LR 3 P & D 37 at 38; *Re Taylor's Estate, National and Provincial and Union Bank of England v Taylor* (1919) 64 Sol Jo 148). As to standard of capacity required, see *Re Sabatini* (1969) 114 Sol Jo 35. Where the destruction is not with consent of the testator, he cannot subsequently ratify such destruction so as to effect a revocation (*Mills v Millward* (1889) 15 PD 20; *Gill v Gill* [1909] P 157), and subsequent acquiescence does not constitute revocation (*Re Booth, Booth v Booth* [1926] P 118). If there is an express revocation clause in a later will which is not in accord with the testator's instructions there is no rule of law that the testator is bound by the draftsman's mistake. The burden of proving on the balance of probabilities that the testator had not intended to revoke the earlier will is on the party seeking to prevent the express clause having effect. The standard of proof is no higher than the usual balance of proof, but the existence of the revocation clause is strong evidence that needs to be overcome (*Lamothe v Lamothe* [2006] EWHC 1387 (Ch), [2006] WTLR 1431). For a later lost will to revoke an earlier will there must be clear, stringent and conclusive evidence that there was either a revocation clause in the lost will or that its provisions were inconsistent with those of the earlier will (*Broadway v Fernandes* [2007] EWHC 684 (Ch), [2007] All ER (D) 485 (Mar)).

(b) *Presumption as to will not forthcoming at testator's death.* Where a will is traced into the testator's custody, and there is no evidence of its having subsequently left his custody, and it is not forthcoming at his death—this will be prima facie evidence of its destruction by him animo revocandi (*Patten v Poulton* (1858) 1 Sw & Tr 55; *Welch v Phillips* (1836) 1 Moo PCC 299 at 302), and it is not necessary for those alleging revocation to show how, in fact, it was lost or destroyed (*Patten v Poulton* (1858) 1 Sw & Tr 55). The presumption may be rebutted by surrounding circumstances, eg declaration of unchanged affection or intention (*Patten v Poulton* (1858) 1 Sw & Tr 55; *Welch v Phillips* (1836) 1 Moo PCC 299 at 302; *Re Mackenzie's Estate* [1909] P 305; *Re Sykes, Drake v Sykes* (1906) 22 TLR 741; affd (1907) 23 TLR 747, CA); *Re Wilson's Estate, Walker v Treasury Solicitor* (1961) 105 Sol Jo 531. The strongest proof of the improbability of revocation by destruction arises from the contents of the document itself (*Saunders v Saunders* (1848) 6 Notes of Cases 518 at 522). Where a will which has been in the custody of a testator at a time when he has been of unsound mind as well as of sound mind, is found torn, or is not forthcoming at his death, the burden of showing that it was revoked by him while of sound mind lies on the party who sets up the revocation (*Harris v Berrall* (1858) 1 Sw & Tr 153). See also *Sprigge v Sprigge* (1868) LR 1 P & D 608 (the presumption of destruction animo revocandi does not apply where the testator became of unsound mind after execution of the will and continued so until his death. The burden of showing that the will was revoked before he became of unsound mind lies on the party asserting revocation); *Re Yule's Estate* (1965) 109 Sol Jo 317 (the presumption of destruction animo revocandi and the contrary presumption, in the case where the testator had lost testamentary capacity, that the will was destroyed unintentionally, were not intended to be rigid rules but as indications of the inferences which would always be drawn from a given state of evidence. But the court was not entitled to depart from *Sprigge v Sprigge*, above). In *Re Dickson* [1984] LS Gaz R 3012, CA; [2002] WTLR 1395 the presumption that a missing will had been destroyed animo revocandi was rebutted where the only reasonable inference from declarations by the testator and other evidence was that he had intended the missing will to be effective and had intended to benefit the beneficiaries thereunder. If the deceased has passed the will to a third party for safe custody no presumption arises (*Chana v Chana* [2001] WTLR 205). In *Rowe v Clarke* [2006] WTLR 347 the presumption was rebutted on the facts, which pointed to the testator having lost or destroyed the will in his lifetime without intending to revoke it. In *Wren v Wren* [2006] EWHC 2243 (Ch), [2007] WTLR 531, the will was not found at death, however, the deceased's clear post-will testamentary declarations rebutted the presumption of revocation. In *Nicholls v Hudson* [2006] EWHC 3006 (Ch), 150 Sol Jo LB 1333 the will made by the deceased was found to have been lost through mistake, accident or inadvertence with no intention of revoking it and a copy of the will was admitted to probate. In *Singh and McDonald v Vozniak* [2016] EWHC 114 (Ch) a wife's assertion that her husband had torn up his will was rejected in circumstances in which the deceased had repeatedly confirmed to one of the executors named in the will, after his wife had found out about the will, that his testamentary wishes were unchanged.

(c) *Revocation by partial destruction.* Where a testator signed his name, which was attested by both the witnesses, on each of the sheets of his will, and at his death only two of the middle sheets were found among his papers, it was held that the will must be presumed to be revoked (*Re Gullan's Goods* (1858) 1 Sw & Tr 23); so, too, where the testator had replaced the three middle sheets of his will (consisting of five sheets) by three other sheets, and the original sheets could not be found (*Treloar v Lean* (1889) 14 PD 49); see also *Clarke v Scripps* (1852) 2 Rob Eccl 563 (the question is whether the portion destroyed is so important as to raise a presumption that the remainder cannot have been intended to stand without it, or whether it is unimportant and independent of the remainder of the will); *Leonard v Leonard* [1902] P 243. Where part of a will is destroyed, but the part preserved contains the signatures of testator and the witnesses, the onus is normally on the party alleging revocation to prove the necessary animus. But if the part preserved is so mutilated as to be unworkable as a testamentary instrument this raises a presumption that the testator could not have intended it to stand as his will (*Re Green's Estate, Ward v Bond* (1962) 106 Sol Jo 1034). In *Re Adams* [1990] Ch 601, [1990] 2 All ER 97 it was held that the obliteration of his signature by the testator, so that it could not be read with a magnifying glass was by itself sufficient evidence of intention to revoke the whole will.

(d) *Revocation of duplicate wills.* Where a will is executed in duplicate the revocation of one is the revocation of both (*Boughey v Moreton* (1758) 3 Hag Ecc 191). But there must be evidence that the will was, in fact, executed in duplicate—subsequent declarations by the testator to this effect are inadmissible (*Atkinson v Morris* [1897] P 40, CA; *Eyre v Eyre* [1903] P 131 at 137). See para **3.209**.

Chapter 36
DISCLOSURE

DNA TESTING

36.27 The High Court has inherent jurisdiction to direct DNA testing in the case of a sample of a deceased's DNA. The power is one that is to be used sparingly[1].

[1] *Spencer v Anderson (Paternity Testing: Jurisdiction)* [2016] EWHC 851 (Fam), [2016] 3 WLR 905, [2016] Fam Law 808.

Chapter 37

COSTS AND CASE MANAGEMENT OF PROBATE CLAIMS

DIRECTIONS QUESTIONNAIRE AND DIRECTIONS

Directions

37.07 The parties are expected to endeavour to agree proposals for the management of the case at the directions stage and submit agreed directions, or their respective proposals, to the court at least seven days before any case management conference in accordance with CPR 29.4 and CPR 29 PD paras 4.6 to 4.8. If the directions are suitable the court may use them as the basis of making an order. Unless both directions and costs budgets are agreed, the claim is likely to be listed for a costs and case management conference. Case and Costs Management is dealt with in Chapter 17 of the Chancery Guide (2016).

37.09 For draft orders commonly made by the Master on allocation and case management conference see the justice.gov website at http://hmctsformfinder.justice.gov.uk/HMCTS/FormFinder.do. The costs and case management conference requires preparation well in advance of the hearing and if this has not been done the hearing may be adjourned and adverse costs orders made[1].

[1] Chancery Guide Ch 17 para 17.6.

OTHER PRE-TRIAL MATTERS

Trial timetable

37.20 Trial timetables have become essential following the introduction of trials with a fixed end date in the Chancery Division. The judge at trial, or at the pre-trial review, will determine the timetable of the trial. The advocates for parties should be ready to assist the court in this respect if so required. The time estimate given for the trial at the case management conference stage should be based on an approximate forecast of the trial timetable, and must be reviewed by each party at the stage of the pre-trial review and as preparation for trial proceeds thereafter[1]. If that review requires a change in the estimate the other parties' advocates and the court must be informed. When a trial timetable is set by the court, it ordinarily fixes the time for the oral submissions and factual and expert evidence, in greater or lesser detail. Trial timetables are

101

37.20 *Costs and case management of probate claims*

always subject to further order by the trial judge[2].

[1] Chancery Guide Ch 17 para 17.25.
[2] Chancery Guide Ch 20 para 20.7.

Pre-trial review

37.21 In cases estimated to take more than five days, a pre-trial review will be directed. The date for the pre-trial review is fixed at the time when the trial date is given[1]. The pre-trial review will, where possible, be heard by the trial judge. This requires the trial judge to have been nominated in advance of the trial. The pre-trial review is usually held between four and eight weeks before the trial date[2].

[1] Chancery Guide Ch 20 para 20.1.
[2] Chancery Guide Ch 20 para 20.3.

37.22 A pre-trial review should be attended by advocates who are to represent the parties at the trial[1].

[1] Chancery Guide Ch 20 para 20.4.

37.23 Not less than seven days before the dated fixed for the review the claimant or some other party if the court so directs must circulate a list of matters to be considered to the other parties who must respond with their comments at least two days before the review[1].

[1] Chancery Guide Ch 20 para 20.5.

37.24 The claimant or another party if so directed should deliver a bundle containing the matters to be considered and the proposals from other parties and the trial timetable and the results of inter party discussions and any other necessary documents to the Listing Officer by 10am on the day before the day fixed for the hearing[1].

[1] Chancery Guide Ch 20 para 20.6.

37.25 At the review the court will review the state of the case and deal with outstanding matters, and give any necessary directions as to how the case is to be tried[1]. Interim applications should not be stored up for the pre-trial review, which is intended primarily to review the issues in the case and the proposed trial timetable.

[1] Chancery Guide Ch 20 para 20.6.

Trial bundle

37.26 Unless the court otherwise orders the claimant must file the trial bundle made as provided in CPR Pt 39 PD paras 3.2–3.9 and Chancery Guide paras 21.34–21.72 not more than seven days nor less than three days before the start of the trial.

Skeleton arguments and reading lists

37.27 As a general rule for the purpose of all hearing before a judge skeleton arguments should be prepared. For trials and applications by order they should be delivered not less than two clear days before the date or first date on

Other pre-trial matters **37.28**

which the application or trial is due to come on for hearing. For guidelines see Chancery Guide paras 21.73–21.81 (skeleton arguments) and 21.82 (reading lists). *Practice Direction on the Citation of Authorities*[1] lays down rules as to the citation of cases. Excessive citation of authority should be avoided and practitioners must have full regard to *Practice Direction (Citation of Authorities)* [2012] 1 WLR 780.

[1] [2001] 1 WLR 1001.

37.28 *Practice Direction (Reading Lists and Time Estimates)*[1] requires that a reading list and an estimated length of reading time and an estimated length of hearing signed by all advocates must be prepared in all matters where the lodging of bundles is required. Time estimates must make a realistic estimate for pre-reading by the judge. All trials in the Chancery Division in London, following practice and procedure successfully adopted in Manchester and elsewhere, are now conducted on a fixed-end trial basis[2].

[1] [2000] 1 All ER 640.
[2] Chancery Guide Ch 21 paras 21.20–21.26.

Chapter 39
TRIAL

LISTS AND DURATION

Estimate of duration

39.06 With the introduction of fixed-end trials, estimates need to be kept under constant review. If after a case is listed in the Royal Courts of Justice the estimated length of the hearing is varied, or if the case is settled, withdrawn or discontinued, the solicitors for the parties must forthwith inform the Chancery Listing Officer in writing. Failure to do so may result in an adverse costs order being made[1].

The parties must inform the court immediately of any material change in a time-estimate[2].

[1] Chancery Guide Ch 21 para 21.11.
[2] Chancery Guide Ch 21 para 21.22.

Time limits

39.08 All cases in the Chancery Division are now to be given fixed-end dates. The court may, either at the outset of the trial or at any other time thereafter fix time limits for oral submissions, speeches and the examination and cross-examination of witnesses[1].

[1] Chancery Guide Ch 21 paras 21.20, 21.29 and 21.30.

THE HEARING

Opening oral submissions

39.09 Generally the claimant opens, unless the burden of proof of all issues in the case lies on the defendant, in which case the defendant has the right to begin. In general and subject to any direction to the contrary by the trial judge there should be a short opening statement on behalf of the claimant, at the conclusion of which the judge will invite short opening statements on behalf of the other parties[1]. Unless notified otherwise advocates should assume that the judge will have read the skeleton arguments and the principal documents referred to in the reading list lodged in advance of the hearing. The judge will state at an early stage how much he or she has read and what arrangements are to be made about reading documents not already read. If additional documents

39.09 *Trial*

need to be read by the judge a list should be provided during the opening[2].

[1] Chancery Guide Ch 21, para 21.90.
[2] Chancery Guide Ch 21 para 21.91.

Witness statements

39.10 Chapter 19 of the Chancery Guide lays down guidelines for the preparation of witness statements.

Closing oral submissions

39.15 After the evidence is concluded, and subject to contrary directions by the judge, the claimant will make closing oral submissions followed by the defendant(s) in the order they appear on the claim form, followed by a reply on behalf of the claimant[1]. This differs from the traditional order of speeches where the defendant made his submissions before the claimant. In a lengthy and complex case each party should provide written summaries of their closing submissions. The court may require the written summaries to set out the principal findings of fact for which a party contends[2].

[1] Chancery Guide Ch 21 para 21.93.
[2] Chancery Guide Ch 21 para 21.94.

Chapter 40
COSTS

COSTS OF PARTIES OPPOSING PROBATE

(a) **Where the litigation has been caused by the testator, or those interested in the residuary estate**

Where conduct of beneficiary under the will caused the litigation

40.30 An unsuccessful party is usually given his costs where one of the principal beneficiaries under a will has been actively engaged in its preparation, and has not shown by disinterested evidence that its dispositions were read over or explained to and approved of by the testator before its execution[1]. The mere fact that someone can be said to be responsible for a will having been executed otherwise than in front of a solicitor cannot make it appropriate to view him as the cause of litigation about it[2].

[1] *Dale v Murrell* (March 1879, unreported). See also *Orton v Smith* (1873) LR 3 P & D 23; and *Wilson v Bassil* [1903] P 239, 72 LJP 89.
[2] *Breslin v Bromley* [2015] EWHC 3760 (Ch), [2015] 6 Costs LR 1115 per Newey J at [4].

(c) **Where the opposing party gives notice to cross-examine under CPR 57.7(5)**

40.37 Under CPR 57.7(5), in probate claims the party opposing a will may give notice in his defence that he does not raise any positive case but insists on the will being proved in solemn form and, for that purpose, will cross-examine the witnesses who attested the will. If a defendant gives such a notice, the court will not make an order for costs against him unless it considers there was no reasonable ground for opposing the will. It does not follow, because a defendant fails, that there was no reasonable ground for opposing the will[1]. On the other hand, once a defendant has sufficient material to form a view as to whether there were any reasonable grounds for opposing a will, he or she becomes at risk for costs incurred from that date and is no longer protected by rule CPR 57.7(5)[2].

[1] *Davies v Jones* [1899] P 161 at 164. For a case under the rule where it was held that there had been no reasonable ground for opposing the will, see *Re Spicer, Spicer v Spicer* [1899] P 38. See also *Perry v Dixon* (1899) 80 LT 297.
[2] *Elliott v Simmonds* [2016] EWHC 962 (Ch), [2016] WTLR 1375.

Chapter 41
ASSOCIATED ACTIONS

FAMILY PROVISION

Costs management of 1975 Act claims

41.41 Claims pursuant to the Inheritance (Provision for Family and Dependants) Act 1975 are specifically referred to as one of the categories of Part 8 claims in which an order for the provision of costs budgets may be particularly appropriate with a view to a costs management order being made[1].

[1] CPR Pt 3 PD 3E para 5(d).

PRESUMPTION OF DEATH

Applications under the Presumption of Death Act 2013

41.42 The Presumption of Death Act 2013 (PDA 2013) came into force on 1 October 2014. It enables applications to be made to the High Court for a declaration that a missing person is presumed to have died.

Jurisdiction

41.43 The court has jurisdiction to hear and determine an application if and only if: (i) the missing person was domiciled in England and Wales on the day on which he or she was last known to be alive; or (ii) the missing person had been habitually resident in England and Wales throughout the period of one year ending with that day; or (iii) if PDA 2013, s 1(4) is satisfied. That sub-section is satisfied if an application is made by the spouse or civil partner of the missing person, and the applicant is domiciled in England and Wales on the day on which the application is made or if the applicant has been habitually resident in England and Wales throughout the period of one year ending with that day. The sub-section cannot be relied on where the application is made by a parent, child or sibling of the missing person. In the case of such an application, jurisdiction must be founded on s 1(3).

41.44 *Associated actions*

The form of declaration made

41.44 Subject to jurisdiction being established, the court must make a declaration if it is satisfied that the missing person has died or has not been known to be alive for a period of at least seven years[1].

Where the court is satisfied that a missing person has died, but is uncertain at which moment during a period the missing person died, a declaration will be made pursuant to s 2(1)(a) that the missing person is presumed to have died at the end of that period.

Where the court is satisfied that the missing person has not been known to be alive for a period of at least seven years, but is not satisfied that the missing person has died, a declaration will be made pursuant to s 2(1)(b) that the missing person is presumed to have died at the end of the period of seven years beginning with the day after the day on which he was last known to be alive[2].

[1] PDA 2013, s 1(3).
[2] This was the form of declaration made in *Re Charles George Bingham* [2015] EWHC 226 (Ch) in relation to Lord Lucan, the Seventh Earl of Lucan.

The effect of a declaration

41.45 A declaration under the Act is conclusive of the missing person's presumed death and the date and time of death[1].

[1] PDA 2013, s 3.

Procedure

41.46 CPR Part 57 Section V and PD 57B sets out detailed rules of court concerning the information to be provided in the claim form, giving of notice of the claim to others who would be entitled themselves to be the claimant, and for advertisement of the claim and for intervening in a claim.

Section 11 of the PDA 2013 permits the missing person's spouse, civil partner, child or sibling to intervene in proceedings on an application under the Act. The Attorney General may intervene. Any other person may only intervene with the permission of the court[1].

The rules provide for a first directions hearing and then a final hearing. If the matter is not opposed, an order may be made by a permanent Master.

[1] An application for permission to intervene must be served on the claimant and must specify the applicant's relationship to the missing person or other interest in the proceedings and the reasons for seeking to intervene: CPR Pt 57 PD57B para 3.2. The prescribed form of advertisement requires any person seeking to intervene do so as soon as possible, and if possible within 21 days of the advertisement.

The Register of Presumed Deaths

41.47 The Act provides for the creation and maintenance by the Registrar General for England and Wales of the Register of Presumed Deaths. A certified copy of an entry in the Register of Presumed Deaths in relation to a person is to be received as evidence of the person's death without further or other proof, if it purports to be sealed or stamped with the seal of the General Register

Office[1].

[1] PDA 2013, s 15 and Sch 1, para 4.

APPENDICES

Appendix I

STATUTES

Contents

Part I – Probate Business

Wills Act 1837	115
Law of Property Act 1925	116
Public Records Act 1958	117
Senior Courts Act 1981	118
Forfeiture Act 1982	119
Children Act 1989	121
Courts and Legal Services Act 1990	130
Adoption and Children Act 2002	133
Marriage (Same Sex Couples) Act 2013	137

Part II – Finance Acts etc

Inheritance Tax Act 1984	139

Note.

The following text contains extracts from Acts of Parliament having a bearing on the probate practice. In general, those enactments, since repealed, which remain applicable in relation to cases where death occurred prior to the relevant date of repeal have been retained for the purpose of reference.

PART I – PROBATE BUSINESS

WILLS ACT 1837

(7 Will 4 & 1 Vict c 26) as amended

A1.01

1 Meaning of certain words in this Act: "Will": "Real estate": "Personal estate": Number: Gender

. . . the words and expressions herein-after mentioned, which in their ordinary signification have a more confined or a different meaning, shall in this Act, except where the nature of the provisions or the context of the Act shall exclude such construction, be interpreted as follows; (that is to say,) the word "will" shall extend to a testament, and to a codicil, and to an appointment by will or by writing in the nature of a will in exercise of a power, [and also to an appointment by will of a guardian of a child], [and also to an appointment by will of a representative under section 4 of the Human Tissue Act 2004 [or section 8 of the Human Transplantation (Wales) Act 2013],] . . . and to any other testamentary disposition; and the words "real estate" shall extend to manors, advowsons, messuages, lands, tithes, rents, and hereditaments, . . . whether corporeal, incorporeal, or personal, . . . and to any estate, right, or interest (other than a chattel interest) therein; and the words "personal estate" shall extend to leasehold estates and other chattels real, and also to monies, shares of government and other funds, securities for money (not being real estates), debts, choses in action, rights, credits, goods, and all other property whatsoever which by law devolves upon the executor or administrator, and to any share or interest therein; and every word importing the singular number only shall extend and be applied to several persons or things as well as one person or thing; and every word importing the masculine gender only shall extend and be applied to a female as well as a male.

Repealed in part, in relation to Northern Ireland, by the Statute Law Revision (Northern Ireland) Act 1954, the Statute Law Revision (Northern Ireland) Act 1976, and the Wills and Administration Proceedings (NI) Order 1994, SI 1994/1899, art 38, Sch 3.

First words omitted repealed by the Statute Law Revision Act 1893, s 1, Schedule.

Words from "and also to" to "of a child," in square brackets substituted by the Children Act 1989, s 108(5), (6), Sch 13, para 1, Sch 14, para 1.

Words from "and also to" to ",", in square brackets inserted by the Human Tissue Act 2004, s 56, Sch 6, para 1. Date in force: 1 September 2006: see SI 2006/1997, art 3(2).

Words "or section 8 of the Human Transplantation (Wales) Act 2013" in square brackets inserted by the Human Transplantation (Wales) Act 2013, s 17. Date in force: 1 December 2015: see SI 2015/1679, art 3(e).

Second and third words omitted repealed by the Statute Law (Repeals) Act 1969, s 1, Schedule, Pt III.

Final words omitted repealed by the Trusts of Land and Appointment of Trustees 1996, s 25(2), Sch 4; for savings in relation to entailed interests created before the commencement of that Act, and savings consequential upon the abolition of the doctrine of conversion, see s 25(4), (5) thereof.

LAW OF PROPERTY (AMENDMENT) ACT 1926

(16 & 17 Geo 5, c 11)

A1.138

3 Meaning of 'trust corporation'

(1) For the purposes of the Law of Property Act 1925, the Settled Land Act 1925, the Trustee Act 1925, the Administration of Estates Act 1925, and the [Senior Courts Act 1981], the expression "Trust Corporation" includes the Treasury Solicitor, the Official Solicitor and any person holding any other official position prescribed by the Lord Chancellor, and, in relation to the property of a bankrupt . . . , includes the trustee in bankruptcy . . . , and, in relation to charitable ecclesiastical and public trusts, also includes any local or public authority so prescribed, and any other corporation constituted under the laws of the United Kingdom or any part thereof which satisfies the Lord Chancellor that it undertakes the administration of any such trusts without remuneration, or that by its constitution it is required to apply the whole of its net income after payment of outgoings for charitable ecclesiastical or public purposes, and is prohibited from distributing, directly or indirectly, any part thereof by way of profits amongst any of its members, and is authorised by him to act in relation to such trusts as a trust corporation.

(2) For the purposes of this provision, the expression "Treasury Solicitor" means the solicitor for the affairs of His Majesty's Treasury, and includes the solicitor for the affairs of the Duchy of Lancaster.

Sub-s (1): words "Senior Courts Act 1981" in square brackets substituted by the Constitutional Reform Act 2005, s 59(5), Sch 11, Pt 1, para 1(2). Date in force: 1 October 2009: see SI 2009/1604, art 2(d).

Sub-s (1): first words omitted repealed by the Deregulation Act 2015, s 19, Sch 6, Pt 1, para 2(1), (5)(a); for effect see para 3. Date in force: 1 October 2015: see SI 2015/1732, art 2(e)(i).

Sub-s (1): second words omitted repealed by the Deregulation Act 2015, s 19, Sch 6, Pt 1, para 2(1), (5)(b); for effect see para 3. Date in force: 1 October 2015: see SI 2015/1732, art 2(e)(i).

PUBLIC RECORDS ACT 1958

(6 & 7 Eliz 2, c 51)

[23rd July 1958]

A1.165

5 Access to public records
* * * * *
(5) The [Secretary of State] shall as respects all public records in places of deposit appointed by him under this Act outside the Public Record Office require arrangements to be made for their inspection by the public comparable to those made for public records in the Public Record Office, ...

Sub-s (5): words "Secretary of State" in square brackets substituted by SI 2015/1897, art 9, Schedule, para 1(1), (3)(f). Date in force: 9 December 2015: see SI 2015/1897, art 1(2).

Sub-s (5): words omitted repealed by the Freedom of Information Act 2000, ss 67, 86, Sch 5, Pt I, para 2(1), (4), Sch 8, Pt III. Date in force: 1 January 2005: see SI 2004/3122, art 2.

A1.166

8 Court records
(1) The Lord Chancellor shall be responsible for the public records of every court of record or magistrates' court which are not in the Public Record Office or a place of deposit appointed by [the Secretary of State] under this Act and shall have power to determine in the case of any such records [other than records of the Supreme Court,] the officer in whose custody they are for the time being to be:

. . .

[(1A) Records of the Supreme Court for which the Lord Chancellor is responsible under subsection (1) shall be in the custody of the chief executive of that court.]

(2), (3) . . .

(4) Where any private documents have remained in the custody of a court in England or Wales for more than fifty years without being claimed, the Keeper of Public Records may, with the approval of the Master of the Rolls, require the documents to be transferred to the Public Record Office and thereupon the documents shall become public records for the purposes of this Act.

(5) Section three of this Act shall not apply to such of the records of ecclesiastical courts described in paragraph (n) of sub-paragraph (1) of paragraph 4 of the First Schedule to this Act as are not held in any office of the [Senior Courts] or in the Public Record Office, but, if the Lord Chancellor after consulting the President of the [Family Division] so directs as respects any of those records, those records shall be transferred to such place of deposit as may be appointed by the [Secretary of State] and shall thereafter be in the custody of such officer as may be so appointed.

(6) The public records which at the commencement of this Act are in the custody of the University of Oxford and which are included in the index a copy of which was transmitted to the principal probate registrar under section two of the Oxford University Act 1860 shall not be required to be transferred under the last foregoing subsection but the Lord Chancellor shall make arrangements with the University of Oxford as to the conditions under which those records may be inspected by the public.

Sub-s (1): words "the Secretary of State" in square brackets substituted by SI 2015/1897, art 9, Schedule, para 1(1), (4). Date in force: 9 December 2015: see SI 2015/1897, art 1(2).

Sub-s (1): words "other than records of the Supreme Court," in square brackets inserted by the Constitutional Reform Act 2005, s 56(1), (2)(a). Date in force: 1 October 2009: see SI 2009/1604, art 2(b).

Sub-s (1): words omitted repealed by the Courts Act 1971, s 56(4), Sch 11, Pt II.

Sub-s (1A): inserted by the Constitutional Reform Act 2005, s 56(1), (2)(b). Date in force: 1 October 2009: see SI 2009/1604, art 2(b).

Sub-s (2): repealed by the Supreme Court Act 1981, s 152(4), Sch 7.

Sub-s (3): repealed by the Administration of Justice Act 1969, ss 27(2), 35(2), Sch 2.

Sub-s (5): words "Senior Courts" in square brackets substituted by the Constitutional Reform Act 2005, s 59(5), Sch 11, Pt 2, para 4(1), (3). Date in force: 1 October 2009: see SI 2009/1604, art 2(d).

Sub-s (5): words "Family Division" in square brackets substituted by the Administration of Justice Act 1970, s 1(6), Sch 2, para 19.

Sub-s (5): words "Secretary of State" in square brackets substituted by SI 2015/1897, art 9, Schedule, para 1(1), (3)(i). Date in force: 9 December 2015: see SI 2015/1897, art 1(2).

[SENIOR COURTS ACT 1981]

(1981, c 54)

[28th July 1981]

PART II
JURISDICTION

The Court of Appeal

* * * * *

A1.304

16 Appeals from High Court

(1) Subject as otherwise provided by this or any other Act (and in particular to the provision in section 13(2)(a) of the Administration of Justice Act 1969 excluding appeals to the Court of Appeal in cases where leave to appeal from the High Court directly to the [Supreme Court] is granted under Part II of that Act), [or as provided by any order made by the Lord Chancellor under section 56(1) of the Access to Justice Act 1999,] the Court of Appeal shall have jurisdiction to hear and determine appeals from any judgment or order of the High Court.

(2) An appeal from a judgment or order of the High Court when acting as a prize court shall not be to the Court of Appeal, but shall be to Her Majesty in Council in accordance with the Prize Acts 1864 to 1944.

Sub-s (1): words 'Supreme Court' in square brackets substituted by the Constitutional Reform Act 2005, s 40(4), Sch 9, Pt 1, para 36(1), (3). Date in force: 1 October 2009: see SI 2009/1604, art 2(d).

Sub-s (1): words from "or as provided" to "Access to Justice Act 1999," in square brackets inserted by SI 2016/917, art 9. Date in force: 3 October 2016: see SI 2016/917, art 1(2); for transitional provisions see art 8.

A1.305

17 Applications for new trial

(1) Where any cause or matter, or any issue in any cause or matter, has been tried in the High Court, any application for a new trial thereof, or to set aside a verdict, finding or judgment therein, shall be heard and determined by the Court of Appeal except where rules of court made in pursuance of subsection (2) provide otherwise.

(2) As regards cases where the trial was by a judge alone and no error of the court at the trial is alleged, or any prescribed class of such cases, rules of court may provide that any such application as is mentioned in subsection (1) shall be heard and determined by the High Court.

(3) Nothing in this section shall alter the practice in bankruptcy.

Sub-ss (1) derived from the Supreme Court of Judicature (Consolidation) Act 1925, s 30.

FORFEITURE ACT 1982

(1982, c 34)

[13 July 1982]

A1.359

2 Power to modify the rule

(1) Where a court determines that the forfeiture rule has precluded a person (in this section referred to as "the offender") who has unlawfully killed another from acquiring any interest in property mentioned in subsection (4) below, the court may make an order under this section modifying [or excluding] the effect of that rule.

(2) The court shall not make an order under this section modifying [or excluding] the effect of the forfeiture rule in any case unless it is satisfied that, having regard to the conduct of the offender and of the deceased and to such other circumstances as appear to the court to be material, the justice of the case requires the effect of the rule to be so modified [or excluded] in that case.

(3) In any case where a person stands convicted of an offence of which unlawful killing is an element, the court shall not make an order under this section modifying [or excluding] the effect of the forfeiture rule in that case unless proceedings for the purpose are brought before the expiry of the *period of three months beginning with his conviction* [relevant period].

[(3A) In subsection (3) above, the "relevant period" is the period of 6 months beginning with—

- (a) the end of the period allowed for bringing an appeal against the conviction, or
- (b) if such an appeal is brought, the conclusion of proceedings on the appeal.]

(4) The interests in property referred to in subsection (1) above are—

- (a) any beneficial interest in property which (apart from the forfeiture rule) the offender would have acquired—
  - (i) under the deceased's will (including, as respects Scotland, any writing having testamentary effect) or the law relating to intestacy or by way of ius relicti, ius relictae or legitim;

>>> (ii) on the nomination of the deceased in accordance with the provisions of any enactment;
>>> (iii) as a donatio mortis causa made by the deceased; or
>>> (iv) under a special destination (whether relating to heritable or moveable property); or
>> (b) any beneficial interest in property which (apart from the forfeiture rule) the offender would have acquired in consequence of the death of the deceased, being property which, before the death, was held on trust for any person.

(5) An order under this section may modify [or exclude] the effect of the forfeiture rule in respect of any interest in property to which the determination referred to in subsection (1) above relates and may do so in either or both of the following ways, that is—
>> (a) where there is more than one such interest, by excluding the application of the rule in respect of any *(but not all)* [or all] of those interests; and
>> (b) in the case of any such interest in property, by excluding the application of the rule in respect of [all or any] part of the property.

(6) On the making of an order under this section [modifying the effect of the forfeiture rule], the forfeiture rule shall have effect for all purposes (including purposes relating to anything done before the order is made) subject to the modifications made by the order.

(7) The court shall not make an order under this section modifying the effect of the forfeiture rule in respect of any interest in property which, in consequence of the rule, has been acquired before the coming into force of this section by a person other than the offender or a person claiming through him.

(8) In this section—
>> "property" includes any chose in action or incorporeal moveable property; and
>> "will" includes codicil.

Sub-s (1): words "or excluding" in square brackets inserted by the Succession (Scotland) Act 2016, s 15(1), (2). Date in force: 1 November 2016: see SSI 2016/210, reg 2(1)(a), (2).

Sub-s (2): words "or excluding" in square brackets inserted by the Succession (Scotland) Act 2016, s 15(1), (3)(a). Date in force: 1 November 2016: see SSI 2016/210, reg 2(1)(a), (2).

Sub-s (2): words "or excluded" in square brackets inserted by the Succession (Scotland) Act 2016, s 15(1), (3)(b). Date in force: 1 November 2016: see SSI 2016/210, reg 2(1)(a), (2).

Sub-s (3): words "or excluding" in square brackets inserted by the Succession (Scotland) Act 2016, s 15(1), (4). Date in force: 1 November 2016: see SSI 2016/210, reg 2(1)(a), (2).

Sub-s (3): words "period of three months beginning with his conviction" in italics repealed and subsequent words in square brackets substituted by the Succession (Scotland) Act 2016, s 16(1), (2). Date in force: 1 November 2016: see SSI 2016/210, reg 2(1)(a), (2).

Sub-s (3A): inserted by the Succession (Scotland) Act 2016, s 16(1), (3). Date in force: 1 November 2016: see SSI 2016/210, reg 2(1)(a), (2).

Sub-s (5): words "or exclude" in square brackets inserted by the Succession (Scotland) Act 2016, s 15(1), (5)(a). Date in force: 1 November 2016: see SSI 2016/210, reg 2(1)(a), (2).

Sub-s (5): in para (a) words "(but not all)" in italics repealed and subsequent words in square brackets substituted by the Succession (Scotland) Act 2016, s 15(1), (5)(b). Date in force: 1 November 2016: see SSI 2016/210, reg 2(1)(a), (2).

Sub-s (5): in para (b) words "all or any" in square brackets inserted by the Succession (Scotland) Act 2016, s 15(1), (5)(c). Date in force: 1 November 2016: see SSI 2016/210, reg 2(1)(a), (2).

Sub-s (6): words "modifying the effect of the forfeiture rule" in square brackets inserted by the Succession (Scotland) Act 2016, s 15(1), (6). Date in force: 1 November 2016: see SSI 2016/210, reg 2(1)(a), (2).

CHILDREN ACT 1989

(1989, c 41)

[16th November 1989]

PART IV
CARE AND SUPERVISION

Care orders

A1.445

33 Effect of care order

(1) Where a care order is made with respect to a child it shall be the duty of the local authority designated by the order to receive the child into their care and to keep him in their care while the order remains in force.

(2) Where—
- (a) a care order has been made with respect to a child on the application of an authorised person; but
- (b) the local authority designated by the order was not informed that that person proposed to make the application,

the child may be kept in the care of that person until received into the care of the authority.

(3) While a care order is in force with respect to a child, the local authority designated by the order shall—
- (a) have parental responsibility for the child; and
- (b) have the power (subject to the following provisions of this section) to determine the extent to which[—
   - (i) a parent, guardian or special guardian of the child; or
   - (ii) a person who by virtue of section 4A has parental responsibility for the child,]

may meet his parental responsibility for him.

(4) The authority may not exercise the power in subsection (3)(b) unless they are satisfied that it is necessary to do so in order to safeguard or promote the child's welfare.

(5) Nothing in subsection (3)(b) shall prevent [a person mentioned in that provision who has care of the child] from doing what is reasonable in all the circumstances of the case for the purpose of safeguarding or promoting his welfare.

(6) While a care order is in force with respect to a child, the local authority designated by the order shall not—
- (a) cause the child to be brought up in any religious persuasion other than that in which he would have been brought up if the order had not been made; or
- (b) have the right—
   - (i) . . .
   - (ii) to agree or refuse to agree to the making of an adoption order, or an order under [section 84 of the Adoption and Children Act 2002], with respect to the child; or
   - (iii) to appoint a guardian for the child.

(7) While a care order is in force with respect to a child, no person may—
- (a) cause the child to be known by a new surname; or
- (b) remove him from the United Kingdom,

without either the written consent of every person who has parental responsibility for the child or the leave of the court.

(8) Subsection (7)(b) does not—
  (a) prevent the removal of such a child, for a period of less than one month, by the authority in whose care he is; or
  (b) apply to arrangements for such a child to live outside England and Wales (which are governed by paragraph 19 of Schedule 2 [in England, and section 124 of the Social Services and Well-being (Wales) Act 2014 in Wales]).

(9) The power in subsection (3)(b) is subject (in addition to being subject to the provisions of this section) to any right, duty, power, responsibility or authority which [a person mentioned in that provision] has in relation to the child and his property by virtue of any other enactment.

Sub-s (3): para (b)(i), (ii) substituted by the Adoption and Children Act 2002, s 139(1), Sch 3, paras 54, 63(a). Date in force: 30 December 2005: see SI 2005/2213, art 2(o).

Sub-s (5): words "a person mentioned in that provision who has care of the child" in square brackets substituted by the Adoption and Children Act 2002, s 139(1), Sch 3, paras 54, 63(b). Date in force: 30 December 2005: see SI 2005/2213, art 2(o).

Sub-s (6): para (b)(i) repealed by the Adoption and Children Act 2002, s 139(1), (3), Sch 3, paras 54, 63(c)(i), Sch 5. Date in force: 30 December 2005: see SI 2005/2213, art 2(o).

Sub-s (6): in para (b)(ii) words "section 84 of the Adoption and Children Act 2002" in square brackets substituted by the Adoption and Children Act 2002, s 139(1), Sch 3, paras 54, 63(c)(ii). Date in force: 30 December 2005: see SI 2005/2213, art 2(o).

Sub-s (8): in para (b) words from "in England, and" to "Social Services and Well-being (Wales) Act 2014 in Wales" in square brackets inserted by SI 2016/413, regs 55, 97. Date in force: 6 April 2016: see SI 2016/413, reg 2(1); for transitional provisions and savings see reg 325, Schedule.

Sub-s (9): words "a person mentioned in that provision" in square brackets substituted by the Adoption and Children Act 2002, s 139(1), Sch 3, paras 54, 63(d). Date in force: 30 December 2005: see SI 2005/2213, art 2(o).

PART XII
MISCELLANEOUS AND GENERAL

* * * * *

Jurisdiction and procedure etc

A1.451

105 Interpretation

(1) In this Act—
  ["activity condition" has the meaning given by section 11C;]
  ["activity direction" has the meaning given by section 11A;]
  "adoption agency" means a body which may be referred to as an adoption agency by virtue of [section 2 of the Adoption and Children Act 2002];
  [. . .]
  "bank holiday" means a day which is a bank holiday under the Banking and Financial Dealings Act 1971;
  ["care home" has the same meaning as in the Care Standards Act 2000;]
  "care order" has the meaning given by section 31(11) and also includes any order which by or under any enactment has the effect of, or is deemed to be, a care order for the purposes of this Act; and any reference to a child who is in the care of an authority is a reference to a child who is in their care by virtue of a care order;
  "child" means, subject to paragraph 16 of Schedule 1, a person under the age of eighteen;

["child arrangements order" has the meaning given by section 8(1);]
"child assessment order" has the meaning given by section 43(2);
"child minder" has the meaning given by section 71;
["child of the family", in relation to parties to a marriage, or to two people who are civil partners of each other, means—
  (a) a child of both of them, and
  (b) any other child, other than a child placed with them as foster parents by a local authority or voluntary organisation, who has been treated by both of them as a child of their family;]
["children's home" has the same meaning as it has for the purposes of the Care Standards Act 2000 (see section 1 of that Act);]
["clinical commissioning group" means a body established under section 14D of the National Health Service Act 2006;]
"community home" has the meaning given by section 53;
[. . .]
[. . .]
. . .
"day care" [*(except in Part XA)*] has the same meaning as in section 18;
"disabled", in relation to a child, has the same meaning as in section 17(11);
. . .
"domestic premises" has the meaning given by section 71(12);
[dwelling-house" includes—
  (a) any building or part of a building which is occupied as a dwelling;
  (b) any caravan, house-boat or structure which is occupied as a dwelling;
 and any yard, garden, garage or outhouse belonging to it and occupied with it;]
["education functions" has the meaning given by section 579(1) of the Education Act 1996;]
"education supervision order" has the meaning given in section 36;
"emergency protection order" means an order under section 44;
["enforcement order" has the meaning given by section 11J;]
"family assistance order" has the meaning given in section 16(2);
"family proceedings" has the meaning given by section 8(3);
"functions" includes powers and duties;
"guardian of a child" means a guardian (other than a guardian of the estate of a child) appointed in accordance with the provisions of section 5;
"harm" has the same meaning as in section 31(9) and the question of whether harm is significant shall be determined in accordance with section 31(10);
[. . .]
"health service hospital" [means a health service hospital within the meaning given by the National Health Service Act 2006 or the National Health Service (Wales) Act 2006];
"hospital" [*(except in Schedule 9A)*] has the same meaning as in the Mental Health Act 1983, except that it does not include a *special hospital within the meaning of that Act* [hospital at which high security psychiatric services within the meaning of that Act are provided];
"ill-treatment" has the same meaning as in section 31(9);
[*"income-based jobseeker's allowance" has the meaning as in the Jobseekers Act 1995;*]
[*"income-related employment and support allowance" means an income-related allowance under Part 1 of the Welfare Reform Act 2007 (employment and support allowance);*]
["independent hospital"—

> > (a) in relation to England, means a hospital as defined by section 275 of the National Health Service Act 2006 that is not a health service hospital as defined by that section; and
> > (b) in relation to Wales, has the same meaning as in the Care Standards Act 2000;]
>
> "independent school" has the same meaning as in [the Education Act 1996];
> "local authority" means, in relation to England . . . , the council of a county, a metropolitan district, a London Borough or the Common Council of the City of London[, in relation to Wales, the council of a county or a county borough] and, in relation to Scotland, a local authority within the meaning of section 1(2) of the Social Work (Scotland) Act 1968;
> ["local authority foster parent" means a person authorised as such in accordance with regulations made by virtue of—
> > (a) paragraph 12F of Schedule 2; or
> > (b) sections 87 and 93 of the Social Services and Well-being (Wales) Act 2014 (regulations providing for approval of local authority foster parents);]
>
> . . .
>
> ["Local Health Board" means a Local Health Board established under section 11 of the National Health Service (Wales) Act 2006;]
> "local housing authority" has the same meaning as in the Housing Act 1985;
> . . .
> . . .
>
> ["officer of the Service" has the same meaning as in the Criminal Justice and Court Services Act 2000;]
> "parental responsibility" has the meaning given in section 3;
> "parental responsibility agreement" has the meaning given in [sections 4(1)[, 4ZA(4)] and 4A(2)];
> "prescribed" means prescribed by regulations made under this Act;
> ["private children's home" means a children's home in respect of which a person is registered under Part II of the Care Standards Act 2000 which is not a community home or a voluntary home;]
> [. . .]
> "privately fostered child" and "to foster a child privately" have the same meaning as in section 66;
> "prohibited steps order" has the meaning given by section 8(1);
> . . .
> . . .
>
> "registered pupil" has the same meaning as in [the Education Act 1996];
> "relative", in relation to a child, means a grandparent, brother, sister, uncle or aunt (whether of the full blood or half blood or [by marriage or civil partnership)] or step-parent;
> . . .
> . . .
>
> "responsible person", in relation to a child who is the subject of a supervision order, has the meaning given in paragraph 1 of Schedule 3;
> "school" has the same meaning as in [the Education Act 1996] or, in relation to Scotland, in the Education (Scotland) Act 1980;
> ["section 31A plan" has the meaning given by section 31A(6);]
> "service", in relation to any provision made under Part III, includes any facility;
> "signed", in relation to any person, includes the making by that person of his mark;
> "special educational needs" has the same meaning as in [the Education Act 1996];

["special guardian" and "special guardianship order" have the meaning given by section 14A;]
["Special Health Authority" means a Special Health Authority established under [section 28 of the National Health Service Act 2006 or section 22 of the National Health Service (Wales) Act 2006,];]
"specific issue order" has the meaning given by section 8(1);
[. . .]
"supervision order" has the meaning given by section 31(11);
"supervised child" and "supervisor", in relation to a supervision order or an education supervision order, mean respectively the child who is (or is to be) under supervision and the person under whose supervision he is (or is to be) by virtue of the order;
"upbringing", in relation to any child, includes the care of the child but not his maintenance;
"voluntary home" has the meaning given by section 60;
"voluntary organisation" means a body (other than a public or local authority) whose activities are not carried on for profit;
["Welsh family proceedings officer" has the meaning given by section 35 of the Children Act 2004].

(2) References in this Act to a child whose father and mother were, or (as the case may be) were not, married to each other at the time of his birth must be read with section 1 of the Family Law Reform Act 1987 (which extends the meaning of such references).

(3) . . .

[(4) References in this Act to a child who is looked after—
- (a) in relation to a child who is looked after by a local authority in England, has the meaning given in section 22; and
- (b) in relation to a child who is looked after by a local authority in Wales, has the meaning given in section 74 of the Social Services and Well-being (Wales) Act 2014 (child or young person looked after by a local authority).]

(5) References in this Act to accommodation provided by or on behalf of a local authority are references to accommodation so provided in the exercise of functions [of that or any other local authority which are social services functions . . .].

[(5A) *References in this Act to a child minder shall be construed—*
- (a) . . . ;
- (b) *in relation to . . . Wales, in accordance with section 79A.]*

[(5B) In subsection (5) "social services functions" means—
- (a) in England, social services functions within the meaning of the Local Authority Social Services Act 1970, and
- (b) in Wales, social services functions within the meaning of the Social Services and Well-being (Wales) Act 2014.]

(6) In determining the "ordinary residence" of a child for any purpose of this Act, there shall be disregarded any period in which he lives in any place—
- (a) which is a school or other institution;
- (b) in accordance with the requirements of a supervision order under this Act . . .
- [(ba) in accordance with the requirements of a youth rehabilitation order under Part 1 of the Criminal Justice and Immigration Act 2008; or]
- (c) while he is being provided with accommodation by or on behalf of a local authority.

(7) References in this Act to children who are in need shall be construed in accordance with section 17.

A1.451 Appendix I – Statutes

[(7A) References in this Act to a hospital or accommodation made available or provided pursuant to arrangements made by the Secretary of State under the National Health Service Act 2006 are references to a hospital or accommodation made available or provided pursuant to arrangements so made in the exercise of the public health functions of the Secretary of State (within the meaning of that Act).

(7B) References in this Act to arrangements made by the National Health Service Commissioning Board or a clinical commissioning group under the National Health Service Act 2006 include references to arrangements so made by virtue of section 7A of that Act.]

(8) Any notice or other document required under this Act to be served on any person may be served on him by being delivered personally to him, or being sent by post to him in a registered letter or by the recorded delivery service at his proper address.

(9) Any such notice or other document required to be served on a body corporate or a firm shall be duly served if it is served on the secretary or clerk of that body or a partner of that firm.

(10) For the purposes of this section, and of section 7 of the Interpretation Act 1978 in its application to this section, the proper address of a person—

(a) in the case of a secretary or clerk of a body corporate, shall be that of the registered or principal office of that body;

(b) in the case of a partner of a firm, shall be that of the principal office of the firm; and

(c) in any other case, shall be the last known address of the person to be served.

Sub-s (1): definition "activity condition" inserted by the Children and Families Act 2014, s 12(4), Sch 2, Pt 1, paras 1, 38(1), (2)(a). Date in force: 22 April 2014: see SI 2014/889, art 4(b), (f).

Sub-s (1): definition "activity direction" inserted by the Children and Families Act 2014, s 12(4), Sch 2, Pt 1, paras 1, 38(1), (2)(a). Date in force: 22 April 2014: see SI 2014/889, art 4(b), (f).

Sub-s (1): in definition "adoption agency" words "section 2 of the Adoption and Children Act 2002" in square brackets substituted by the Adoption and Children Act 2002, s 139(1), Sch 3, paras 54, 70(a). Date in force: 30 December 2005: see SI 2005/2213, art 2(o).

Sub-s (1): definition "appropriate children's home" inserted by the Care Standards Act 2000, s 116, Sch 4, para 14(1), (23)(a)(i). Date in force (in relation to England): 1 April 2002: see SI 2001/4150, art 3(3)(a); for transitional provisions see SI 2001/4150, arts 3(2), 4(1), (3), (4) and SI 2002/1493, art 4 (as amended by SI 2002/1493, art 6). Date in force (in relation to Wales): 1 April 2002: see SI 2002/920, art 3(3)(d); for transitional provisions see arts 2, 3(2), (4), (6)–(10), Sch 1 thereto.

Sub-s (1): definition "appropriate children's home" (omitted) repealed by the Children and Young Persons Act 2008, ss 8(2), 42, Sch 1, para 3(1), (2), Sch 4. Date in force (in relation to England): 1 April 2011: see SI 2010/2981, art 4(a). Date in force (in relation to Wales): 6 April 2016: see SI 2016/452, art 2(b).

Sub-s (1): definition "care home" inserted by the Care Standards Act 2000, s 116, Sch 4, para 14(1), (23)(a)(ii). Date in force (in relation to England): 1 April 2002: see SI 2001/4150, art 3(3)(a); for transitional provisions see SI 2001/4150, arts 3(2), 4(1), (3), (4) and SI 2002/1493, art 4 (as amended by SI 2002/1493, art 6). Date in force (in relation to Wales): 1 April 2002: see SI 2002/920, art 3(3)(d); for transitional provisions see arts 2, 3(2), (4), (6)–(10), Sch 1 thereto.

Sub-s (1): definition "child arrangements order" inserted by the Children and Families Act 2014, s 12(4), Sch 2, Pt 1, paras 1, 38(1), (2)(b). Date in force: 22 April 2014: see SI 2014/889, art 4(b), (f).

Sub-s (1): definition "child minder" repealed by the Care Standards Act 2000, s 117(2), Sch 6. Date in force (in relation to Wales): 1 April 2002: see SI 2002/920, art 3(3)(g)(vi); for transitional provisions see arts 2, 3(2), (5)–(10), Schs 1, 2 thereto. Date in force (in relation to England): to be appointed: see the Care Standards Act 2000, s 122.

Sub-s (1): definition "child of the family" substituted by the Civil Partnership Act 2004, s 75(1), (3). Date in force: 5 December 2005: see SI 2005/3175, art 2(1), Sch 1.

Sub-s (1): definition "children's home" substituted by the Children and Young Persons Act 2008, s 8(2), Sch 1, para 3(1), (3). Date in force (in relation to England): 1 April 2011: see SI 2010/2981, art 4(a). Date in force (in relation to Wales): 6 April 2016: see SI 2016/452, art 2(b).

Sub-s (1): definition "clinical commissioning group" inserted by the Health and Social Care Act 2012, s 55(2), Sch 5, paras 47, 56(1), (2)(a). Date in force: 1 April 2013: see SI 2013/160, art 2; for transitional provisions and savings see arts 5–7 thereof.

Sub-s (1): definition "contact activity condition" (omitted) inserted by the Children and Adoption Act 2006, s 15(1), Sch 2, paras 7, 11. Date in force: 8 December 2008: see SI 2008/2870, art 2(2)(e).

Sub-s (1): definition "contact activity condition" (omitted) repealed by the Children and Families Act 2014, s 12(4), Sch 2, Pt 1, paras 1, 38(1), (2)(c). Date in force: 22 April 2014: see SI 2014/889, art 4(b), (f).

Sub-s (1): definition "contact activity direction" (omitted) inserted by the Children and Adoption Act 2006, s 15(1), Sch 2, paras 7, 11. Date in force: 8 December 2008: see SI 2008/2870, art 2(2)(e).

Sub-s (1): definition "contact activity direction" (omitted) repealed by the Children and Families Act 2014, s 12(4), Sch 2, Pt 1, paras 1, 38(1), (2)(c). Date in force: 22 April 2014: see SI 2014/889, art 4(b), (f).

Sub-s (1): definition "contact order" (omitted) repealed by the Children and Families Act 2014, s 12(4), Sch 2, Pt 1, paras 1, 38(1), (2)(c). Date in force: 22 April 2014: see SI 2014/889, art 4(b), (f).

Sub-s (1): in definition "day care" words "(except in Part XA)" in square brackets inserted by the Care Standards Act 2000, s 116, Sch 4, para 14(1), (23)(a)(iv). Date in force (in relation to England): 2 July 2001: see SI 2001/2041, art 2(1)(d)(ii). Date in force (in relation to Wales): 1 April 2002: see SI 2002/920, art 3(3)(d); for transitional provisions see arts 2, 3(2), (4), (6)–(10), Schs 1, 2 thereto.

Sub-s (1): in definition "day care" words "(except in Part XA)" in italics repealed, in relation to Wales, by the Children and Families (Wales) Measure 2010, s 72, Sch 1, paras 5, 7(a)(i). Date in force: 1 April 2011: see SI 2010/2582, art 2, Sch 1; for savings see art 4, Schs 2, 3 thereto.

Sub-s (1): definition "district health authority" (omitted) repealed by the Health Authorities Act 1995, ss 2(1), 5(1), Sch 1, para 118(10)(a), Sch 3.

Sub-s (1): definition "dwelling house" inserted by the Family Law Act 1996, s 52, Sch 6, para 5. Date in force: 1 October 1997: see SI 1997/1892, art 3(1)(a).

Sub-s (1): definition "education functions" inserted by SI 2010/1158, art 5(1), Sch 2, Pt 2, para 37(1), (13)(a). Date in force: 5 May 2010: see SI 2010/1158, art 1.

Sub-s (1): definition "enforcement order" inserted by the Children and Adoption Act 2006, s 15(1), Sch 2, paras 7, 11. Date in force: 8 December 2008: see SI 2008/2870, art 2(2)(e).

Sub-s (1): definition "Health Authority" (omitted) repealed by the National Health Service (Consequential Provisions) Act 2006, s 2, Sch 1, paras 124, 125(a). Date in force: 1 March 2007: see the National Health Service (Consequential Provisions) Act 2006, s 8(2).

Sub-s (1): in definition "health service hospital" words from "means a health" to "National Health Service (Wales) Act 2006" in square brackets substituted by the National Health Service (Consequential Provisions) Act 2006, s 2, Sch 1, paras 124, 125(b). Date in force: 1 March 2007: see the National Health Service (Consequential Provisions) Act 2006, s 8(2).

Sub-s (1): in definition "hospital" words "(except in Schedule 9A)" in square brackets inserted by the Care Standards Act 2000, s 116, Sch 4, para 14(1), (23)(a)(v). Date in force (in relation to England): 2 July 2001: see SI 2001/2041, art 2(1)(d)(ii). Date in force (in relation to Wales): 1 April 2002: see SI 2002/920, art 3(3)(d); for transitional provisions see arts 2, 3(2), (4), (6)–(10), Schs 1, 2 thereto.

Sub-s (1): in definition "hospital" words "(except in Schedule 9A)" in italics repealed, in relation to Wales, by the Children and Families (Wales) Measure 2010, s 72, Sch 1, paras 5, 7(a)(ii). Date in force: 1 April 2011: see SI 2010/2582, art 2, Sch 1; for savings see art 4, Schs 2, 3 thereto.

Sub-s (1): in definition "hospital" words "special hospital within the meaning of that Act" in italics repealed and subsequent words in square brackets substituted, in relation to England and Wales only, by SI 2000/90, arts 2(1), 3(2), Sch 2, para 5. Date in force: 1 April 2000: see SI 2000/90, art 1.

Sub-s (1): definition "income-based jobseeker's allowance" inserted by the Jobseekers Act 1995, s 41(4), Sch 2, para 19(4).

A1.451 *Appendix I – Statutes*

Sub-s (1): definition "income-based jobseeker's allowance" repealed by the Welfare Reform Act 2012, s 147, Sch 14, Pt 1. Date in force: to be appointed: see the Welfare Reform Act 2012, s 150(3).

Sub-s (1): definition "income-related employment and support allowance" inserted, in relation to England and Wales, by the Welfare Reform Act 2007, s 28(1), Sch 3, para 6(1), (5). Date in force: 27 October 2008: see SI 2008/787, art 2(4)(b), (f).

Sub-s (1): definition "income-related employment and support allowance" repealed by the Welfare Reform Act 2012, s 147, Sch 14, Pt 1. Date in force: to be appointed: see the Welfare Reform Act 2012, s 150(3).

Sub-s (1): definition "independent hospital" (as inserted by the Care Standards Act 2000, s 116, Sch 4, para 14(1), (23)(a)(vi)) substituted by SI 2010/813, art 7(1), (3). Date in force: 1 October 2010: see SI 2010/813, art 1.

Sub-s (1): in definitions "independent school", "registered pupil", "school" and "special educational needs" words "the Education Act 1996" in square brackets substituted by the Education Act 1996, s 582(1), Sch 37, para 91.

Sub-s (1): in definition "local authority" words omitted repealed by the Local Government (Wales) Act 1994, ss 22(4), 66(8), Sch 10, para 13, Sch 18.

Sub-s (1): in definition "local authority" words ", in relation to Wales, the council of a county or a county borough" in square brackets inserted by the Local Government (Wales) Act 1994, ss 22(4), 66(8), Sch 10, para 13.

Sub-s (1): definition "local authority foster parent" substituted by SI 2016/413, regs 55, 106(a). Date in force: 6 April 2016: see SI 2016/413, reg 2(1); for transitional provisions and savings see reg 325, Schedule.

Sub-s (1): definition "local education authority" (omitted) repealed by SI 2010/1158, art 5(1), (2), Sch 2, Pt 2, para 37(1), (13)(b), Sch 3, Pt 2. Date in force: 5 May 2010: see SI 2010/1158, art 1.

Sub-s (1): definition "Local Health Board" inserted by SI 2007/961, art 3, Schedule, para 20(1), (3). Date in force: 1 April 2007: see SI 2007/961, art 1(1).

Sub-s (1): definition "mental nursing home" (omitted) repealed by the Care Standards Act 2000, s 117(2), Sch 6. Date in force (in relation to England): 1 April 2002: see SI 2001/4150, art 3(3)(c)(viii); for transitional provisions see SI 2001/4150, arts 3(2), 4(1)–(3), (5) and SI 2002/1493, art 4 (as amended by SI 2002/1493, art 6). Date in force (in relation to Wales): 1 April 2002: see SI 2002/920, art 3(3)(g)(vi); for transitional provisions see arts 2, 3(2), (5)–(10), Sch 1 thereto.

Sub-s (1): definition "nursing home" (omitted) repealed by the Care Standards Act 2000, s 117(2), Sch 6. Date in force (in relation to England): 1 April 2002: see SI 2001/4150, art 3(3)(c)(viii); for transitional provisions see SI 2001/4150, arts 3(2), 4(1)–(3), (5) and SI 2002/1493, art 4 (as amended by SI 2002/1493, art 6). Date in force (in relation to Wales): 1 April 2002: see SI 2002/920, art 3(3)(g)(vi); for transitional provisions see arts 2, 3(2), (5)–(10), Sch 1 thereto.

Sub-s (1): definition "officer of the Service" inserted by the Criminal Justice and Court Services Act 2000, s 74, Sch 7, Pt II, paras 87, 95. Date in force: 1 April 2001: see SI 2001/919, art 2(f)(ii).

Sub-s (1): in definition "parental responsibility agreement" words "sections 4(1) and 4A(2)" in square brackets substituted by the Adoption and Children Act 2002, s 139(1), Sch 3, paras 54, 70(c). Date in force: 30 December 2005: see SI 2005/2213, art 2(o).

Sub-s (1): in definition "parental responsibility agreement" reference to ", 4ZA(4)" in square brackets inserted by the Human Fertilisation and Embryology Act 2008, s 56, Sch 6, Pt 1, para 31. Date in force (for certain purposes): 6 April 2009: see SI 2009/479, art 6(1)(e). Date in force (for remaining purposes): 1 September 2009: see SI 2009/479, art 6(2).

Sub-s (1): definition "private children's home" inserted by the Care Standards Act 2000, s 116, Sch 4, para 14(1), (23)(a)(vii). Date in force (in relation to England): 1 April 2002: see SI 2001/4150, art 3(3)(a); for transitional provisions see SI 2001/4150, arts 3(2), 4(1), (3), (4) and SI 2002/1493, art 4 (as amended by SI 2002/1493, art 6). Date in force (in relation to Wales): 1 April 2002: see SI 2002/920, art 3(3)(d); for transitional provisions see arts 2, 3(2), (4), (6)–(10), Sch 1 thereto.

Sub-s (1): definition "Primary Care Trust" (omitted) inserted, in relation to England and Wales only, by SI 2000/90, arts 2(1), 3(1), Sch 1, para 24(1), (10). Date in force: 8 February 2000: see SI 2000/90, art 1.

Sub-s (1): definition "Primary Care Trust" (omitted) repealed by the Health and Social Care Act 2012, s 55(2), Sch 5, paras 47, 56(1), (2)(b). Date in force: 1 April 2013: see SI 2013/160, art 2; for transitional provisions and savings see arts 5–7 thereof.

Sub-s (1): definition "protected child" (omitted) repealed by the Adoption and Children Act 2002, s 139(1), (3), Sch 3, paras 54, 70(d), Sch 5. Date in force: 30 December 2005: see SI 2005/2213, art 2(o).

Sub-s (1): definition "registered children's home" (omitted) repealed by the Care Standards Act 2000, s 117(2), Sch 6. Date in force (in relation to England): 1 April 2002: see SI 2001/4150, art 3(3)(c)(viii); for transitional provisions see SI 2001/4150, arts 3(2), 4(1)–(3), (5) and SI 2002/1493, art 4 (as amended by SI 2002/1493, art 6). Date in force (in relation to Wales): 1 April 2002: see SI 2002/920, art 3(3)(g)(vi); for transitional provisions see arts 2, 3(2), (5)–(10), Schs 1, 3 thereto.

Sub-s (1): in definition "relative" words "by marriage or civil partnership)" in square brackets substituted by the Civil Partnership Act 2004, s 75(1), (4). Date in force: 5 December 2005: see SI 2005/3175, art 2(1), Sch 1.

Sub-s (1): definition "residence order" (omitted) repealed by the Children and Families Act 2014, s 12(4), Sch 2, Pt 1, paras 1, 38(1), (2)(c). Date in force: 22 April 2014: see SI 2014/889, art 4(b), (f).

Sub-s (1): definition "residential care home" (omitted) repealed by the Care Standards Act 2000, s 117(2), Sch 6. Date in force (in relation to England): 1 April 2002: see SI 2001/4150, art 3(3)(c)(viii); for transitional provisions see SI 2001/4150, arts 3(2), 4(1)–(3), (5) and SI 2002/1493, art 4 (as amended by SI 2002/1493, art 6). Date in force (in relation to Wales): 1 April 2002: see SI 2002/920, art 3(3)(g)(vi); for transitional provisions see arts 2, 3(2), (5)–(10), Sch 1 thereto.

Sub-s (1): definition "section 31A plan" inserted by the Adoption and Children Act 2002, s 139(1), Sch 3, paras 54, 70(b). Date in force: 30 December 2005: see SI 2005/2213, art 2(o).

Sub-s (1): definition "special guardian" and "special guardianship order" inserted by the Adoption and Children Act 2002, s 139(1), Sch 3, paras 54, 70(e). Date in force: 30 December 2005: see SI 2005/2213, art 2(o).

Sub-s (1): definition "Special Health Authority" substituted by the Health Authorities Act 1995, ss 2(1), 5(1), Sch 1, para 118(10)(c).

Sub-s (1): in definition "Special Health Authority" words from "section 28 of" to "National Health Service (Wales) Act 2006," in square brackets substituted by the National Health Service (Consequential Provisions) Act 2006, s 2, Sch 1, paras 124, 125(d). Date in force: 1 March 2007: see the National Health Service (Consequential Provisions) Act 2006, s 8(2).

Sub-s (1): definition "Strategic Health Authority" (omitted) inserted by SI 2002/2469, reg 4, Sch 1, Pt 1, para 16(1), (3). Date in force: 1 October 2002: see SI 2002/2469, reg 1.

Sub-s (1): definition "Strategic Health Authority" (omitted) repealed by the Health and Social Care Act 2012, s 55(2), Sch 5, paras 47, 56(1), (2)(c). Date in force: 1 April 2013: see SI 2013/160, art 2; for transitional provisions and savings see arts 5–7 thereof.

Sub-s (1): definition "Welsh family proceedings officer" inserted by the Children Act 2004, s 40, Sch 3, paras 5, 11. Date in force: 1 April 2005: by virtue of SI 2005/700, art 2(2).

Sub-s (3): repealed by the Children and Families Act 2014, s 12(4), Sch 2, Pt 1, paras 1, 38(1), (3). Date in force: 22 April 2014: see SI 2014/889, art 4(b), (f).

Sub-s (4): substituted by SI 2016/413, regs 55, 106(b). Date in force: 6 April 2016: see SI 2016/413, reg 2(1); for transitional provisions and savings see reg 325, Schedule.

Sub-s (5): words from "of that or any other" to "within the meaning of" in square brackets substituted by the Local Government Act 2000, s 107, Sch 5, para 22. Date in force (in relation to England): 26 October 2000: see SI 2000/2849, art 2(f). Date in force (in relation to Wales): 28 July 2001 (unless the National Assembly for Wales by order provides for this amendment to come into force before that date): see the Local Government Act 2000, s 108(4), (6)(b).

Sub-s (5): words omitted repealed by SI 2016/413, regs 55, 106(c). Date in force: 6 April 2016: see SI 2016/413, reg 2(1); for transitional provisions and savings see reg 325, Schedule.

Sub-s (5A): inserted by the Care Standards Act 2000, s 116, Sch 4, para 14(1), (23)(b). Date in force (in relation to England): 2 July 2001: see SI 2001/2041, art 2(1)(d)(ii). Date in force (in relation to Wales): 1 April 2002: see SI 2002/920, art 3(3)(d); for transitional provisions see arts 2, 3(2), (4), (6)–(10), Schs 1, 2 thereto.

Sub-s (5A): repealed, in relation to Wales, by the Children and Families (Wales) Measure 2010, ss 72, 73, Sch 1, paras 5, 7(b), Sch 2. Date in force: 1 April 2011: see SI 2010/2582, arts 2, 4, Schs 1, 2; for savings see art 4, Sch 2 thereto.

Sub-s (5A): para (a) repealed, in relation to Scotland, by the Regulation of Care (Scotland) Act 2001, s 79, Sch 3, paras 15(1), (2)(a). Date in force: 1 April 2002: see the Regulation of Care

A1.451 *Appendix I – Statutes*

(Scotland) Act 2001, s 81(2) and SSI 2002/162, arts 1(2), 2(f), (h); for transitional provisions see SSI 2002/162, arts 3, 4(6), (9), (10), 7, 8(c), 12, 13.

Sub-s (5A): in para (b) words omitted repealed by the Childcare Act 2006, s 103, Sch 2, para 17, Sch 3, Pt 2. Date in force: 1 September 2008: see SI 2008/2261, art 2; for transitional provisions and savings see arts 3, 4, Schs 1, 2 thereto.

Sub-s (5B): inserted in relation to England and Wales by SI 2016/413, reg 106(d); a corresponding amendment has been made in relation to Scotland by the Regulation of Care (Scotland) Act 2001, s 79, Sch 3, paras 15(1), (2)(b). Date in force (in relation to Scotland): 1 April 2002: see the Regulation of Care (Scotland) Act 2001, s 81(2) and SSI 2002/162, arts 1(2), 2(f), (h); for transitional provisions see SSI 2002/162, arts 3, 4(6), (9), (10), 7, 8(c), 12, 13. Date in force (in relation to England and Wales): 6 April 2016: see SI 2016/413, reg 2(1).

Sub-s (6): in para (b) words omitted repealed by the Criminal Justice and Immigration Act 2008, ss 6(2), 149, Sch 4, Pt 1, paras 33, 36(a), Sch 28, Pt 1. Date in force: 30 November 2009: see SI 2009/3074, art 2(f), (k), (l), (p)(v), (t)(i), (u)(xi); for transitional provisions and savings see the Criminal Justice and Immigration Act 2008, s 148(2), Sch 27, Pt 1, paras 1(1), 5.

Sub-s (6): para (ba) inserted by the Criminal Justice and Immigration Act 2008, s 6(2), Sch 4, Pt 1, paras 33, 36(b). Date in force: 30 November 2009: see SI 2009/3074, art 2(f), (k), (p)(v), (t)(i); for transitional provisions and savings see the Criminal Justice and Immigration Act 2008, s 148(2), Sch 27, Pt 1, paras 1(1), 5.

Sub-ss (7A), (7B): inserted by the Health and Social Care Act 2012, s 55(2), Sch 5, paras 47, 55(1), (3). Date in force: 1 April 2013: see SI 2013/160, art 2; for transitional provisions and savings see arts 5–7 thereof.

COURTS AND LEGAL SERVICES ACT 1990

(1990, c 41)

[1 November 1990]

PART II
LEGAL SERVICES

Licensed conveyancers

A1.469

53 The Council for Licensed Conveyancers

[(1) The Council for Licensed Conveyancers has the powers necessary to enable it to become designated as an approved regulator in relation to one or more of the reserved legal activities within subsection (1A).

(1A) The reserved legal activities to which this subsection applies are—
    (a)   the exercise of a right of audience;
    (b)   the conduct of litigation;
    (c)   probate activities.

(2) If the Council becomes an approved regulator in relation to one or more of those activities, it may, in that capacity, authorise a person to carry on a relevant activity . . . .

(3) Where the Council authorises [a person] to carry on a relevant activity, it is to do so by issuing a licence to [the person in respect of that activity].]

(4) [If the person granted a licence under this section is a licensed conveyancer, the] licence may be granted as a separate licence or as part of a composite licence comprising the licensed conveyancer's licence issued under Part II of the Administration of Justice Act 1985 and any other licence which the Council may grant to the licensed conveyancer concerned.

[(4A) If the person granted a licence under this section is not a licensed conveyancer, the licence may be granted as a separate licence or as part of a composite licence comprising that and any other licence under this section which the Council may grant to the person.

(4B) A licence under this section granted to a person who is not a licensed conveyancer ceases to have effect if the person becomes a licensed conveyancer.]

(5) . . .

[(6) Where the Council exercises any of its powers in connection with—
- (a) an application for designation as an approved regulator in relation to a reserved legal activity within subsection (1A), or
- (b) the authorising of a person to carry on a relevant activity,

it is to do so subject to any requirements to which it is subject in accordance with the provisions of the Legal Services Act 2007.]

(7) Schedule 8 makes further provision in connection with the powers given to the Council by this section and the provision made by the Act of 1985 in relation to licensed conveyancers, including amendments of Part II of that Act.

(8) The [Lord Chancellor] may by order make such—
- (a) amendments of, or modifications to, the provisions of Part II of the Act of 1985; or
- (b) transitional or consequential provision,

as he considers necessary or expedient in connection with the provision made by this section and Schedule 8.

(9) Subject to any provision made by this section, Schedule 8 or any order made by the [Lord Chancellor] under subsection (8), the provisions of Part II of the Act of 1985 shall, with the necessary modifications, apply with respect to [persons who apply for, or hold, an advocacy, litigation or probate licence and]—
- (a) any application for an advocacy, litigation or probate licence;
- (b) any such licence;
- (c) the practice of any [person] which is carried on by virtue of any such licence;
- (d) rules made by the Council under Schedule 8;
- [(da) any case of an individual who describes himself or herself, or holds himself or herself out, as a licensed CLC practitioner without holding a licence in force under this section;]
- (e) . . .
- (f) any other matter dealt with by this section or Schedule 8,

as they apply with respect to [persons who apply for, or hold, a licence under Part 2 of the Act of 1985 and] the corresponding matters dealt with by Part II of that Act.

[(9A) The modifications mentioned in subsection (9) may differ depending on whether the person applying for, or holding, an advocacy, litigation or probate licence is or is not a licensed conveyancer.

(9B) Subsection (9) does not apply to section 34 of the Act of 1985 (modification of existing enactments relating to conveyancing etc).]

[(10) For the purposes of this section—
- (a) "right of audience", "conduct of litigation", "probate activities" and "reserved legal activity" have the same meaning as in the Legal Services Act 2007;
- (b) references to designation as an approved regulator are to designation as an approved regulator—
  - (i) by Part 1 of Schedule 4 to the Legal Services Act 2007, by virtue of an order under paragraph 5 of Schedule 22 to that Act, or
  - (ii) under Part 2 of Schedule 4 to that Act;
- (c) "relevant activity" means an activity which is a reserved legal activity—

(i) which is within subsection (1A), and
(ii) in relation to which the Council is designated as an approved regulator by Part 1 of Schedule 4 to that Act (by virtue of an order under paragraph 5 of Schedule 22 to that Act) or under Part 2 of that Schedule.]

[(11) In this section—

"advocacy licence" means a licence issued under this section by which the Council authorises the person concerned to exercise a right of audience;

"CLC practitioner services" has the same meaning as in section 32B of the Act of 1985;

"licensed CLC practitioner" means a person, other than a licensed conveyancer, who holds a licence under this section;

"litigation licence" means a licence issued under this section by which the Council authorises the person concerned to carry on activities which constitute the conduct of litigation;

"the practice of a licensed CLC practitioner" means the provision by a person, as the holder of a licence under this section, of CLC practitioner services in accordance with the licence; and

"probate licence" means a licence issued under this section by which the Council authorises the person concerned to carry on activities that constitute probate activities.]

Sub-ss (1), (1A), (2), (3): substituted, for sub-ss (1)–(3) as originally enacted, by the Legal Services Act 2007, s 182, Sch 17, Pt 2, paras 33, 34(1), (2). Date in force: 1 January 2010: see SI 2009/3250, art 2(f)(iii).

Sub-s (2): words omitted repealed by the Deregulation Act 2015, s 87(1), (2). Date in force: 29 June 2015: see SI 2015/1402, art 2(a).

Sub-s (3): words "a person" in square brackets substituted by the Deregulation Act 2015, s 87(1), (3)(a). Date in force: 29 June 2015: see SI 2015/1402, art 2(a).

Sub-s (3): words "the person in respect of that activity" in square brackets substituted by the Deregulation Act 2015, s 87(1), (3)(b). Date in force: 29 June 2015: see SI 2015/1402, art 2(a).

Sub-s (4): words from "If the person" to "licensed conveyancer, the" in square brackets substituted by the Deregulation Act 2015, s 87(1), (4). Date in force: 29 June 2015: see SI 2015/1402, art 2(a).

Sub-ss (4A), (4B): inserted by the Deregulation Act 2015, s 87(1), (5). Date in force: 29 June 2015: see SI 2015/1402, art 2(a).

Sub-s (5): repealed by the Legal Services Act 2007, ss 182, 210, Sch 17, Pt 2, paras 33, 34(1), (3), Sch 23. Date in force: 1 January 2010: see SI 2009/3250, art 2(f)(iii).

Sub-s (6): substituted by the Legal Services Act 2007, s 182, Sch 17, Pt 2, paras 33, 34(1), (4). Date in force: 1 January 2010: see SI 2009/3250, art 2(f)(iii).

Sub-s (8): words "Lord Chancellor" in square brackets substituted by the Legal Services Act 2007, s 182, Sch 17, Pt 2, paras 33, 34(1), (5). Date in force: 31 March 2009: see SI 2009/503, art 2(c)(ii).

Sub-s (9): words "Lord Chancellor" in square brackets substituted by the Legal Services Act 2007, s 182, Sch 17, Pt 2, paras 33, 34(1), (6)(a). Date in force: 31 March 2009: see SI 2009/503, art 2(c)(ii).

Sub-s (9): words from "persons who apply" to "probate licence and" in square brackets inserted by the Deregulation Act 2015, s 87(1), (6)(a). Date in force: 29 June 2015: see SI 2015/1402, art 2(a).

Sub-s (9): in para (c) word "person" in square brackets substituted by the Deregulation Act 2015, s 87(1), (6)(b). Date in force: 29 June 2015: see SI 2015/1402, art 2(a).

Sub-s (9): para (da) inserted by the Deregulation Act 2015, s 87(1), (6)(c). Date in force: 29 June 2015: see SI 2015/1402, art 2(a).

Sub-s (9): para (e) repealed by the Legal Services Act 2007, ss 182, 210, Sch 17, Pt 2, paras 33, 34(1), (6)(b), Sch 23. Date in force: 31 March 2009: see SI 2009/503, art 2(c)(ii).

Sub-s (9): words from "persons who apply" to "of 1985 and" in square brackets inserted by the Deregulation Act 2015, s 87(1), (6)(d). Date in force: 29 June 2015: see SI 2015/1402, art 2(a).

Sub-ss (9A), (9B): inserted by the Deregulation Act 2015, s 87(1), (7). Date in force: 29 June 2015: see SI 2015/1402, art 2(a).

Sub-s (10): inserted by the Legal Services Act 2007, s 182, Sch 17, Pt 2, paras 33, 34(1), (7). Date in force: 1 January 2010: see SI 2009/3250, art 2(f)(iii).

Sub-s (11): inserted by the Deregulation Act 2015, s 87(1), (8). Date in force: 29 June 2015: see SI 2015/1402, art 2(a).

ADOPTION AND CHILDREN ACT 2002

(2002, c 38)

[7th November 2002]

CHAPTER 3

PLACEMENT FOR ADOPTION AND ADOPTION ORDERS
Placement and adoption: general

A1.508

53 Modification of 1989 Act [and 2014 Act] in relation to adoption

(1) Where—

    (a)   a local authority are authorised to place a child for adoption, or

    (b)   a child who has been placed for adoption by a local authority is less than six weeks old,

regulations may provide for the following provisions . . . to apply with modifications, or not to apply, in relation to the child.

[(2) The provisions are—

    (a)   section 22(4)(b), (c) and (d) and (5)(b) of the 1989 Act (duty to ascertain wishes and feelings of certain persons);

    (b)   sections 6(4)(b) and 78(3)(a) of the 2014 Act (duty to ascertain wishes and feelings of certain persons);

    (c)   paragraphs 15 and 21 of Schedule 2 to the 1989 Act (promoting contact with parents and parents' obligations to contribute towards maintenance);

    (d)   section 95 of and paragraph 1 of Schedule 1 to the 2014 Act (promoting contact with parents and parents' obligations to contribute towards maintenance).]

(3) Where a registered adoption society is authorised to place a child for adoption or a child who has been placed for adoption by a registered adoption society is less than six weeks old, regulations may provide—

    (a)   for section 61 of [the 1989 Act] to have effect in relation to the child whether or not he is accommodated by or on behalf of the society,

    (b)   for subsections (2)(b) to (d) and (3)(b) of that section (duty to ascertain wishes and feelings of certain persons) to apply with modifications, or not to apply, in relation to the child.

(4) Where a child's home is with persons who have given notice of intention to adopt, no contribution is payable (whether under a contribution order or otherwise) under Part 3 of Schedule 2 to [the 1989 Act (contributions towards maintenance of

A1.508 *Appendix I – Statutes*

children looked after by local authorities) or under Schedule 1 to the 2014 Act (contributions towards maintenance of looked after children)] in respect of the period referred to in subsection (5).

(5) That period begins when the notice of intention to adopt is given and ends if—
   (a) the period of four months beginning with the giving of the notice expires without the prospective adopters applying for an adoption order, or
   (b) an application for such an order is withdrawn or refused.

(6) In this section, "notice of intention to adopt" includes notice of intention to apply for a Scottish or Northern Irish adoption order.

Section heading: words "and 2014 Act" in square brackets inserted by SI 2016/413, regs 188, 197(e). Date in force: 6 April 2016: see SI 2016/413, reg 2(1); for transitional provisions and savings see reg 325, Schedule.

Sub-s (1): words omitted repealed by SI 2016/413, regs 188, 197(a). Date in force: 6 April 2016: see SI 2016/413, reg 2(1); for transitional provisions and savings see reg 325, Schedule.

Sub-s (2): substituted by SI 2016/413, regs 188, 197(b). Date in force: 6 April 2016: see SI 2016/413, reg 2(1); for transitional provisions and savings see reg 325, Schedule.

Sub-s (3): in para (a) words "the 1989 Act" in square brackets substituted by SI 2016/413, regs 188, 197(c). Date in force: 6 April 2016: see SI 2016/413, reg 2(1); for transitional provisions and savings see reg 325, Schedule.

Sub-s (4): words from "the 1989 Act" to "looked after children)" in square brackets substituted by SI 2016/413, regs 188, 197(d). Date in force: 6 April 2016: see SI 2016/413, reg 2(1); for transitional provisions and savings see reg 325, Schedule.

See further, the application of this section, with modifications, in relation to an external adoption order effected within the period of six months of the making of the adoption, and in respect of adoptions under the 1993 Hague Convention on Protection of Children and Co-operation in respect of Intercountry Adoption: the Adoptions with a Foreign Element Regulations 2005, SI 2005/392, regs 11(1)(q), 52, 55.

A1.537

SCHEDULE 6
GLOSSARY

Section 147

In this Act, the expressions listed in the left-hand column below have the meaning given by, or are to be interpreted in accordance with, the provisions of this Act or (where stated) of the 1989 Act [or the 2014 Act] listed in the right-hand column.

Expression	*Provision*
the 1989 Act	section 2(5)
[the 2014 Act	section 2(5)]
Adopted Children Register	section 77
Adoption and Children Act Register	section 125
adoption (in relation to Chapter 4 of Part 1)	section 66
adoption agency	section 2(1)
adoption agency placing a child for adoption	section 18(5)
Adoption Contact Register	section 80
adoption order	section 46(1)
Adoption Service	section 2(1)
adoption society	section 2(5)
adoption support agency	section 8

Expression	Provision
adoption support services	section 2(6)
appointed day (in relation to Chapter 4 of Part 1)	section 66(2)
appropriate Minister	section 144
Assembly	section 144
body	section 144
by virtue of	section 144
care order	section 105(1) of the 1989 Act
child	sections 49(5) and 144
[child arrangements order	section 8(1) of the 1989 Act]
child assessment order	section 43(2) of the 1989 Act
child in the care of a local authority	section 105(1) of the 1989 Act
[child looked after by a local authority (in relation to a local authority in England)	section 22 of the 1989 Act
child looked after by a local authority (in relation to a local authority in Wales)	section 74 of the 2014 Act]
child placed for adoption by an adoption agency	section 18(5)
child to be adopted, adopted child	section 49(5)
consent (in relation to making adoption orders or placing for adoption)	section 52
the Convention	section 144
Convention adoption	section 66(1)(c)
Convention adoption order	section 144
Convention country	section 144
couple	section 144(4)
court	section 144
disposition (in relation to Chapter 4 of Part 1)	section 73
enactment	section 144
fee	section 144
guardian	section 144
information	section 144
interim care order	section 38 of the 1989 Act
local authority	section 144
[local authority foster parent	section 105(1) of the 1989 Act]
Northern Irish adoption agency	section 144
Northern Irish adoption order	section 144
notice	section 144
notice of intention to adopt	section 44(2)
overseas adoption	section 87
parental responsibility	section 3 of the 1989 Act
partner, in relation to a parent of a child	section 144(7)
placement order	section 21
placing, or placed, for adoption	sections 18(5) and 19(4)

A1.537 *Appendix I – Statutes*

Expression	*Provision*
prohibited steps order	section 8(1) of the 1989 Act
records (in relation to Chapter 5 of Part 1)	section 82
registered adoption society	section 2(2)
registers of live-births (in relation to Chapter 5 of Part 1)	section 82
registration authority (in Part 1)	section 144
regulations	section 144
relative	section 144, read with section 1(8)
...	...
rules	section 144
Scottish adoption agency	section 144(3)
Scottish adoption order	section 144
specific issue order	section 8(1) of the 1989 Act
subordinate legislation	section 144
supervision order	section 31(11) of the 1989 Act
unitary authority	section 144
voluntary organisation	section 2(5)

Words "or the 2014 Act" in square brackets inserted by SI 2016/413, regs 188, 198(a). Date in force: 6 April 2016: see SI 2016/413, reg 2(1); for transitional provisions and savings see reg 325, Schedule.

Entry "the 2014 Act" inserted by SI 2016/413, regs 188, 198(b). Date in force: 6 April 2016: see SI 2016/413, reg 2(1); for transitional provisions and savings see reg 325, Schedule.

Entry "child arrangements order" inserted by the Children and Families Act 2014, s 12(4), Sch 2, Pt 2, paras 59, 65(1), (2). Date in force: 22 April 2014: see SI 2014/889, art 4(b), (f).

Entries "child looked after by a local authority (in relation to a local authority in England)" and "child looked after by a local authority (in relation to a local authority in Wales)" substituted, for definition "child looked after by a local authority" as originally enacted, by SI 2016/413, regs 188, 198(c). Date in force: 6 April 2016: see SI 2016/413, reg 2(1); for transitional provisions and savings see reg 325, Schedule.

Entry "local authority foster parent" substituted by SI 2016/413, regs 188, 198(d). Date in force: 6 April 2016: see SI 2016/413, reg 2(1); for transitional provisions and savings see reg 325, Schedule.

In entry relating to "local authority foster parent" reference to "23(3)" in italics repealed and subsequent reference in square brackets substituted by the Children and Young Persons Act 2008, s 8(2), Sch 1, para 14. Date in force (in relation to England): 1 April 2011: see SI 2010/2981, art 4(a). Date in force (in relation to Wales): to be appointed: see the Children and Young Persons Act 2008, s 44(3), (4), (5)(a).

Entry "residence order" (omitted) repealed by the Children and Families Act 2014, s 12(4), Sch 2, Pt 2, paras 59, 65(1), (3). Date in force: 22 April 2014: see SI 2014/889, art 4(b), (f).

MARRIAGE (SAME SEX COUPLES) ACT 2013

2013 Chapter 30

[17th July 2013]

PART 1

MARRIAGE OF SAME SEX COUPLES IN ENGLAND AND WALES

Other provisions relating to marriages of same sex couples

9 Conversion of civil partnership into marriage

(1) The parties to an England and Wales civil partnership may convert their civil partnership into a marriage under a procedure established by regulations made by the Secretary of State.

(2) The parties to a civil partnership within subsection (3) may convert their civil partnership into a marriage under a procedure established by regulations made by the Secretary of State.

(3) A civil partnership is within this subsection if—

    (a) it was formed outside the United Kingdom under an Order in Council made under Chapter 1 of Part 5 of the Civil Partnership Act 2004 (registration at British consulates etc or by armed forces personnel), and

    (b) the part of the United Kingdom that was relevant for the purposes of section 210(2)(b) or (as the case may be) section 211(2)(b) of that Act was England and Wales.

(4) Regulations under this section may in particular make—

    (a) provision about the making by the parties to a civil partnership of an application to convert their civil partnership into a marriage;

    (b) provision about the information to be provided in support of an application to convert;

    (c) provision about the making of declarations in support of an application to convert;

    (d) provision for persons who have made an application to convert to appear before any person or attend at any place;

    (e) provision conferring functions in connection with applications to convert on relevant officials, relevant armed forces personnel, the Secretary of State, or any other persons;

    (f) provision for fees, of such amounts as are specified in or determined in accordance with the regulations, to be payable in respect of—

        (i) the making of an application to convert;

        (ii) the exercise of any function conferred by virtue of paragraph (e).

(5) Functions conferred by virtue of paragraph (e) of subsection (4) may include functions relating to—

    (a) the recording of information on the conversion of civil partnerships;

    (b) the issuing of certified copies of any information recorded;

    [(ba) the carrying out, on request, of searches of any information recorded and the provision, on request, of records of any information recorded (otherwise than in the form of certified copies);]

    (c) the conducting of services or ceremonies (other than religious services or ceremonies) following the conversion of a civil partnership.

[(5A) Subsection (5B) applies where regulations under this section provide for a fee to be payable to a superintendent registrar or registrar.

(5B) The regulations may provide for such part of the fee as may be specified in or determined in accordance with the regulations to be payable by the superintendent registrar or registrar to the Registrar General in such circumstances as may be set out in the regulations.

(5C) The regulations may provide for the reduction, waiver or refund of part or all of a fee whether by conferring a discretion or otherwise.]

(6) Where a civil partnership is converted into a marriage under this section—
- (a) the civil partnership ends on the conversion, and
- (b) the resulting marriage is to be treated as having subsisted since the date the civil partnership was formed.

(7) In this section—

"England and Wales civil partnership" means a civil partnership which is formed by two people registering as civil partners of each other in England or Wales (see Part 2 of the Civil Partnership Act 2004);

"relevant armed forces personnel" means—
- (a) a member of Her Majesty's forces;
- (b) a civilian subject to service discipline (within the meaning of the Armed Forces Act 2006);

and for this purpose "Her Majesty's forces" has the same meaning as in the Armed Forces Act 2006;

"relevant official" means—
- (a) the Registrar General;
- (b) a superintendent registrar;
- (c) a registrar;
- (d) a consular officer in the service of Her Majesty's government in the United Kingdom;
- (e) a person authorised by the Secretary of State in respect of the solemnization of marriages or formation of civil partnerships in a country or territory in which Her Majesty's government in the United Kingdom has for the time being no consular representative.

Sub-s (5): para (ba) inserted by the Deregulation Act 2015, s 99(1), (3). Date in force: 26 May 2015: see the Deregulation Act 2015, s 115(3)(k).

Sub-ss (5A)–(5C): inserted by the Immigration Act 2016, s 89(1), (2)(a), Sch 15, Pt 1, para 5. Date in force: 12 July 2016: see SI 2016/603, reg 3(r), (w).

PART II – FINANCE ACTS ETC.

Note.

For the earlier statutes, since repealed, relating to estate duty, see Appendix I to the Twenty-fifth edition of this work; the provisions of the Finance Acts 1975 et seq, consolidated in the Inheritance Tax/Capital Transfer Tax Act 1984, are to be found in Appendix 1 to the Twenty-sixth edition of this work.

For Tables of Rates of Inheritance Tax and Capital Transfer Tax, see Appendix IV.

For Inheritance Tax and Capital Transfer Tax (Delivery of Accounts) Regulations, see Appendix II.

INHERITANCE TAX ACT 1984
(1984, c 51)

[31 July 1984]

PART I
GENERAL

Rates

A1.727

7 Rates

(1) [Subject to subsections (2), (4) and (5) below] [and to [section 8D and] Schedule 1A] the tax charged on the value transferred by a chargeable transfer made by any transferor shall be charged at the following rate or rates, that is to say—

- (a) if the transfer is the first chargeable transfer made by that transferor in the period of [seven years] ending with the date of the transfer, at the rate or rates applicable to that value under the . . . Table in Schedule 1 to this Act;
- (b) in any other case, at the rate or rates applicable under that Table to such part of the aggregate of—
  - (i) that value, and
  - (ii) the values transferred by previous chargeable transfers made by him in that period,

as is the highest part of that aggregate and is equal to that value.

[(2) Except as provided by subsection (4) below, the tax charged on the value transferred by a chargeable transfer made before the death of the transferor shall be charged at one half of the rate or rates referred to in subsection (1) above.]

(3) In [the Table] in Schedule 1 to this Act any rate shown in the third column is that applicable to such portion of the value concerned as exceeds the lower limit shown in the first column but does not exceed the upper limit (if any) shown in the second column.

[(4) Subject to subsection (5) below, subsection (2) above does not apply in the case of a chargeable transfer made at any time within the period of seven years ending with the death of the transferor but, in the case of a chargeable transfer made within that period but more than three years before the death, the tax charged on the value transferred shall be charged at the following percentage of the rate or rates referred to in subsection (1) above—

- (a) where the transfer is made more than three but not more than four years before the death, 80 per cent;
- (b) where the transfer is made more than four but not more than five years before the death, 60 per cent;
- (c) where the transfer is made more than five but not more than six years before the death, 40 per cent; and
- (d) where the transfer is made more than six but not more than seven years before the death, 20 per cent.

(5) If, in the case of a chargeable transfer made before the death of the transferor, the tax which would fall to be charged in accordance with subsection (4) above is less than the tax which would have been chargeable (in accordance with subsection (2) above) if the transferor had not died within the period of seven years beginning with the date of the transfer, subsection (4) above shall not apply in the case of that transfer.]

Sub-s (1): words "Subject to subsections (2), (4) and (5) below" in square brackets inserted by the Finance Act 1986, s 101(1), (3), Sch 19, Pt I, para 2, with respect to transfers of value made, and other events occurring, on or after 18 March 1986.

Sub-s (1): words in square brackets beginning with the words "and to" inserted by the Finance Act 2012, s 209, Sch 33, paras 2, 3. Date in force: this amendment has effect in cases where D's death occurs on or after 6 April 2012: see the Finance Act 2012, s 209, Sch 33, para 10(1).

Sub-s (1): words "section 8D and" in square brackets inserted by the Finance (No 2) Act 2015, s 9(1), (2). Date in force: this amendment came into force on 18 November 2015 (date of Royal Assent of the Finance (No 2) Act 2015) in the absence of any specific commencement provision.

Sub-s (1): in para (a) words "seven years" in square brackets substituted by the Finance Act 1986, s 101(1), (3), Sch 19, Pt I, para 2, with respect to transfers of value made, and other events occurring, on or after 18 March 1986.

Sub-s (1): in para (a) word omitted repealed by the Finance Act 1986, ss 101(1), (3), 114(6), Sch 19, Pt I, para 2, Sch 23, Pt X, with respect to transfers of value made, and other events occurring, on or after 18 March 1986.

Sub-s (2): substituted by the Finance Act 1986, s 101(1), (3), Sch 19, Part I, para 2, with respect to transfers of value made, and other events occurring, on or after 18 March 1986.

Sub-s (3): words in square brackets substituted by the Finance Act 1986, s 101(1), (3), Sch 19, Part I, para 2, with respect to transfers of value made, and other events occurring, on or after 18 March 1986.

Sub-ss (4), (5): inserted by the Finance Act 1986, s 101(1), (3), Sch 19, Part I, para 2, with respect to transfers of value made, and other events occurring, on or after 18 March 1986.

Appendix II

RULES, ORDERS AND REGULATIONS

Contents

Part 1 – Non-Contentious Business

SI 1987/2024 The Non-Contentious Probate Rules 1987 — 141

SI 2007/1253 Lasting Powers of Attorney, Enduring Powers of Attorney and Public Guardian Regulations 2007 — 143

PART I – NON-CONTENTIOUS BUSINESS

THE NON-CONTENTIOUS PROBATE RULES 1987

SI 1987/2024

Note.

Shown as amended by the Non-Contentious Probate (Amendment) Rules 1991 (SI 1991/1876), Non-Contentious Probate (Amendment) Rules 1998 (SI 1998/1903), Non-Contentious Probate (Amendment) Rules 1999 (SI 1999/1015), Non-Contentious Probate (Amendment) Rules 2003 (SI 2003/185), Non-Contentious Probate (Amendment) Rules 2004 (SI 2004/2985), Civil Partnership Act 2004 (Amendments to Subordinate Legislation) Order 2005 (SI 2005/2114), Adoption and Children Act (Consequential Amendments) Order 2005 (SI 2005/3504), Mental Capacity Act 2005 (Transitional and Consequential Provisions) Order 2007 (SI 2007/1898), Constitutional Reform Act 2005 (Commencement No 11) Order 2009 (SI 2009/1604), Non-Contentious Probate (Amendment) Rules 2009 (SI 2009/1893), Legal Services Act 2007 (Consequential Amendments) Order 2009 (SI 2009/3348), Child Arrangements Order (Consequential Amendments to Subordinate Legislation) Order 2014 (SI 2014/852) and Non-Contentious Probate (Amendment) Rules 2016 (SI 2016/972). New/inserted text is inside square brackets.

A2.44

5 Personal applications.—
(1) A personal applicant may apply for a grant at any registry or sub-registry.
(2) Save as provided for by rule 39 a personal applicant may not apply through an agent, whether paid or unpaid, and may not be attended by any person acting or appearing to act as his adviser.
(3) No personal application shall be proceeded with if—
    (a) it becomes necessary to bring the matter before the court by action or summons, [unless a judge, district judge or registrar so permits];
    (b) an application has already been made by a solicitor [or probate practitioner] on behalf of the applicant and has not been withdrawn; or
    (c) the [district judge or] registrar so directs.

A2.44 Appendix II – Rules, Orders and Regulations

(4) After a will has been deposited in a registry by a personal applicant, it may not be delivered to the applicant or to any other person unless in special circumstances the [district judge or] registrar so directs.

(5) A personal applicant shall produce a certificate of the death of the deceased or such other evidence of the death as the [district judge or] registrar may approve.

(6) A personal applicant shall supply all information necessary to enable the papers leading to the grant to be prepared in the registry.

(7) Unless the [district judge or] registrar otherwise directs, every oath or affidavit required on a personal application shall be sworn or executed by all the deponents before an authorised officer.

(8) No legal advice shall be given to a personal applicant by any officer of a registry and every such officer shall be responsible only for embodying in proper form the applicant's instructions for the grant.

[(9) In any case where an application is made under rule 5A (alternative procedure for personal applications), this rule applies with the exceptions and modifications provided by that rule.]

Para (3): in sub-para (a) words ', unless a judge, district judge or registrar so permits' in square brackets inserted by SI 1998/1903, r 5 from 14 September 1998: see SI 1998/1903, r 1(1).

Para (3): in sub-para (b) words 'or probate practitioner' in square brackets inserted by SI 1998/1903, r 6 from 14 September 1998: see SI 1998/1903, r 1(1).

Para (3): in sub-para (c) words 'district judge or' in square brackets inserted by SI 1991/1876, r 7(1).

Para (4): words 'district judge or' in square brackets inserted by SI 1991/1876, r 7(1).

Para (5): words 'district judge or' in square brackets inserted by SI 1991/1876, r 7(1).

Para (7): words 'district judge or' in square brackets inserted by SI 1991/1876, r 7(1).

Para (9): inserted by SI 2016/972, r 2(1). Date in force: 1 November 2016: see SI 2016/972, r 1(1).

A2.44A

[**5A Alternative procedure for personal applications**]

[(1) A personal applicant may apply for a grant at any registry under this rule if invited to do so by that registry.

(2) An application under this rule must be made by completing and sending an online application form in accordance with instructions given by the registry.

(3) Where an application is made under this rule, rule 5 applies with the following exceptions and modifications—
- (a) paragraphs (1), (7) and (8) do not apply;
- (b) paragraph (5) applies as if for the words "the district judge or registrar may approve" there were substituted "required by instructions given by the registry"; and
- (c) paragraph (6) applies as if for the words after "information" there were substituted "required by instructions given by the registry".

(4) Where an application is made under this rule, rule 8 does not apply, and—
- (a) the application must be verified by a statement of truth by the applicant in the online application form;
- (b) rule 10(1)(a) applies as if for "signatures of the applicant and the person before whom the oath is sworn" there were substituted "signature of the applicant";
- (c) rule 27(1) applies as if at the end there were inserted "or, where the application is made under rule 5A, the applicant shall confirm in accordance with instructions given by the registry that such notice has been given".

(5) Where original documents are required by instructions given by the registry to be sent in support of the application, they must be sent separately to the registry in accordance with such instructions.]

Inserted by SI 2016/972, r 2(2). Date in force: 1 November 2016: see SI 2016/972, r 1(1).

LASTING POWERS OF ATTORNEY, ENDURING POWERS OF ATTORNEY AND PUBLIC GUARDIAN REGULATIONS 2007

SI 2007/1253

PART 1
PRELIMINARY

A2.145

2 Interpretation

(1) In these Regulations—

"the Act" means the Mental Capacity Act 2005;

"court" means the Court of Protection;

"LPA certificate", in relation to an instrument made with a view to creating a lasting power of attorney, means the certificate which is required to be included in the instrument by virtue of paragraph 2(1)(e) of Schedule 1 to the Act;

"[person to notify]", in relation to an instrument made with a view to creating a lasting power of attorney, means a person who[, under Schedule 1, paragraph 2(1)(c)(i) of the Act,] is named in the instrument as being a person to be notified of any application for the registration of the instrument;

"prescribed information", in relation to any instrument intended to create a lasting power of attorney, means the information contained in the form used for the instrument which appears under the heading ["Section 8—Your legal rights and responsibilities"].

Para (1): in definition "person to notify" words "person to notify" in square brackets substituted by SI 2015/899, regs 2, 4(a)(i). Date in force: 1 July 2015: see SI 2015/899, reg 1(2); for transitional provisions see regs 17–19.

Para (1): in definition "person to notify" words ", under Schedule 1, paragraph 2(1)(c)(i) of the Act," in square brackets inserted by SI 2015/899, regs 2, 4(a)(ii). Date in force: 1 July 2015: see SI 2015/899, reg 1(2); for transitional provisions see regs 17–19.

Para (1): in definition "prescribed information" words ""Section 8—Your legal rights and responsibilities"" in square brackets substituted by SI 2015/899, regs 2, 4(b). Date in force: 1 July 2015: see SI 2015/899, reg 1(2); for transitional provisions see regs 17–19.

PART 2
LASTING POWERS OF ATTORNEY

Instruments intended to create a lasting power of attorney

A2.148

6 Maximum number of [people to notify]

The maximum number of [people to notify] that the donor of a lasting power of attorney may specify in the instrument intended to create the power is 5.

A2.148 *Appendix II – Rules, Orders and Regulations*

Provision heading: words "people to notify" in square brackets substituted by SI 2015/899, regs 2, 5. Date in force: 1 July 2015: see SI 2015/899, reg 1(2); for transitional provisions see regs 17–19.

Words "person to notify" in square brackets substituted by SI 2015/899, regs 2, 5. Date in force: 1 July 2015: see SI 2015/899, reg 1(2); for transitional provisions see regs 17–19.

A2.149

7 . . .

. . .

Revoked by SI 2015/899, regs 2, 6. Date in force: 1 July 2015: see SI 2015/899, reg 1(2); for transitional provisions see regs 17–19.

A2.151

9 Execution of instrument

(1) An instrument intended to create a lasting power of attorney must be executed in accordance with this regulation.

(2) The donor must read (or have read to him) all the prescribed information.

(3) As soon as reasonably practicable after the steps required by paragraph (2) have been taken, the donor must—
- (a) complete the provisions of [Sections 1 to 7] of the instrument that apply to him (or direct another person to do so); and
- [(b) subject to paragraph (7), in the presence of a witness—
   - (i) sign Section 9 of the instrument if the instrument is intended to create a lasting power of attorney for property and financial affairs (Form LP1F); or
   - (ii) sign Sections 5 and 9 of the instrument if the instrument is intended to create a lasting power of attorney for health and welfare (Form LP1H)].

(4) As soon as reasonably practicable after the steps required by paragraph (3) have been taken—
- (a) the person giving an LPA certificate . . .
- (b) . . .

must complete the LPA certificate at [Section 10] of the instrument and sign it.

(5) As soon as reasonably practicable after the steps required by paragraph (4) have been taken—
- (a) the donee, or
- (b) if more than one, each of the donees,

must read (or have read to him) all the prescribed information.

(6) As soon as reasonably practicable after the steps required by paragraph (5) have been taken, the donee or, if more than one, each of them—
- (a) must complete the provisions of [Section 11] of the instrument that apply to him (or direct another person to do so); and
- (b) subject to paragraph (7), must sign [Section 11] of the instrument in the presence of a witness.

(7) If the instrument is to be signed by any person at the direction of the donor, or at the direction of any donee, the signature must be done in the presence of two witnesses.

(8) For the purposes of this regulation—
- (a) the donor may not witness any signature required for the power;
- (b) a donee may not witness any signature required for the power apart from that of another donee.

(9) A person witnessing a signature must—

(a) sign the instrument; and
(b) give his full name and address.

(10) Any reference in this regulation to a person signing an instrument (however expressed) includes his signing it by means of a mark made on the instrument at the appropriate place.

Para (3): in sub-para (a) words "Sections 1 to 7" in square brackets substituted by SI 2015/899, regs 2, 7(a). Date in force: 1 July 2015: see SI 2015/899, reg 1(2); for transitional provisions see regs 17–19.

Para (3): sub-para (b) substituted by SI 2015/899, regs 2, 7(b). Date in force: 1 July 2015: see SI 2015/899, reg 1(2); for transitional provisions see regs 17–19.

Para (4): in sub-para (a) word omitted revoked by SI 2015/899, regs 2, 7(c). Date in force: 1 July 2015: see SI 2015/899, reg 1(2); for transitional provisions see regs 17–19.

Para (4): sub-para (b) revoked by SI 2015/899, regs 2, 7(d). Date in force: 1 July 2015: see SI 2015/899, reg 1(2); for transitional provisions see regs 17–19.

Para (4): words "Section 10" in square brackets substituted by SI 2015/899, regs 2, 7(e). Date in force: 1 July 2015: see SI 2015/899, reg 1(2); for transitional provisions see regs 17–19.

Para (6): in sub-paras (a), (b) words "Section 11" in square brackets substituted by SI 2015/899, regs 2, 7(f). Date in force: 1 July 2015: see SI 2015/899, reg 1(2); for transitional provisions see regs 17–19.

Registering the instrument

A2.152

10 Notice to be given by a person about to apply for registration of lasting power of attorney

Schedule 2 to these Regulations sets out the form of notice [(Form LPA3)] which must be given by a donor or donee who is about to make an application for the registration of an instrument intended to create a lasting power of attorney.

Words "(Form LPA3)" in square brackets substituted by SI 2015/899, regs 2, 8. Date in force: 1 July 2015: see SI 2015/899, reg 1(2); for transitional provisions see regs 17–19.

A2.153

11 Application for registration

[(1) An application to the Public Guardian for the registration of an instrument intended to create a lasting power of attorney that is in Form LP1F or LP1H must be made by completion of Sections 12 and 13, the relevant parts of Section 14 and Section 15 of that Form.

(2) An application to the Public Guardian for the registration of an instrument intended to create a lasting power of attorney that is in a pre-July 2015 form must be made by using Form LP2 set out in Schedule 3 to these Regulations.

(3) An application to the Public Guardian for the registration of an instrument intended to create a lasting power of attorney where the application is a repeat application ("a reduced fee repeat application") may only be made if—
(a) the initial application for the registration of a lasting power of attorney is made on or after 1st October 2011;
(b) the initial application was returned to the applicant as invalid;
(c) the reduced fee repeat application is submitted for registration within three months of the date on which the initial application was returned to the applicant as invalid; and
(d) the reduced fee for such applications applies.

(4) Where the initial application for the registration of the lasting power of attorney was made in accordance with paragraph (1) using Form LP1F or LP1H, a reduced fee

A2.153 Appendix II – Rules, Orders and Regulations

repeat application must also be made by the completion of Form LP1F or LP1H as appropriate, including completion of the repeat application option in Section 14 of that Form.

(5) Where the initial application for the registration of the lasting power of attorney was made in accordance with paragraph (2) using a pre-July 2015 form, a reduced fee repeat application must be made by the completion of Form LP1F or LP1H as appropriate, including completion of the repeat application option in Section 14 of that Form.

(6) Where the instrument to be registered which is sent with the application is neither—
    (a)   the original instrument intended to create the power; nor
    (b)   a certified copy of it,
the Public Guardian must not register the instrument unless the court directs the Public Guardian to do so.

(7) In this regulation—
    (a)   "pre-July 2015 form" means a valid instrument intended to create a lasting power of attorney that is not in Form LP1F or LP1H but that complies with these Regulations as they were in force immediately before 1st July 2015; and
    (b)   "certified copy" means a photographic or other facsimile copy which is certified as an accurate copy by—
        (i)   the donor; or
        (ii)   a solicitor or notary.]

Substituted by SI 2015/899, regs 2, 9. Date in force: 1 July 2015: see SI 2015/899, reg 1(2); for transitional provisions see regs 17–19.

Appendix III

FEES (NON-CONTENTIOUS BUSINESS)

THE NON-CONTENTIOUS PROBATE FEES ORDER 2004

SI 2004/3120

Note.
1. Shown as amended by the Non-Contentious Probate Fees (Amendment) Orders, SI 2007/2174, SI 2011/588, SI 2013/2302, SI 2014/513, SI 2014/590, SI 2014/876 and SI 2016/211. New/inserted text is inside square brackets.

2. At the time of publication of this supplement the Government has announced that it will implement proposals for reforming fees payable for applications for grants of probate. The proposals now contained in the draft Non-Contentious Probate Fees Order 2017 will take effect sometime in May 2017. For the draft Fees Order see para **A3.12** below. In addition, the proposed reform of fees will remove probate fees from the scheme for fees remission set out in Schedule 1A of the current Fees Order.

A3.04

[4. Remission of fees
Schedule 1A applies for the purpose of ascertaining whether a party is entitled to a remission or part remission of a fee prescribed by this Order.]

Amendment
Substituted by SI 2007/2174, art 3. Date in force: 1 October 2007: see SI 2007/2174, art 1.

SCHEDULE 1

FEES TO BE TAKEN

A3.09

[Column 1	Column 2
Number and description of fee	Amount of fee
1. Application for a grant	
On an application for a grant (or for resealing a grant) other than on an application to which fee 3 applies, where the assessed value of the estate exceeds £5,000	[£155]
2. Personal application fee	
Where the application under fee 1 is made by a personal applicant (not being an application to which fee 3 applies) fee 2 is payable in addition to fee 1, where the assessed value of the estate exceeds £5,000	£60

A3.09 *Appendix III – Fees (Non-Contentious Business)*

[Column 1	Column 2
Number and description of fee	Amount of fee
3. Special applications	
3.1 For a duplicate or second or subsequent grant (including one following a revoked grant) in respect of the same deceased person, other than a grant preceded only by a grant limited to settled land, to trust property, or to part of the estate	£20
3.2 On an application for a grant relating to a death occurring on or after 20th March 2003 and in respect of an estate exempt from inheritance tax by virtue of section 154 of the Inheritance Tax Act 1984 (exemption for members of the armed forces etc)	£10
4. Caveats	
For the entry or the extension of a caveat	£20
5. Search	
On an application for a standing search to be carried out in an estate, for each period of six months including the issue of a copy grant and will, if any (irrespective of the number of pages)	[£10]
6. Deposit of wills	
On depositing a will for safe custody in the principal registry or a district registry	£20
7. Inspection	
On inspection of any will or other document retained by the registry (in the presence of an officer of the registry)	£20
8. Copy documents	
On a request for a copy of any document whether or not provided as a certified copy:	
(a) for the first copy	[£10]
(b) for every subsequent copy of the same document if supplied at the same time	[50p]
(c) where copies of any document are made available on a computer disk or in other electronic form, for each such copy	[£10]
(d) where a search of the index is required, in addition to fee 8(a), (b) or (c) as appropriate, for each period of 4 years searched after the first 4 years	£4
9. Oaths	
Except on a personal application for a grant, for administering an oath,	
9.1 for each deponent to each affidavit	[£11]
9.2 for marking each exhibit	£2
10. Determination of costs For determining costs	The same fees as are payable from time to time for determining costs under the Civil Proceedings Fees Order 2004, (the relevant fees are set out in fee 5 in Schedule 1 to that Order)

Appendix III – Fees (Non-Contentious Business) **A3.10**

[Column 1	Column 2
Number and description of fee	Amount of fee
11. Settling documents	
For perusing and settling citations, advertisements, oaths, affidavits, or other documents, for each document settled	£12]

Substituted by SI 2011/588, arts 2, 3, Schedule. Date in force: 4 April 2011: see SI 2011/588, art 1.

Item 1: in column 2 sum "£155" in square brackets substituted by SI 2014/876, art 2(1), (2)(a). Date in force: 22 April 2014: see SI 2014/876, art 1.

Item 5: in column 2 sum "£10" in square brackets substituted by SI 2014/876, art 2(1), (2)(b). Date in force: 22 April 2014: see SI 2014/876, art 1.

Item 8: in para (a) in column 2 sum "£10" in square brackets substituted by SI 2014/876, art 2(1), (2)(c). Date in force: 22 April 2014: see SI 2014/876, art 1.

Item 8: in para (b) in column 2 sum "50p" in square brackets substituted by SI 2014/876, art 2(1), (2)(d). Date in force: 22 April 2014: see SI 2014/876, art 1.

Item 8: in para (c) in column 2 sum "£10" in square brackets substituted by SI 2014/876, art 2(1), (2)(e). Date in force: 22 April 2014: see SI 2014/876, art 1.

Item 9.1: in column 2 sum "£11" in square brackets substituted by SI 2014/876, art 2(1), (2)(f). Date in force: 22 April 2014: see SI 2014/876, art 1.

[SCHEDULE 1A

REMISSIONS AND PART-REMISSIONS]

[Article 4]

A3.10

1 [Interpretation

(1) In this Schedule—

"child" means a person—

    (a) whose main residence is with a party and who is aged—

        (i) under 16 years; or

        (ii) 16 to 19 years; and is—

            (aa) not married or in a civil partnership; and

            (bb) enrolled or accepted in full-time education that is not advanced education, or approved training; or

    (b) in respect of whom a party or their partner pays child support maintenance or periodic payments in accordance with a maintenance agreement,

and "full-time education", "advanced education" and "approved training" have the meaning given by the Child Benefit (General) Regulations 2006;

"child support maintenance" has the meaning given in section 3(6) of the Child Support Act 1991;

"couple" has the meaning given in section 3(5A) of the Tax Credits Act 2002;

"disposable capital" has the meaning given in paragraph 5;

["excluded benefits" means any of the following—

    (a) any of the following benefits payable under the Social Security Contributions and Benefits Act 1992 or the corresponding provisions of the Social Security Contributions and Benefits (Northern Ireland) Act 1992—

        (i) attendance allowance under section 64;

        (ii) severe disablement allowance;

        (iii) carer's allowance;

A3.10 Appendix III – Fees (Non-Contentious Business)

(iv) disability living allowance;
(v) constant attendance allowance under section 104 as an increase to a disablement pension;
(vi) any payment made out of the social fund;
(vii) housing benefit;
(viii) widowed parents allowance;

(b) any of the following benefit payable under the Tax Credits Act 2002—
(i) any disabled child element or severely disabled child element of the child tax credit;
(ii) any childcare element of the working tax credit;

(c) any direct payment made under the Community Care, Services for Carers and Children's Services (Direct Payments) (England) Regulations 2009, . . . the Carers and Direct Payments Act (Northern Ireland) 2002, . . . [the Social Care (Self-directed Support) (Scotland) Act 2013] [or under regulations made under sections 50 to 53 of the Social Services and Well-being (Wales) Act 2014];

(d) a back to work bonus payable under section 26 of the Jobseekers Act 1995, or article 28 of the Jobseekers (Northern Ireland) Order 1995;

(e) any exceptionally severe disablement allowance paid under the Personal Injuries (Civilians) Scheme 1983;

(f) any payments from the Industrial Injuries Disablement Benefit;

(g) any pension paid under the Naval, Military and Air Forces etc (Disablement and Death) Service Pension Order 2006;

(h) any payment made from the Independent Living Funds;

(i) any payment made from the Bereavement Allowance;

(j) any financial support paid under an agreement for the care of a foster child;

(k) any housing credit element of pension credit;

(l) any armed forces independence payment;

(m) any personal independence payment payable under the Welfare Reform Act 2012;

(n) any payment on account of benefit as defined in the Social Security (Payments on Account of Benefit) Regulations 2013;

(o) any of the following amounts, as defined by the Universal Credit Regulations 2013, that make up an award of universal credit—
(i) an additional amount to the child element in respect of a disabled child;
(ii) a housing costs element;
(iii) a childcare costs element;
(iv) a carer element;
(v) a limited capability for work or limited capacity for work and work -related activity element;]

"family help (higher)" has the meaning given in paragraph 15(3) of the Civil Legal Aid (Merits Criteria) Regulations 2013;
"family help (lower)" has the meaning given in paragraph 15(2) of the Civil Legal Aid (Merits Criteria) Regulations 2013;
"gross monthly income" has the meaning given in paragraph 13;
"Independent Living Funds" means the funds listed at regulation 20(2)(b) of the Criminal Legal Aid (Financial Resources) Regulations 2013;

"legal representation" has the meaning given in paragraph 18(2) of the Civil Legal Aid (Merits Criteria) Regulations 2013;
"maintenance agreement" has the meaning given in subsection 9(1) of the Child Support Act 1991;
"partner" means a person with whom the party lives as a couple and includes a person with whom the party is not currently living but from whom the party is not living separate and apart;
"party" means the individual who would, but for this Schedule, be liable to pay a fee under this Order;
"restraint order" means—

    (a)   an order under section 42(1A) of the Senior Courts Act 1981;
    (b)   an order under section 33 of the Employment Tribunals Act 1996;
    (c)   a civil restraint order made under rule 3.11 of the Civil Procedure Rules 1998, or a practice direction made under that rule; or
    (d)   a civil restraint order under rule 4.8 of the Family Procedure Rules 2010, or the practice direction referred to in that rule.

(2) References to remission of a fee are to be read as including references to a part remission of a fee as appropriate and remit and remitted shall be construed accordingly.

2 Fee remission

If a party satisfies the disposable capital test, the amount of any fee remission is calculated by applying the gross monthly income test.

Disposable capital test

3 Disposable capital test

(1) Subject to paragraph 4, a party satisfies the disposable capital test if—

    (a)   the fee payable by the party and for which an application for remission is made, falls within a fee band set out in column 1 of Table 1; and
    (b)   the party's disposable capital is less than the amount in the corresponding row of column 2.

Table 1

Column 1 (fee band)	Column 2 (disposable capital)
Up to and including £1,000	£3,000
£1,001 to £1,335	£4,000
£1,336 to £1,665	£5,000
£1,666 to £2,000	£6,000
£2,001 to £2,330	£7,000
£2,331 to £4,000	£8,000
£4,001 to £5,000	£10,000
£5,001 to £6,000	£12,000
£6,001 to £7,000	£14,000
£7,001 or more	£16,000

4
Subject to paragraph 14, if a party or their partner is aged 61 or over, that party satisfies the disposable capital test if that party's disposable capital is less than £16,000.

A3.10 Appendix III – Fees (Non-Contentious Business)

5 Disposable capital
Subject to paragraph 14, disposable capital is the value of every resource of a capital nature belonging to the party on the date on which the application for remission is made, unless it is treated as income by this Order, or it is disregarded as excluded disposable capital.

6 Disposable capital—non-money resources
The value of a resource of a capital nature that does not consist of money is calculated as the amount which that resource would realise if sold, less—
- (a) 10% of the sale value; and
- (b) the amount of any borrowing secured against that resource that would be repayable on sale.

7 Disposable capital—resources held outside the United Kingdom
(1) Capital resources in a country outside the United Kingdom count towards disposable capital.
(2) If there is no prohibition in that country against the transfer of a resource into the United Kingdom, the value of that resource is the amount which that resource would realise if sold in that country, in accordance with paragraph 6.
(3) If there is a prohibition in that country against the transfer of a resource into the United Kingdom, the value of that resource is the amount that resource would realise if sold to a buyer in the United Kingdom.

8 Disposable capital—foreign currency resources
Where disposable capital is held in currency other than sterling, the cost of any banking charge or commission that would be payable if that amount were converted into sterling, is deducted from its value.

9 Disposable capital—jointly owned resources
Where any resource of a capital nature is owned jointly or in common, there is a presumption that the resource is owned in equal shares, unless evidence to the contrary is produced.

10 Excluded disposable capital
The following things are excluded disposable capital—
- (a) a property which is the main or only dwelling occupied by the party;
- (b) the household furniture and effects of the main or only dwelling occupied by the party;
- (c) articles of personal clothing;
- (d) any vehicle, the sale of which would leave the party, or their partner, without motor transport;
- (e) tools and implements of trade, including vehicles used for business purposes;
- (f) the capital value of the party's or their partner's business, where the party or their partner is self-employed;
- (g) the capital value of any funds or other assets held in trust, where the party or their partner is a beneficiary without entitlement to advances of any trust capital;
- (h) a jobseeker's back to work bonus;
- (i) a payment made as a result of a determination of unfair dismissal by a court or tribunal, or by way of settlement of a claim for unfair dismissal;
- (j) any compensation paid as a result of a determination of medical negligence or in respect of any personal injury by a court, or by way of settlement of a claim for medical negligence or personal injury;
- (k) the capital held in any personal or occupational pension scheme;

Appendix III – Fees (Non-Contentious Business) **A3.10**

(l) any cash value payable on surrender of a contract of insurance;
(m) any capital payment made out of the Independent Living Funds;
(n) any bereavement payment;
(o) any capital insurance or endowment lump sum payments that have been paid as a result of illness, disability or death;
(p) any student loan or student grant;
(q) any payments under the criminal injuries compensation scheme.

Gross monthly income test

11 Remission of fees—gross monthly income
(1) If a party satisfies the disposable capital test, no fee is payable under this Order if, at the time when the fee would otherwise be payable, the party or their partner has the number of children specified in column 1 of Table 2 and—
(a) if the party is single, their gross monthly income does not exceed the amount set out in the appropriate row of column 2; or
(b) if the party is one of a couple, the gross monthly income of that couple does not exceed the amount set out in the appropriate row of column 3.

Table 2

Column 1 Number of children of party	Column 2 Single	Column 3 Couple
no children	£1,085	£1,245
1 child	£1,330	£1,490
2 children	£1,575	£1,735

(2) If a party or their partner has more than 2 children, the relevant amount of gross monthly income is the appropriate amount specified in Table 2 for 2 children, plus the sum of £245 for each additional child.
(3) For every £10 of gross monthly income received above the appropriate amount in Table 2, including any additional amount added under sub-paragraph (2), the party must pay £5 towards the fee payable, up to the maximum amount of the fee payable.
(4) This paragraph is subject to paragraph 12.

12 Gross monthly income cap
(1) No remission is available if a party or their partner has the number of children specified in column 1 of Table 3 and—
(a) if the party is single, their gross monthly income exceeds the amount set out in the appropriate row of column 2 of Table 3; or
(b) if the party is one of a couple, the gross monthly income of that couple exceeds the amount set out in the appropriate row of column 3 of Table 3.

Table 3

Column 1 Number of children of party	Column 2 Single	Column 3 Couple
no children	£5,085	£5,245
1 child	£5,330	£5,490
2 children	£5,575	£5,735

(2) If a party or their partner has more than 2 children, the relevant amount of gross monthly income is the appropriate amount specified in Table 3 for 2 children, plus the sum of £245 for each additional child.

13 Gross monthly income
(1) Subject to paragraph 14, gross monthly income means the total monthly income, for the month preceding that in which the application for remission is made, from all sources, other than receipt of any of the excluded benefits.
(2) Income from a trade, business or gainful occupation other than an occupation at a wage or salary is calculated as—
   (a) the profits which have accrued or will accrue to the party; and
   (b) the drawings of the party;
in the month preceding that in which the application for remission is made.
(3) In calculating profits under sub-paragraph (2)(a), all sums necessarily expended to earn those profits are deducted.

General

14 Resources and income treated as the party's resources and income
(1) Subject to sub-paragraph (2), the disposable capital and gross monthly income of a partner of a party is to be treated as disposable capital and gross monthly income of the party.
(2) Where the partner of a party has a contrary interest to the party in the matter to which the fee relates, the disposable capital and gross monthly income of that partner, if any, is not treated as the disposable capital and gross monthly income of the party.

15 Application for remission of a fee
(1) An application for remission of a fee must be made at the time when the fee would otherwise be payable.
(2) Where an application for remission of a fee is made, the party must—
   (a) indicate the fee to which the application relates;
   (b) declare the amount of their disposable capital; and
   (c) provide documentary evidence of their gross monthly income and the number of children relevant for the purposes of paragraphs 11 and 12.
(3) Where an application for remission of a fee is made on or before the date on which a fee is payable, the date for payment of the fee is disapplied.
(4) Where an application for remission is refused, or if part remission of a fee is granted, the amount of the fee which remains unremitted must be paid within the period notified in writing to the party.

16 Remission in exceptional circumstances
A fee specified in this Order may be remitted where the Lord Chancellor is satisfied that there are exceptional circumstances which justify doing so.

17 Refunds
(1) Subject to sub-paragraph (3), where a party pays a fee at a time when that party would have been entitled to a remission if they had provided the documentary evidence required by paragraph 15, the fee, or the amount by which the fee would have been reduced as the case may be, must be refunded if documentary evidence relating to the time when the fee became payable is provided at a later date.
(2) Subject to sub-paragraph (3), where a fee has been paid at a time when the Lord Chancellor, if all the circumstances had been known, would have remitted the fee under paragraph 15, the fee or the amount by which the fee would have been reduced, as the case may be, must be refunded to the party.

Appendix III – Fees (Non-Contentious Business) **A3.10**

(3) No refund shall be made under this paragraph unless the party who paid the fee applies within 3 months of the date on which the fee was paid.

(4) The Lord Chancellor may extend the period of 3 months mentioned in sub-paragraph (3) if the Lord Chancellor considers that there is a good reason for a refund being made after the end of the period of 3 months.

18 Legal Aid

A party is not entitled to a fee remission if, under Part 1 of the Legal Aid, Sentencing and Punishment of Offenders Act 2012, they are in receipt of the following civil legal services—

- (a) Legal representation; or
- (b) Family help (higher); or
- (c) Family help (lower) in respect of applying for a consent order.

19 Vexatious litigants

(1) This paragraph applies where—
- (a) a restraint order is in force against a party; and
- (b) that party makes an application for permission to—
  - (i) issue proceedings or take a step in proceedings as required by the restraint order;
  - (ii) apply for amendment or discharge of the order; or
  - (iii) appeal the order.

(2) The fee prescribed by this Order for the application is payable in full.

(3) If the party is granted permission, they are to be refunded the difference between—
- (a) the fee paid; and
- (b) the fee that would have been payable if this Schedule had been applied without reference to this paragraph.

20 Exceptions

No remissions or refunds are available in respect of the fee payable for—
- (a) copy or duplicate documents;
- (b) searches.]

Substituted by SI 2013/2302, art 3(1), (2), Schedule. Date in force: 7 October 2013: see SI 2013/2302, art 1; for transitional provisions see art 13 thereof.

Para 1: in sub-para (1) definition "excluded benefits" substituted by SI 2014/590, art 6(1), (2). Date in force: 6 April 2014: see SI 2014/590, art 1.

Para 1: in sub-para (1) in definition "excluded benefits" in para (c) first words omitted revoked by SI 2016/211, reg 3, Sch 3, Pt 2, para 189(a). Date in force: 6 April 2016: see SI 2016/211, reg 1(2).

Para 1: in sub-para (1) in definition "excluded benefits" in para (c) second word omitted revoked by SI 2016/211, reg 3, Sch 3, Pt 2, para 189(b). Date in force: 6 April 2016: see SI 2016/211, reg 1(2).

Para 1: in sub-para (1) in definition "excluded benefits" para (c) words "the Social Care (Self—directed Support) (Scotland) Act 2013" in square brackets substituted by SI 2014/513, art 2, Schedule, para 9. Date in force: 1 April 2014: see SI 2014/513, art 1(2).

Para (1): in sub-para (1) in definition "excluded benefits" in para (c) words from "or under regulations" to "Social Services and Well-being (Wales) Act 2014" in square brackets inserted by SI 2016/211, reg 3, Sch 3, Pt 2, para 189(c). Date in force: 6 April 2016: see SI 2016/211, reg 1(2).

A3.12 *Appendix III – Fees (Non-Contentious Business)*

THE NON-CONTENTIOUS PROBATE FEES ORDER 2017

(An Order of which this is a draft has been laid before Parliament for approval by resolution of each House of Parliament and a commencement date is to be set).

A3.12

1. Citation and commencement

This Order may be cited as the Non-Contentious Probate Fees Order 2017 and comes into force 21 days after the day on which the Order is made.

A3.13

2. Interpretation: general

(1) In this Order—

"the assessed value of an estate" has the meaning given in article 3;

"authorised place of deposit" means any place where, in accordance with a direction given under section 124 of the Senior Courts Act 1981 (place for deposit of original wills and other documents), original wills and other documents under the control of the High Court (either in the Principal Registry or a district registry) are deposited and preserved;

"district registry" means—
- (a) the probate registry of Wales and any sub-registry attached to it;
- (b) any district probate registry, or
- (c) any sub-registry attached to a district probate registry;

"grant" means a grant of probate or letters of administration;

"the Principal Registry" means the Principal Registry of the Family Division and any subregistry attached to it;

"the registrar" means the district probate registrar of the district probate registry to which an application for a grant is made.

(2) Any reference in this Order to a fee by number is to the fee so numbered in Schedule 1.

A3.14

3. Interpretation: assessed value of an estate

(1) For the purposes of this Order, "the assessed value of an estate" means—
- (a) in the case of an application for a grant, the value of the net real and personal estate (excluding any settled land and any relevant death gratuity) passing under the grant as shown—
    - (i) in the Inland Revenue affidavit (for a death occurring before 13th March 1975);
    - (ii) in the account required to be delivered under section 216 of the Inheritance Tax Act 1984 (for a death occurring on or after 13th March 1975), or
    - (iii) where paragraph (2) applies, in the oath which is sworn to lead to the grant;
- (b) in the case of an application to reseal, the value as shown in the document referred to in paragraph (a)(i) to (iii), passing under the grant upon its being resealed.

Appendix III – Fees (Non-Contentious Business) **A3.18**

(2) This paragraph applies in any case in which, in accordance with arrangements made under section 109 of the Senior Courts Act 1981 (refusal of grant where capital transfer tax unpaid) or regulations made under section 256(1)(a) or (aa) of the Inheritance Tax Act 1984 (regulations about accounts, etc.), the affidavit or account referred to in paragraph (a)(i) or (ii) is not required to be delivered.

(3) In this article "relevant death gratuity" means a death gratuity payable—

- (a) under section 17(2) of the Judicial Pensions Act 1981 (lump sum on retirement or death);
- (b) under section 4(3) of the Judicial Pensions and Retirement Act 1993 (lump sum on the judicial officer's retirement or death), or
- (c) to the personal representatives of a deceased civil servant by virtue of a scheme made under section 1 of the Superannuation Act 1972 (superannuation schemes as respects civil servants, etc.).

A3.15

4. Fees to be taken

The fees prescribed in column 2 of Schedule 1 are to be taken in the Principal Registry and each district registry in respect of the items described in column 1 in accordance with and subject to any directions specified in column 1.

A3.16

5 Exemptions: general

If any convention entered into by Her Majesty with any foreign power provides that no fee is to be required to be paid in respect of any proceedings, the fees prescribed by this Order are not to be taken in respect of those proceedings.

A3.17

6. Exemption: search made for documents over 100 years old

Fee 6 (inspection) is not to be taken where—

- (a) a search is made for research, or a similar purpose, for a document over 100 years old filed in any authorised place of deposit, and
- (b) the President of the Family Division gives permission for no fee to be taken.

A3.18

7. Refunds: armed forces

Where a fee has been taken on an application for a grant or resealing of a grant and that application was in respect of—

- (a) an estate which, on the date on which that fee was taken, was exempt from inheritance tax by virtue of section 154 of the Inheritance Tax Act 1984 (death on active service, etc.), and
- (b) a death occurring before 20th March 2003,

the Lord Chancellor must, on receipt of a written application from the person who paid the fee, refund to that person the difference between the fee taken and fee 2.2 (application for grant in respect of death in active service, etc.).

A3.19 Appendix III – Fees (Non-Contentious Business)

A3.19

8. Remissions and refunds: Indian Ocean Tsunami and London Terrorist Bombings
(1) The Lord Chancellor must remit in full any fee prescribed in this Order where it appears to the Lord Chancellor that an application for a grant or resealing of a grant is in respect of—
- (a) a death occurring as a result of the earthquake and tsunami in the Indian Ocean on 26th December 2004;
- (b) a death occurring as a result of another person's detonation of a bomb in London on 7th July 2005, or
- (c) a death occurring as a result of action taken in a police operation following another person's attempted detonation of a bomb in London on 21st July 2005.

(2) Where a fee has been taken under the Non-Contentious Probate Fees Order 2004—
- (a) after 26th December 2004 but before 4th March 2005, in respect of a death occurring in the circumstance described in paragraph (1)(a), or
- (b) after 7th July 2005 but before 29th December 2005, in respect of a death occurring in the circumstances described in paragraph (1)(b) or (c),

the Lord Chancellor must, on receipt of a written application from the person who paid the fee, refund the fee to that person.

A3.20

9. Refund of fees on withdrawal of application for grant
Where an application for a grant is withdrawn before the issue of the grant, the registrar must refund to the applicant the difference between the fee taken and £50.

A3.21

10. Remission of fees in exceptional circumstances
The Lord Chancellor may remit a fee prescribed in this Order where satisfied that there are exceptional circumstances which justify doing so.

A3.22

11. Revocation
The Orders specified in Schedule 2 are revoked.

A3.23

12. Transitional and savings provisions
The Non-Contentious Probate Order 2004 continues to have effect where an application described in column 1 of Schedule 1 has been received by the Principal Registry or a district registry before the coming into force of this Order.

SCHEDULE 1
FEES TO BE TAKEN

A3.24

[Column 1	Column 2
Number and description of fee	Amount of fee
1. Application for a grant or resealing of a grant	

Appendix III – Fees (Non-Contentious Business) **A3.24**

[Column 1	Column 2
Number and description of fee	*Amount of fee*
On an application for a grant or resealing of a grant where the assessed value of the estate:	
(a) exceeds £50,000 but does not exceed £300,000;	£300
(b) exceeds £300,000 but does not exceed £500,000;	£1,000
(c) exceeds £500,000 but does not exceed £1,000,000;	£4,000
(d) exceeds £1,000,000 but does not exceed £1,600,000;	£8,000
(e) exceeds £1,600,000 but does not exceed £2,000,000;	£12,000
(f) exceeds £2,000,000	£20,000
Fee 1 is not payable on any application on which fee 2.1 or 2.2 is payable	
2. Special applications	
2.1 On an application for a duplicate or second or subsequent grant (including a grant following a revoked grant) in respect of the same estate as the original grant	£20
Fee 2.1 is not payable if the application for the grant was preceded only by a grant limited to settled land, to trust property or to part of the estate	
2.2 On an application for a grant or resealing of a grant in respect of—	£10
(a) a death occurring on or after 20th March 2003; and	
(b) an estate exempt from inheritance tax by virtue of section 154 of the Inheritance Tax Act 1984 (death in active service etc.)	
3. Caveats	
On an application for the entry or extension of a caveat	£20
4. Search	
On an application for a standing search to be carried out in an estate, for each period of six months and including the issue of a copy grant and will (if any) (irrespective of the number of pages)	£10
5. Deposit of wills	
On depositing a will for safe custody in the Principal Registry or a district registry	£20
6. Inspection	
On inspection of any will or other document retained by the Principal Registry or a district registry and in the presence of an official of that registry	£20
7. Copy documents	
On a request for a copy of any document:	
(a) for the first copy;	£10
(b) for every subsequent copy if supplied at the same time as the first copy;	50p
(c) where the copy or copies are made available on a computer disk or in any other electronic form, for each such copy	£10
Fees 7(a), (b) and (c) are payable whether or not the copy is provided as a certified copy	
8. Oaths	
For administering an oath:	
(a) for each deponent to each affidavit;	£11

A3.24 *Appendix III – Fees (Non-Contentious Business)*

[Column 1	Column 2
Number and description of fee	Amount of fee
(b) for marking each exhibit Fees 8(a) and (b) are not payable on an application for a grant which is a personal application	£2
9. Determination of costs For determining costs	The same fees as are payable under the Civil Proceedings Fees Order 2008 for determining costs (see Fee 5 (Determining costs in the Senior and County Court) in Schedule 1)
10. Settling documents For perusing and settling citations, advertisements, oaths, affidavits or other documents, for each document settled	£12

SCHEDULE 2

ORDERS REVOKED

A3.25

Title	S.I. number
Non-Contentious Probate Fees Order 2004	S.I. 2004/3120
Non-Contentious Probate Fees (Indian Ocean Tsunami) Order 2005	S.I. 2005/266
Non-Contentious Probate Fees (London Terrorist Bombings) Order 2005	S.I. 2005/3359
Non-Contentious Probate Fees (Amendment) Order 2007	S.I. 2007/2174
Non-Contentious Probate Fees (Amendment) Order 2008	S.I. 2008/2854
Non-Contentious Probate Fees (Amendment) Order 2009	S.I. 2009/1497
Non-Contentious Probate Fees (Amendment) Order 2011	S.I. 2011/588
Non-Contentious Probate Fees (Amendment) Order 2013	S.I. 2013/1408
Non-Contentious Probate Fees (Amendment) Order 2014	S.I. 2014/876

Appendix IV

RATES OF INHERITANCE TAX AND CAPITAL TRANSFER TAX

A4.10 For deaths on or after 15 March 1988.

Effective dates	Taxable threshold	Rate of tax	Legislation
15/3/88–5/4/89	£110,000	40%	FA 1988, s 136
6/4/89–5/4/90	£118,000	40%	SI 1989/468
6/4/90–5/4/91	£128,000	40%	SI 1990/680
6/4/91–9/3/92	£140,000	40%	SI 1991/735
10/3/95–5/4/95	£150,000	40%	FA [No2] 1992, s 72
6/4/95–5/4/96	£154,000	40%	SI1994/3011
6/4/96–5/4/97	£200,000	40%	FA 1996, s 183
6/4/97–5/4/98	£215,000	40%	FA 1997, s 93
6/4/98–5/4/99	£223,000	40%	SI 1998/756
6/4/99–5/4/00	£231,000	40%	SI 1999/596
6/4/00–5/4/01	£234,000	40%	SI 2000/967
6/4/01–5/4/02	£242,000	40%	SI 2001/639
6/4/02–5/4/03	£250,000	40%	FA 2002, s 118
6/4/03–5/4/04	£255,000	40%	SI 2003/841
6/4/04–5/4/05	£263,000	40%	SI 2004/771
6/4/05–5/4/06	£275,000	40%	FA 2005, s 98
6/4/06–5/4/07	£285,000	40%	FA 2005, s 98
6/4/07–5/4/08	£300,000	40%	FA 2005, s 98
6/4/08–5/4/09	£312,000	40%	FA 2006, s 155
6/4/09–5/4/21	£325,000	40%	FA (No2) 2015, s 10 negated the indexation provisions for a further 3 years up to 5 April 2021. FA 2014, Sch 25 negated the indexation provisions for a further 3 years up to 5 April 2018.

A4.10 *Appendix IV – Rates of Inheritance Tax and Capital Transfer Tax*

Effective dates	Taxable threshold	Rate of tax	Legislation
			FA 2006, s 155, subject to the potential application of IHTA 1984, s 8. FA 2010, s 8 extended the use of the threshold of £325,000 until 5 April 2015 by negating the indexation provisions until that date. FA 2012, s 208 revised the content of s 8(1) of the IHTA 1984 by substituting 'consumer prices index for the month of September in any year' for 'retail prices index for the month of September in any year' with effect from 6 April 2015. Section 8(2) IHTA 1984 was amended to 'consumer prices index' instead of 'retail prices index'. Section 8(3) of the IHTA 1984 was amended to read 'consumer prices index' and means the all items consumer prices index published by the Statistics Board.

Appendix VI

FORMS

Contents

    Part I – Forms for use in Non-contentious Probate Matters

Affidavits / witness statement

Appearance

Appointment

Caveat

Citations

Consents

County court form

Disclaimer

Inventory and account

Motion

Nomination

Notices

Oaths

Order

Powers of Attorney

Pre-lodgement enquiry

Renunciations

Standing search

Subpoenas

Summonses

Warning

Appendix VI – Forms

Part II – Forms for use in Probate Claims

Acknowledgments of service

Administrator's account

Affidavits and witness statements

Claim form

Guarantee

Notices

Orders

Statements of case

I. Indorsements of interest and brief details of claim

II. Particulars of claim

III. Defences

IV. Replies and defences to counterclaims

Subpoena

* denotes a form included in this Supplement.

No	Description	Para
Part I – Forms for use in Non-contentious Probate Matters		
1	General heading of affidavit (and other forms)	A6.01
2	General heading of witness statement	A6.02
3	Affidavit of execution of a will or codicil	A6.03
3A	Will signed in attestation clause or testimonium clause	A6.04
3B	Execution by acknowledgment of signature	A6.05
3C	Imperfect signature, or will signed by mark, or in foreign characters: knowledge of contents	A6.06
3D	Will signed by another person by direction of testator	A6.07
3E	Signature of testator appears below those of the witnesses	A6.08
4	Affidavit in support of due execution (evidence of execution not available)	A6.09
5	Affidavit of handwriting	A6.10
6	Affidavit of plight and condition and finding	A6.11
7	Affidavit of search for will	A6.12
8	Affidavit as to alterations in a will (deponent an attesting witness)	A6.13
9	Affidavit verifying alterations in a will (deposed to by the writer of it)	A6.14
10	Affidavit as to foreign law	A6.15
11	Affidavit of facts: Wills Act 1963	A6.16
12	Affidavit verifying the translation of a will	A6.17

Contents

No	Description	Para
13	Affidavit as to military service	A6.18
14	Affidavit of identity of executor	A6.19
15	Affidavit as to alias (will)	A6.20
16	Affidavit as to alias (administration)	A6.21
17	Affidavit to lead order for grant under s 116 of the Senior Courts Act 1981	A6.22
18	Affidavit to lead district judge's or registrar's order appointing persons to obtain administration for the use and benefit of a minor	A6.23
19	Affidavit to lead district judge's or registrar's order for appointment of a person for the purpose of renouncing on behalf of a minor	A6.24
20	Affidavit as to the insertion of advertisements for kin	A6.25
21	Affidavit as to the insertion of advertisements for the recovery of a lost will	A6.26
22	Affidavit of medical officer in proof of lack of capacity	A6.27
23	Affidavit to lead amendment of grant	A6.28
24	Affidavit to lead amendment to 'save and except settled land'	A6.29
25	Affidavit to lead order for notation of domicile (estate in Scotland)	A6.30
26	Affidavit to lead order for notation of domicile (estate in Northern Ireland)	A6.31
27	Affidavit to lead citation to accept or refuse probate (NCPR SI 1987/2024 r 47(1))	A6.32
28	Affidavit to lead citation to accept or refuse administration (NCPR SI 1987/2024 r 47(1))	A6.33
29	Affidavit of creditor to lead citation (no known kin) (NCPR SI 1987/2024 r 47(1))	A6.34
30	Affidavit to lead citation against executor to whom power is reserved to accept or refuse double probate (NCPR SI 1987/2024 r 47(2))	A6.35
31	Affidavit to lead citation requiring an intermeddling executor to take probate (NCPR SI 1987/2024 r 47(3))	A6.36
32	Affidavit to lead citation to propound a will (NCPR SI 1987/2024 r 48)	A6.37
33	Affidavit of party cited – accepting grant	A6.38
34	Affidavit to lead summons to exhibit an inventory and account	A6.39
35	Affidavit to lead subpoena to bring in testamentary document (NCPR SI 1987/2024 r 50(2))	A6.40
36	Affidavit to lead revocation of grant by consent	A6.41
37	Affidavit of service of citation	A6.42
38	Affidavit of service of warning (NCPR SI 1987/2024 rr 44, 67)	A6.43
39*	Non-Contentious Probate Rules 1987 Form 5: Appearance to warning or citation NCPR SI 1987/2024 rr 44(10), 46(6)	A6.44
40	Appointment of nominee of a county council to take grant	A6.45
41*	Non-contentious Probate Rules 1987 Form 4: Caveat... NCPR SI 1987/2024 r 44(2)	A6.46
42	Citation to accept or refuse probate (NCPR SI 1987/2024 r 47(1))	A6.47

Appendix VI – Forms

No	Description	Para
43*	Citation to accept or refuse administration (NCPR SI 1987/2024 r 47(1))	A6.48
44*	Citation by creditor against kin (if any) to accept or refuse administration (NCPR SI 1987/2024 r 47(1))	A6.49
45*	Citation by creditor against a minor to accept or refuse administration (NCPR SI 1987/2024 r 47(1); RSC Order 80, r 16(2))	A6.50
46*	Citation, by executor of executor, against executor to whom power was reserved, to accept or refuse probate (NCPR SI 1987/2024 r 47(2))	A6.51
47*	Citation to take probate against an executor who has intermeddled (NCPR SI 1987/2024 r 47(3))	A6.52
48*	Citation to propound paper writing (NCPR SI 1987/2024 r 48)	A6.53
49	Abstract of citation for advertisement	A6.54
50	Consent to proof of will	A6.55
51	Consent by assignee to grant to other assignees	A6.56
52	Consent to trust corporation applying	A6.57
52A*	Disclaimer on intestacy	A6.57A
52B*	Disclaimer of interest under a will	A6.57B
53	Notice to Leeds District Probate Registry to produce documents	A6.58
54	Inventory and account	A6.59
55	Notice of motion (RSC Order 8, r 3)	A6.60
56	Nomination of a second administrator; minority interest (NCPR SI 1987/2024 r 32(3))	A6.61
57	Nomination of a second administrator; lack of mental capacity within the meaning of the Mental Capacity Act 2005 and minority or life interest (NCPR SI 1987/2024 r 35(3))	A6.62
58	Form 7: A6.12 Notice of Election to Redeem Life Interest Rule 56	A6.63
59	Notice of application for probate to executor to whom power is to be reserved	A6.64
60	Oath for probate (general form)	A6.65
61	Oath for probate to a trust corporation	A6.66
62	Oath for probate to the Public Trustee	A6.67
63	Oath for probate where partners in a firm (probate practitioners) appointed as executors by reference to them being such partners	A6.68
64	Oath for probate where partners in a successor firm (probate practitioners) appointed as executors	A6.69
65	Oath for probate where partners in a firm (probate practitioners) appointed as executors and firm has converted to limited liability partnership (llp) or other incorporated practice	A6.70
66	Oath for probate where directors/members of an incorporated practice/limited liability partnership appointed as executors by reference to them being such directors/members	A6.71
67	Oath of executor, former probate having been revoked	A6.72
68	Oath after judgment pronouncing for a will as contained in a draft	A6.73

Contents

No	Description	Para
69	Oath on proving a lost will as contained in a copy or draft etc	A6.74
70	Oath for double probate, where not more than four executors were appointed	A6.75
71	Oath for double probate, where more than four executors were appointed	A6.76
72	Oath for probate 'save and except'	A6.77
73	Oath for probate caeterorum	A6.78
74	Oath for cessate probate to a substituted executor	A6.79
75	Oath for cessate probate, the executor having attained his majority	A6.80
76	Oath for cessate probate to executor where attorney has proved	A6.81
77	Oath of special executors for letters of administration limited to settled land after probate 'save and except', or letters of administration (with will) 'save and except'	A6.82
78	Oath for administration limited to settled land to the trustees where deceased died intestate	A6.83
79	Oath for administration limited to settled land to trustees (no former grant) where deceased left a will	A6.84
80	Oath for letters of administration limited to settled land to personal representatives of the settlor as special executors (after grant 'save and except')	A6.85
81	Oath for probate save and except settled land (after grant limited to settled land)	A6.86
82	Oath for administration (with will) (will admissible only as to part of estate)	A6.87
83	Oath for administration to husband or widow or civil partner* – net estate not exceeding £250,000 (where deceased left issue surviving) or £450,000 (where deceased left no issue or other kin entitled) for death on or after 1 February 2009	A6.88
84	Oath for administrators where net value of the estate exceeds £250,000 for death on or after 1 February 2009 and there are issue (husband or widow applying with next person entitled under NCPR SI 1987/2024 r 22)	A6.89
85	Oath for administrators – net estate exceeding £250,000 for death on or after 1 February 2009: widow (or husband) and minor child survive: application by spouse and nominated co-administrator	A6.90
86	Oath for administrators – net estate exceeding £250,000 for death on or after 1 February 2009: civil partner and minor child survive: application by civil partner who has parental responsibility for minor and nominated co-administrator	A6.91
87	Oath for administrator – spouse or civil partner applies alone on assignment by children (net estate exceeding £250,000 for death on or after 1 February 2009)	A6.92
88	Oath for administrator (husband's, or widow's, or civil partner's representative applies, whole estate having passed to surviving spouse or civil partner)	A6.93
89	Oath for administrator where net estate exceeds in value £250,000 for death on or after 1 February 2009 – issue apply on renunciation of surviving spouse [surviving civil partner]	A6.94

Appendix VI – Forms

No	Description	Para
90	Oath for administrator where the net estate is under £250,000 for death on or after 1 February 2009 – son or daughter applies on renunciation of surviving spouse [or surviving civil partner]	A6.95
91	Oath for administration to child, or other issue having a beneficial interest – spouse [or civil partner] survived but has since died	A6.96
92	Oath for administration to child, or other issue having a beneficial interest – spouse [civil partner] survived but has since died without acquiring a beneficial interest	A6.97
93	Oath for administration to child (on assignment by surviving spouse [civil partner])	A6.98
94	Oath for administration to child or other issue having a beneficial interest – no surviving spouse [civil partner]	A6.99
95	Oath for administration to issue having a beneficial interest – no surviving spouse [civil partner] and forfeiture rule precludes a child from acquiring a benefit in the estate (death on or after 1 February 2012)	A6.100
96	Oath for administration to a person entitled, jointly with attorney of person equally entitled	A6.101
97	Oath for administration to child or children the only issue, save and except others alienated by adoption order made during the lifetime of intestate	A6.102
98*	Oath for administration to person entitled, issue being alienated by adoption order made during the lifetime of intestate	A6.103
99	Oath for administration to adopted child	A6.104
100	Oath for administration to adopter or adopters	A6.105
101	Oath for administrator: deceased a divorced man or woman	A6.106
102	Oath for administrator: deceased's civil partnership dissolved	A6.107
103	Oath for administrator (father or mother takes)	A6.108
104	Oath for administration to personal representative of father or mother	A6.109
105	Oath for administration to brother and sister of the whole blood	A6.110
106	Oath for administration to nephew or niece of the whole blood	A6.111
107	Oath for administration to brother or sister of the half blood	A6.112
108	Oath for administration to nephew or niece of the half blood	A6.113
109	Oath for administration to grandparent	A6.114
110	Oath for administration to uncle or aunt	A6.115
111	Oath for administration to cousin german	A6.116
112	Oath for administration to a trust corporation	A6.117
113	Oath for administration to a creditor (on the renunciation of the persons entitled)	A6.118
114	Oath for administration to assignee of persons entitled on intestacy (NCPR SI 1987/2024 r 24)	A6.119
115	Oath for administration upon disclaimer of person entitled on intestacy to a beneficial interest in the residuary estate death on or after 1 February 2012	A6.120
116	Oath for administration to attorneys of intestate's husband or widow or civil partner	A6.121

Contents

No	Description	Para
117	Oath for administration to attorney of intestate's father or mother	A6.122
118	Oath for administration to attorneys of intestate's child – another child being a minor	A6.123
119	Oath for administration (leave having been given to swear to the death)	A6.124
120	Oath for administrator (grantee having become mentally incapable) or (grantee subsequently lacks capacity within the meaning of the Mental Capacity Act 2005 to manage his affairs)	A6.125
121	Oath for administrator (a former grant having been revoked)	A6.126
122	Oath for administration to mother of minor and nominated co-administrator	A6.127
123	Oath for administration to mother of minor and nominated co-administrator (beneficial interest saved by virtue of s 47, Administration of Estates Act as amended by the Estate of Deceased Persons (Forfeiture Rule and Law of Succession) Act 2011) (death on or after 1 February 2012)	A6.128
124	Oath for administration to father of minor and nominated co-administrator	A6.129
125	Oath for administration to step-parent of minor and nominated co-administrator	A6.130
126	Oath for administration to guardian of minor and nominated co-administrator	A6.131
127	Oath for administration to special guardians of minor	A6.132
128	Oath for persons who have acquired parental responsibility for minors following the making of a residence order	A6.133
129	Oath for persons appointed to obtain administration for the use of minors	A6.134
130	Oath for administration to adopters of minor (adopted subsequent to death of parent on or after 1 October 2014)	A6.135
131*	Oath for administration to guardians of a minor as personal representatives of the person entitled	A6.136
132	Oath for person appointed by the Court of Protection for use of a person who lacks capacity to manage his affairs within the meaning of the Mental Capacity Act 2005	A6.137
133	Oath for administrator by attorney acting under a registered enduring power of attorney / registered lasting power of attorney	A6.138
134	Oath for administrators appointed by district judge or registrar for the use of a person who lacks capacity	A6.139
135	Oath for administrator pending determination of a probate claim	A6.140
136	Oath for administrator, after citation to accept or refuse a grant	A6.141
137	Oath for administrator, after citation to propound will (NCPR SI 1987/2024 r 48)	A6.142
138	Oath for administrator (commorientes) to representative of person deemed to have survived	A6.143
139	Oath for administration (with will) (commorientes)	A6.144
140	Oath for cessate administration to person entitled on attaining his majority	A6.145

Appendix VI – Forms

No	Description	Para
141	Oath for cessate administration, the attorney administrator having died	A6.146
142	Oath for cessate administration, following a grant limited to a claim	A6.147
143	Oath for administration limited to prosecuting or defending a claim	A6.148
144	Oath for administration ad colligenda bona	A6.149
145	Oath for administration under s 116 of the Senior Courts Act 1981	A6.150
146	Oath for administration under s 113 of the Senior Courts Act 1981	A6.151
147	Oath for administration – judicially separated spouse (death on or after 1 August 1970)	A6.152
148	Oath for administration – judicially separated civil partner (death on or after 5 December 2005)	A6.153
149	Oath for administration (will) to residuary legatee and devisee	A6.154
150	Oath for administration (will) to residuary legatee and devisee for life and residuary legatee and devisee substituted	A6.155
151	Oath for administration (will) to residuary legatee and devisee and a specific legatee or devisee, or a creditor	A6.156
152	Oath for administration (will) to representative of residuary legatee and devisee	A6.157
153	Oath for administration (will) to substituted residuary legatees	A6.158
154*	Oath for administration (will) to person entitled to estate not disposed of	A6.159
155*	Oath for administration (will) to person entitled to estate not disposed of following disclaimer (death on or after 1 February 2012)	A6.160
156	Oath for administration (will) to legatee, devisee or creditor	A6.161
157	Oath for administration (will) to legatee in accordance with NCPR SI 1987/2024 r 20(c)(ii); whole, or substantially whole, of known estate disposed of by enumeration	A6.162
158	Oath for administration (will) to the Public Trustee	A6.163
159*	Oath for administration (will) to testator's widow and a person entitled to share in estate (there being no executor or residuary legatee or devisee)	A6.164
160	Oath for administration (will) to a person interested in the event of an accretion (estate below £250,000 (where deceased left issue), or £450,000 (where deceased left no issue)) for death on or after 1 February 2009	A6.165
161	Oath for administration (will) – gift to child or other issue saved by s 33 of the Wills Act 1837	A6.166
162	Oath for administration (will): gift to issue saved by s 33A of the Wills Act 1837 (amended by Estate of Deceased Persons (Forfeiture Rule and Law of Succession Act 2011) upon disclaimer (Death on or after 1 February 2012)	A6.167
163	Oath for administration (will) – gift to child or other issue saved from the effect of the forfeiture rule by s 33A of the Wills Act 1837 (amended by Estate of Deceased Persons (Forfeiture Rule and Law of Succession Act 2011) (Death on or after 1 February 2012)	A6.168

Contents

No	Description	Para
164	Oath for administration (will) to assignee (NCPR SI 1987/2024 r 24)	A6.169
165	Oath for administration (will) to the attorney of an executor	A6.170
166	Oath for administration (will) to nominee of an executor or residuary legatee or devisee (a non-trust corporation)	A6.171
167	Oath for administration (will) to both parents of a minor jointly	A6.172
168	Oath for administration (will) to person authorised by Court of Protection where executor is lacks capacity to manage his affairs	A6.173
169	Oath for administration (will) to attorney acting under a registered enduring power of attorney or registered lasting power of attorney; for the use executor who lacks capacity	A6.174
170	Oath for administration (will) to person entitled to the residuary estate; for the use of executor who lacks capacity within the meaning of the Mental Capacity Act 2005	A6.175
171	Oath for administration (will) under s 116 of the Senior Courts Act 1981	A6.176
172	Oath for administration (will) where deceased died domiciled out of England and Wales; attorney of person entrusted with administration by court of domicile	A6.177
173	Oath for administration (will) where deceased died domiciled out of England and Wales; person beneficially entitled to the estate by the law of the place where the deceased died domiciled	A6.178
174	Oath for administration or administration (with will) where deceased died domiciled out of England and Wales – discretionary order made under NCPR SI 1987/2024 r 30(1)(c)	A6.179
175	Oath for administration (will) to legatee in accordance with NCPR SI 1987/2024 r 30(3)(b); whole or substantially whole estate in England and Wales consists of immoveable property	A6.180
176	Oath – limited administration (with will) – will made under power and not revoked by subsequent marriage (Wills Act 1837, s 18)	A6.181
177	Oath for cessate administration (will) to residuary legatee [or devisee] on his attaining his majority	A6.182
178	Oath for administration de bonis non to intestate's child	A6.183
179	Oath for administration de bonis non to personal representative of spouse [civil partner]	A6.184
180	Oath for administration de bonis non to personal representative of only person entitled	A6.185
181	Oath for administration de bonis non to another person sharing on intestacy	A6.186
182	Oath for administration (will) de bonis non to residuary legatee or devisee	A6.187
183	Oath for administration (will) de bonis non to representative of residuary legatee and devisee	A6.188
184	Oath for administration (will) de bonis non to specific legatee or devisee or creditor	A6.189
185	Oath for administration caeterorum to only person entitled to the estate, after limited administration	A6.190
186	Order for grant after caveat	A6.191
187	Power of attorney to take administration	A6.192

Appendix VI – Forms

No	Description	Para
188	Power of attorney to take administration (will) given by executors	A6.193
189	Power of attorney to take administration (will) given by residuary legatee	A6.194
190	Power of attorney where further grant to attorney in his representative capacity is required	A6.195
190A	Pre-lodgement enquiry	A6.195A
191	Renunciation of probate	A6.196
192	Renunciation of administration	A6.197
193	Renunciation by two members of a partnership	A6.198
194	Renunciation of administration (with will annexed)	A6.199
195	Renunciation and consent to grant to a trust corporation	A6.200
196	Renunciation, by person appointed for the purpose, of minor's right to a grant (NCPR SI 1987/2024 r 34(2))	A6.201
197	Retraction of renunciation	A6.202
198	Retraction of renunciation by (two) members of a partnership	A6.203
199	Form 2: A6.02 Standing Search Rule 43(1)	A6.204
200	Subpoena to bring in a testamentary document	A6.205
201*	Order for examination of person with knowledge of testamentary document	A6.206
202	Summons (general form) (Family Division)	A6.207
203	Summons for discontinuance of caveat after appearance to warning (Family Division)	A6.208
204	Warning to caveat (NCPR SI 1987/2024 r 44(5))	A6.209
Part II – Forms for use in Probate Claims		
CP0	Heading for all claims (hereinafter called 'Heading')	A6.210
CP1	Acknowledgement of service (probate claim) (Form N3)	A6.211
CP2	Administrator's cash account	A6.212
CP3	Administrator's inventory	A6.213
CP4	Witness statement or affidavit about testamentary documents (CPR 57.5)	A6.214
CP4A*	Handing out Testamentary Documents for examination (Form CH27)	A6.214A
CP5	Witness statement or affidavit verifying administrator's account	A6.215
CP6	Claim form (probate claim) (Form N2)	A6.216
CP7	Guarantee for the acts and defaults of an administrator pending determination of probate claim	A6.217
CP8	Notice of proceedings (CPR 19.8A)	A6.218
CP9	Notice which may be given in a defence under CPR 57.7(5)	A6.219
CP10*	Order in probate action involving compromise (Form CH26)	A6.220
CP11	Order appointing administrator pending determination of the claim	A6.221
CP12	Order staying proceedings in 'Tomlin' form	A6.222
CP13	Order for discontinuance of action and grant	A6.223
CP13A*	Revocation/refusal of revocation of grant of probate (Form CH28)	A6.223A

Contents

No	Description	Para
CP13B*	Order pronouncing for some words, against others (Form CH29)	A6.223B
CP14	Executor or residuary legatee propounds will – defendant interested on an intestacy	A6.224
CP15	Residuary legatee propounds will omitting interlineation – defendants interested (1) in the interlineation, and (2) on intestacy	A6.225
CP16	Executor propounds lost will – defendants executors under earlier will	A6.226
CP17	Executors propound will and codicil – defendant a beneficiary under an alleged second codicil	A6.227
CP18	Executor or residuary legatee under an earlier will claims revocation – defendant the executor under a later will	A6.228
CP19	Party entitled on an intestacy claims revocation – defendants executors and beneficiaries under a will	A6.229
CP20	Executor or residuary legatee propounds will and claims revocation of grant of administration – defendant the party who has obtained the grant	A6.230
CP21	Residuary legatee propounds privileged will – defendants entitled on an intestacy	A6.231
CP22	Interest action	A6.232
CP23	Executor propounds will	A6.233
CP24	Executor propounds a lost will	A6.234
CP25	Executrix propounds will destroyed by deceased whilst incapable	A6.235
CP26	Executor propounds will of person domiciled abroad	A6.236
CP27	Executor propounds will under Wills Act 1963 (death on or after 1 January 1964)	A6.237
CP28	Claimant (entitled on an intestacy) claims revocation of probate, and grant of administration	A6.238
CP29	Claimant (executor) claims revocation of probate and grant of probate of earlier will	A6.239
CP30	Executor propounds will which has been revoked, and codicil reviving the same (or as re-executed)	A6.240
CP31	Interest action	A6.241
CP32	Plea – will not duly executed	A6.242
CP33	Plea – testator not of sound mind, memory and understanding	A6.243
CP34	Plea – undue influence	A6.244
CP35	Plea – fraud	A6.245
CP36	Plea – want of knowledge and approval	A6.246
CP37	Plea – pretended will	A6.247
CP38	Plea – testator not of age	A6.248
CP39	Plea – testator prevented by force and threats from making a fresh will	A6.249
CP40	Defendant pleads that will propounded by claimant was revoked by destruction	A6.250
CP41	Defendant pleads against will propounded by claimant and claims probate of earlier will	A6.251
CP42	Defendant pleads against will propounded by claimant and claims an intestacy	A6.252

No	Description	Para
CP43	Claimant propounds will under Wills Act 1963: defendant pleads that it was not duly executed	A6.253
CP44	Claimant propounds privileged will	A6.254
CP45	Defendant sets up further testamentary document in addition to those propounded by claimant	A6.255
CP46	Interest action	A6.256
CP47	Defendant having pleaded against will and claimed an intestacy – claimant sets up earlier will in the alternative	A6.257
CP48	Defendant having propounded earlier will, claimant pleads that it was revoked by a later will which was in turn revoked by last will	A6.258
CP49	Claimants propound will – defendants propound later will revoking it– claimants reply that later will was executed while deceased was not of sound mind; alternatively that it was in its turn revoked	A6.259
CP50	Claimant propounds will – defendants claim intestacy: claimant in reply claims in the alternative probate of earlier will destroyed by testator (dependent relative revocation)	A6.260
CP51	Witness summons (Form N20) to bring in a testamentary document in a probate action	A6.261

PART I – FORMS FOR USE IN NON-CONTENTIOUS PROBATE MATTERS

Appearance

A6.44

39. Non-Contentious Probate Rules 1987
Form 5: Appearance to warning or citation
NCPR SI 1987/2024 rr 44(10), 46(6)

In the High Court of Justice

Family Division

The Principal [or. . . . . District Probate] Registry

  Caveat No. . . . . . dated the. . . . . . day of. . . . . 20. . . . . .

   [Citation dated the day of. . . . . 20. . . . . . .]

Full name and address of deceased:. . . . .

Full name and address of person warning [or citor]:

[Here set out the interest of the person warning, or citor, as shown in warning or citation.]

Full name and address of caveator [or person cited].

[Here set out the interest of the caveator or person cited, stating the date of the will [if any] under which such interest arises.]

Enter an appearance for the above-named caveator [*or* person cited] in this matter.

Dated the. . . . . . day of. . . . . 20. . . . . . .

[Signed]

whose address for service is:

Solicitor (*or* 'In person').

Caveat

A6.46

41. Non-contentious Probate Rules 1987
Form 4: Caveat...
NCPR SI 1987/2024 r 44(2)

In the High Court of Justice

Family Division

The Principal [*or*. . . . . District Probate] Registry.

Let no grant be sealed in the estate of [*full name and address*] deceased, who died on the. . . . . . day of. . . . . 20. . . . . . without notice to [*name of party by whom or on whose behalf the caveat is entered*].

Dated this. . . . . . day of. . . . . 20. . . . . . .

[Signed] [to be signed by the caveator's probate practitioner or by the caveator if acting in person]

whose address for service is:. . . . .

Probate Practitioner for the. . . . . [*If the caveator is acting in person, substitute 'In person'.*]

Citations

A6.48

43. Citation to accept or refuse administration (NCPR SI 1987/2024 r 47(1))

(*Heading as in Form 1:* **A6.01**)

Elizabeth the Second etc (*as in Form 42:* **A6.47**).

To E B of. . . . .

Take notice that C B and D B have stated in a joint affidavit, sworn the. . . . . . day of. . . . . 20. . . . . . that A B of. . . . . died on the. . . . . . day of. . . . . 20. . . . . . domiciled in England and Wales intestate, leaving you E B his lawful widow and one of the persons entitled to share in his estate and C B and D B his lawful* [*or* natural*] sons and two of the persons entitled to share in the estate of the deceased:

Now this is to command you E B that within eight days after service of this citation on you, inclusive of the day of such service, you do cause an appearance to be entered in the Principal Registry of the Family Division of the High Court of Justice at First Avenue House, 42–49 High Holborn, London WC1V 6NP [*or* in the . . . . District Probate Registry at. . . . .] and accept or refuse letters of administration of all the estate which by law devolves to and vests in the personal representative of the deceased, or show cause why they should not be granted to C B and D B. And take further notice that, in default of your so appearing and accepting and extracting the letters of administration, our court will proceed to grant letters of administration of the estate to C B and D B, your absence notwithstanding.

Dated at. . . . . this. . . . . . day of. . . . . 20. . . . . . .

Extracted by. . . . .

of. . . . . *(Signed)*

Solicitor.   District Judge/Registrar.

[*If the deceased died on or after 4 April 1988 the word 'lawful' or 'natural' can be omitted.]

[Note.–
This form may be adapted for use in cases where specific persons are cited by a creditor.]
(Form of affidavit to lead citation, *Form 28:* **A6.33**.)

A6.49

**44. Citation by creditor against kin (if any) to accept or refuse administration
(NCPR SI 1987/2024 r 47(1))**

(*Heading as in Form 1:* A6.01)

Elizabeth the Second etc *(as in Form 42)*: A6.47

To the kin (if any) who are entitled to share and all other persons having or claiming any interest in the estate of A B deceased.

Take notice that C D has stated in an affidavit sworn the. . . . . . day of . . . . 20. . . . . . that AB of. . . . . died on the. . . . . . day of. . . . . 20. . . . . . domiciled in England and Wales intestate, a widower/surviving civil partner without known issue or parent, brother or sister of the whole or half blood or their issue, grandparent, uncle or aunt of the whole or half blood or their issue, or any other person entitled in priority to share in his estate by virtue of any enactment, and that C D is a creditor of the deceased:

Now this is to command you that within one month after service by publication of this citation on you, inclusive of the day of such service, you do cause an appearance to be entered in the Principal Registry of the Family Division of the High Court of Justice at First Avenue House, 42–49 High Holborn, London WC1V 6NP [*or in the*. . . . . District Probate Registry at. . . . .] and accept or refuse letters of administration of all the estate which by law devolves to and vests in the personal representative of the deceased, or show cause why letters of administration of his estate should not be granted to C D. And take further notice that, in default of your so appearing and accepting and extracting letters of administration as aforesaid, our court will proceed to grant letters of administration of the estate of the deceased to C D, your absence notwithstanding.

Dated at. . . . . this. . . . . . day of. . . . . . . 20. . . . . . .

Extracted by. . . . .

of. . . . . *(Signed)*

Solicitor.   District Judge/Registrar.

[Note.–

If the applicant is the nominee of a county council, he should be so described, and the sealed or certified appointment lodged (see *Form 40*: **A6.45**).]

(Form of affidavit to lead citation, *Form 29*: **A6.34**.)

A6.50

**45. Citation by creditor against a minor to accept or refuse administration
(NCPR SI 1987/2024 r 47(1); RSC Order 80, r 16(2))**

(*Heading as in Form 1:* A6.01)

A6.50 *Appendix VI – Forms*

Elizabeth the Second etc (*as in Form 42:* **A6.47**):

To G H of. . . . .

Take notice that E F has stated in an affidavit sworn the. . . . . . day of . . . . 20. . . . . . that A B of. . . . . died on the. . . . . . day of. . . . . 20. . . . . . domiciled in England and Wales intestate, a bachelor without issue or parent or any other person entitled in priority to share in his estate by virtue of any enactment, leaving you G H, his lawful* brother of the whole blood and the only person entitled to his estate, that E F is a creditor of the deceased, that you G H are a minor, and that C D is your lawful father [*or* your guardian or the person with whom you reside *or* under whose care you are [*as the case may be*]]:

Now this is to command you G H that within eight days after service of this citation on you, inclusive of the day of such service, you do cause an appearance to be entered in the Principal Registry of the Family Division of the High Court of Justice at First Avenue House, 42–49 High Holborn, London WC1V 6NP [*or* in the . . . . District Probate Registry at. . . . .] and accept or refuse letters of administration of all the estate which by law devolves to and vests in the personal representative of the deceased, or show cause why they should not be granted to E F and another. And take further notice that, in default of your so appearing and accepting and extracting the letters of administration, our said court will proceed to grant letters of administration of the estate to E F and another, your absence notwithstanding.

Dated at. . . . . this. . . . . . day of. . . . . 20. . . . . . .

Extracted by. . . . .

of. . . . . (Signed)

Solicitor.   District Judge/Registrar.

[*If the deceased died on or after 4 April 1988 the relationship, except in the case of a spouse, need not be lawful and, with that exception, the word 'lawful' may be omitted.]

A6.51

46. Citation, by executor of executor, against executor to whom power was reserved, to accept or refuse probate
(NCPR SI 1987/2024 r 47(2))

(*Heading as in Form 1:* **A6.01**)

Elizabeth the Second etc (*as in Form 42:* **A6.47**):

To E F of. . . . .

Take notice that G H has stated in an affidavit sworn the. . . . . . day of . . . . 20. . . . . . that probate of the will of A B of. . . . . deceased, was on the. . . . . . day of. . . . . granted by our High Court of Justice at the Principal Registry of the Family Division [*or* at the. . . . . District Probate Registry] to C D one of the executors named therein, power being reserved of making a like grant to you E F the other executor named therein, that C D died on the. . . . . . day of. . . . . . . leaving part of the estate of the deceased unadministered and that on the. . . . . . day of . . . . 20. . . . . . probate of the will of C D deceased, was granted by this court at the registry [*or* at the. . . . . District Probate Registry] to G H the sole executor thereof:

Now this is to command you E F that within eight days after service of this citation on you, inclusive of the day of such service, you do cause an appearance to be entered in the Principal Registry of the Family Division of this court at First Avenue House, 42–49 High Holborn, London WC1V 6NP [*or* in the. . . . . District Probate Registry at. . . . .] and accept or refuse probate of the will of A B deceased. And take further notice that, in default of your so appearing and accepting and extracting probate of the will, your rights as such executor will wholly cease, and the representation to the estate of A B deceased will devolve as if you had not been appointed executor.

Dated at. . . . . this. . . . . . day of. . . . . 20. . . . . . .

Extracted by. . . . .

of. . . . . *(Signed)*

Solicitor.   District Judge/Registrar.

(Form of affidavit to lead citation, *Form 30*: **A6.35**.)

A6.52

47. Citation to take probate against an executor who has intermeddled (NCPR SI 1987/2024 r 47(3))

(*Heading as in Form 1:* **A6.01**)

Elizabeth the Second etc (*as in Form 42:* **A6.47**):

To E F of. . . . .

Take notice that C D has stated in an affidavit sworn the. . . . . . day of . . . . 20. . . . . . that A B of. . . . . died on the. . . . . . day of. . . . . . . 20. . . . . . domiciled in England and Wales, having made and duly executed his last will and testament bearing date the. . . . . . day of . . . . 20. . . . . . [now remaining in the Principal Registry of the Family Division of the High Court of Justice *or* in the. . . . . District Probate Registry], that you E F are appointed sole executor in that will, that C D is interested in the estate of the deceased under the will and that you E F have intermeddled in the estate of the deceased:

Now this is to command you E F that within eight days after service of this citation on you, inclusive of the day of such service, you do cause an appearance to be entered in the Principal Registry of the Family Division at First Avenue House, 42–49 High Holborn, London WC1V 6NP [*or* in the. . . . . District Probate

A6.52 Appendix VI – Forms

Registry at. . . . .] and show cause why you should not be ordered to take probate of the will.

Dated at. . . . . this. . . . . . day of. . . . . 20. . . . . . .

                                                        Extracted by. . . . .

                                          of. . . . . *(Signed)*

                        Solicitor.   District Judge/Registrar.

(Form of affidavit to lead citation, *Form 31*: **A6.36**.)

A6.53

48. Citation to propound paper writing (NCPR SI 1987/2024 r 48)

(Heading as in Form 48: **A6.53***)*

Elizabeth the Second etc (*as in Form 42:* **A6.47**):

To E F of. . . . .

Take notice that C D has stated in an affidavit sworn the. . . . . . day of . . . . 20. . . . . . that A B of. . . . . died on the. . . . . . day of. . . . . 20. . . . . . domiciled in England and Wales a widower leaving C D, his lawful* [*or* natural*] son and the only person entitled to his estate and that the deceased left a certain paper writing dated the. . . . . . day of. . . . . 20. . . . . . purporting to be a will [now remaining in the Principal Registry of the Family Division or in the. . . . . District Probate Registry] whereby he appointed you E F sole executrix and residuary legatee and devisee:

Now this is to command you E F that within eight days after service of this citation on you, inclusive of the day of such service, you do cause an appearance to be entered in the Principal Registry of the Family Division of the High Court of Justice at First Avenue House, 42–49 High Holborn, London WC1V 6NP [*or* in the . . . . District Probate Registry at. . . . .] and propound the paper writing should you think it for your interest so to do, or show cause why letters of administration of all the estate which by law devolves to and vests in the personal representative of the deceased should not be granted to C D. And take further notice that in default of your so appearing and doing as aforesaid our court will proceed to issue a grant of representation of the said estate as if the purported will were invalid, your absence notwithstanding.

Dated at. . . . . this. . . . . . day of. . . . . 20. . . . . . .

                                                        Extracted by. . . . .

                                          of. . . . . *(Signed)*

                        Solicitor.   District Judge/Registrar.

Forms **A6.57A**

[*If the deceased died on or after 4 April 1988 the word 'lawful' or 'natural' can be omitted.]

(Form of affidavit to lead citation, *Form 32*: **A6.37**.)

Disclaimer

A6.57A

52A. Deed of disclaimer of interest under intestacy

(*Heading as in Form 1:* **A6.01** *optional*)

THIS DEED OF DISCLAIMER is made the. . . . . . day of. . . . . 20 . . . .

BY A B of . . . .

WHEREAS

1. C D ('the Intestate') late of. . . . . died on the. . . . . day of. . . . . . 20. . . . . . .
2. A B is the spouse/civil partner of the Intestate and is the sole beneficiary/one of statutory beneficiaries entitled to the estate of the Intestate under section 46, Administration of Estates Act 1925.
3. A B has not taken or accepted any share in the estate.
4. A B desires and intends to disclaim all that is his/her interest in the estate of the Intestate.

NOW THIS DEED WITNESSES that A B hereby disclaims all that is his/her interest in and right to and title over the property comprised in the estate of the Intestate or any part of it

AND A B hereby acknowledges that on the execution of this disclaimer he/she will be treated for the purpose of section 46A, Administration of Estates Act 1925 as having died immediately before the Intestate.

AS WITNESS of which A B has set his/her hand the day and date first written

(Signed)

In the presence of

[Name and address of witness]

A6.57B Appendix VI – Forms

A6.57B

52B. Deed of disclaimer of interest under a will

(*Heading as in Form 1:* **A6.01** *optional*)

THIS DEED OF DISCLAIMER is made on the. . . . . . day of. . . . . . . 20 . . . .

By A B of . . . .

WHEREAS

1.   C D ('the Testator') late of. . . . . died on the. . . . . . day of . . . . 20. . . . . . having made a will dated the. . . . . . day of . . . . 20. . . . . . (the Will).
2.   A B is the sole beneficiary/one of the beneficiaries named in the Will.
3.   A B has not accepted any share in the estate.
4.   A B desires and intends to disclaim all his/her interest under the Will or otherwise in the estate of the Testator.

NOW THIS DEED WITNESSES that A B hereby disclaims all that may be his/her interest in and right to and title over the property or any part of it given to him/her under the Will

AND A B hereby acknowledges that on the execution of this disclaimer he/she will be treated for the purposes of section 33A, Wills Act 1837 as having died immediately before the testator.

AS WITNESS of which A B has set his/her hand the day and date first written

(Signed)

In the presence of

[Name and address of witness]

Oaths

A6.103

98. Oath for administration to person entitled, issue being alienated by adoption order made during the lifetime of intestate

(*Death on or after 1 January 1950*)

(*Heading as in Form 1:* **A6.01**)

I, E F, of. . . . . make oath and say that:

1.   A B of. . . . . deceased, was born on the. . . . . . day of . . . . 19. . . . . and died on the. . . . . . day

of. . . . . 20. . . . . . aged. . . . . . years, domiciled in England and Wales intestate a widow[er][surviving civil partner*] without issue entitled to her [his] estate or any other person entitled in priority to share in the estate by virtue of any enactment;

2. By virtue of an adoption order made under the authority of the Adoption Act 1958 [or as the case may be] during the lifetime of the deceased, which order is still subsisting, C D, the son [or daughter] and only issue of the deceased was duly adopted and the estate of the deceased devolves in all respects as if C D were the lawful child of the adopter [or adopters] and not the child of the deceased;

3. [Clear off any intervening classes.]

4. No life or minority interest arises under the intestacy.

5. [add statement as to settled land];

6. I am the. . . . . and only person entitled to [or one of the persons entitled to share in] the estate of the deceased;

7. I will:

    (i) collect, get in and administer [etc – complete as in Form 83: **A6.88**].

* Deaths on or after 5 December 2006

[Note.–

The adoption order should not be exhibited to the oath, and the child should be referred to by the name by which he was known prior to the adoption (Registrar's Circular, 2 March 1966).]

A6.136

131. Oath for administration to guardians of a minor as personal representatives of the person entitled

(Heading as in Form 1: **A6.01**)

We, C D of. . . . . and R F of. . . . . make oath and say that:

1. A B of. . . . . deceased, was born on the. . . . . . day of . . . . 19. . . . . . and died on the. . . . . . day of. . . . . 20. . . . . . aged. . . . . . years, domiciled in England and Wales intestate, a widower [or as the case may be], leaving E B, his son and the only person entitled to his estate, who has since died without having taken upon himself letters of administration of the estate of the intestate;

2. No minority or life interest arises under the intestacy;

3. [add statement as to settled land];

4. E B died intestate a bachelor leaving F B his son and only person entitled to his estate;

5. We are the administrators (as guardians and for the use and benefit of F B, who is now a minor) of the estate of E B, letters of administration of his estate having been granted to us at the Principal [or. . . . . District Probate] Registry on the. . . . . . day of. . . . . 20. . . . . . ;

6. We will:

    (i) collect, get in and administer according to law the real and personal estate of the deceased, for the use and benefit of F B until he attains the age of eighteen years and until further representation be granted;

(ii) when required to do so by the Court, exhibit in the Court a full inventory of the estate and render an account thereof to the Court; and

(iii) when required to do so by the High Court, deliver up to that Court the grant of letters of administration;

[etc – as in Form 60: A6.65].

A6.159

154. Oath for administration (will) to person entitled to estate not disposed of

(Heading as in Form 1: A6.01)

I, C D, of. . . . . make oath and say that:

1. I believe the paper writing now produced to and marked by me to contain the true and original last will and testament of A B of. . . . . deceased, who was born on the. . . . . . day of. . . . . 19. . . . . . and who died on the. . . . . . day of . . . . 20. . . . . . aged. . . . . . years, domiciled in England and Wales;

2. No executor or residuary legatee or devisee is named in the will which does not dispose of the whole estate of the deceased;

3. The deceased died a bachelor [spinster] [widower] [widow] without issue or parent or any other person entitled in priority to share in the estate by virtue of any enactment [or as the case may be];

4. I am the brother of the whole blood and only person entitled to [or one of the persons entitled to share in] the estate of the deceased not disposed of by the will;

5. No life or minority interest arises in the estate of the deceased;

6. [add statement as to settled land];

7. I will:

(i) collect, get in and administer [etc – complete as in Form 149: A6.154].

[Note.–

If a residuary gift in a will fails by reason of s 15 of the Wills Act 1837, the following wording, adapted as necessary, should be used: 'The residuary bequest and devise to E F in the will is void by reason that he was an attesting witness to the will [or that at the date of the will he was the lawful husband of G F, an attesting witness to the will].']

A6.160

155. Oath for administration (will) to person entitled to estate not disposed of following disclaimer (death on or after 1 February 2012)

(Heading as in Form 1: A6.01)

I, C D, of. . . . . make oath and say that:

1. I believe the paper writing now produced to and marked by me to contain the true and original last will and testament of A B of. . . . . deceased, who was born on the. . . . . day of. . . . . 19. . . . . . and who died on the. . . . . day of . . . . 20. . . . . . aged. . . . . . years, domiciled in England and Wales;

2. E F the sole executor and residuary legatee or devisee named in the will has renounced probate thereof and administration (with will) of the estate of the deceased; further by a deed dated the . . . . . . day of . . . . 20. . . . . . E F has disclaimed all his right and title to the estate and is treated by virtue of the s 33A of the Wills Act 1837 (amended by the Estate of Deceased Persons (Forfeiture Rule and Law of Succession) Act 2011) as having died immediately before the deceased;

3. The deceased died a bachelor [spinster] [widower] [widow] without issue or parent or any other person entitled in priority to share in the estate by virtue of any enactment [*or as the case may be*];

4. I am the brother of the whole blood and only person now entitled to [*or* one of the persons entitled to share in] the estate of the deceased now not disposed of by the will;

5. No life or minority interest arises in the estate of the deceased;

6. [*add statement as to settled land*];

7. I will:

    (i) collect, get in and administer [etc– *complete as in* Form 149: **A6.154**].

A6.164

159. Oath for administration (will) to testator's widow and a person entitled to share in estate (there being no executor or residuary legatee or devisee)

(Heading as in Form 1: **A6.01**)

We, E B of. . . . . and C B of. . . . . make oath and say that:

1. We believe the paper writing now produced to and marked by us to contain the true and original last will and testament of A B of. . . . . deceased, who was born on the. . . . . day of. . . . . 19. . . . . . and who died on the. . . . . day of . . . . 19. . . . . . /20. . . . . . aged. . . . . years, domiciled in England and Wales;

2. No executor or residuary legatee or devisee is named in the will;

3. No minority but a life interest arises in the estate of the deceased;

4. [*add statement as to any settled land*];

5. We are respectively the lawful widow, and a son and two of the persons entitled to share in the estate of the deceased not disposed of by the will;

6. We will:

    (i) collect, get in and administer [etc – *complete as in Form 149*: **A6.154**].

A6.164 *Appendix VI – Forms*

Subpoenas

A6.206

201. Order for examination of person with knowledge of testamentary document

(Heading as in Form 1: **A6.01**)

Elizabeth the Second, [etc *as in Form 200:* **A6.205**]:

To. . . . . of

We command you to appear before the [Right] Honourable Sir. . . . . Knight, the President [or Judge] of the Family Division of our High Court of Justice at the Royal Courts of Justice, Strand, London WC2 on the . . . . . . day of. . . . . 20. . . . . . at. . . . . . o'clock, to testify the truth according to your knowledge [*or* to answer any question to be put to you], relating to a certain document, being or purporting to be testamentary, namely [*here describe the document, and give its date as accurately as possible*], of which said document there are reasonable grounds for believing that you have knowledge.

Witness the Right Honourable [Lord Chancellor], the. . . . . day of. . . . . 20. . . . . . .

(Signed)

District Judge/Registrar.

[*Name and address of solicitor.*]

[Note.–
To be indorsed prominently on the front of the copy to be served:] You the within-named . . . . are warned that disobedience to this order would be a contempt of court punishable by imprisonment.

PART II – FORMS FOR USE IN PROBATE CLAIMS

Affidavits and witness statements

A6.214A

CP4A. Handing out Testamentary Documents for examination1 (Form CH27)[1]

(Heading: **A6.210**)

UPON the application of the [*party*] by application notice dated [. . . . .]

Forms A6.220

AND UPON HEARING [. . . . .] for the Claimant and [. . . . .] for the Defendant

AND . . . . [*name*], the Solicitors for the [*party*] having undertaken (1) that they will on or before [*date*] or earlier if so directed by this Court return the testamentary documents specified in the attached Schedule to Masters' Appointments, Ground Floor, Rolls Building, Fetter Lane, London EC4A 1NL and (2) that until the specified testamentary documents are returned as stated above they will remain in the possession of [*name*] and [*name*] who are handwriting experts

IT IS ORDERED that

1. the testamentary documents be handed out to [*name*] the Solicitors for the Claimant/Defendant for the purpose of handwriting analysis being examined by microscope and immersion tests
2. an officer of the Chancery Division attend [*name*] at [*address*] and produce to him for the purpose of handwriting analysis the testamentary documents specified in the attached Schedule
3. [*name*] return the specified testamentary documents to Masters' Appointments, Ground Floor, Rolls Building, Fetter Lane, London EC4A 1NL on or before [*date*] or earlier if so directed by the Court
4. the costs of the Application shall be costs in the case
5. this order shall be served by the [*Claimant*] on the [*Defendant*]

Service of the order

The court has provided a sealed copy of this order to the serving party:

ABC Solicitors LLP at [*address*] [*reference*]

SCHEDULE

[*Identify the testamentary documents the subject of the order*]

[1] Note CPR 57.5(5) provides that except with the permission of the court, a party is not allowed to inspect the testamentary documents or written evidence lodged or filed by any other party until he himself has lodged his testamentary document and filed his evidence.

Orders

A6.220

CP10. Order in probate action involving compromise (Form CH26)

(*Heading:* A6.210)

UPON the application of [. . . . .]

by application notice dated [. . . . .]

A6.220 Appendix VI – Forms

AND upon hearing [. . . . .] for the [. . . . .] and for the [. . . . .]

AND upon reading the written evidence filed

AND UPON [probate of the alleged last will and testament of the above named deceased bearing date. . . . . having been granted on. . . . . to. . . . .] [or letters of administration of the estate of the above named deceased having been granted on. . . . . to . . . .]

AND UPON the parties having agreed the terms set out in the attached schedule

And the Court being satisfied

(1) that consents by or on behalf of every relevant beneficiary (as defined by s 49, Administration of Justice Act 1985) have been given to the making of this order hereinafter made and

(2) that the said order is for the benefit of those relevant beneficiaries who are children

The Court pronounces for [against] the force and validity of the last will and testament of the above named deceased a completed copy of which is the script bearing the date [. . . . .] being the exhibit marked [. . . . .] referred to in the [witness statement] [affidavit] of testamentary documents of [. . . . .] dated [. . . . .] and against the force and validity of the last will and testament of the above named deceased a completed copy of which is the script bearing the date [. . . . .] being the exhibit marked [. . . . .] referred to in the [witness statement] [affidavit] of testamentary documents of [. . . . .] dated [. . . . .]

AND it is ordered that

(1) this claim [and counterclaim] be discontinued

(2) the said probate [letters of administration] be revoked

(3) the terms set out in the Schedule be carried into effect

(4) [probate of the will] [and. . . . . codicil] [letters of administration of the estate] of the above named deceased late of [. . . . .] be granted to the claimant/the defendant [. . . . .] the executor named therein [*if entitled thereto – see Note*]

(5) on application for such a grant the caveat numbered [. . . . .] and entered on [. . . . .] do if still subsisting cease to have effect

(6) there be assessed if not agreed

(a) the costs of this claim [and counterclaim] of the claimant/defendant [. . . .] the executor named in the said will

(b) the costs of this claim [and counterclaim] of the claimant/defendant [. . . . .] and [. . . . .]

(7) that the costs specified in (a) and (b) above be paid out of the estate of the said deceased in the due course of administration.

Service of the order

Forms **A6.223A**

The court has provided a sealed copy of this order to the serving party:

ABC Solicitors LLP at [address] [reference]

Schedule

[Set out the agreed terms]

[Note.–
The words 'if entitled thereto' must be included unless it is proved that the named person is solely entitled without the exercise of any discretion under the Non-Contentious Probate Rules or unless all persons to whom a grant could be made are before the Court ([1972] 1 WLR 1217).]

A6.223A

CP13A. Revocation/refusal of revocation of grant of probate (Form CH28)

(Heading: A6.210)

UPON the application of the [party] by application notice dated [date]

UPON THE TRIAL of this Claim and Counterclaim

AND UPON HEARING [names of the advocates and/or those given permission to address the court] for the Claimant / the Defendant

AND UPON READING [Probate of the alleged last Will and Testament of the deceased dated [date] granted on [date] to [name] or Letters of Administration of the estate of the deceased granted on . . . . [date] to . . . . [name]]

THE COURT PRONOUNCES FOR the force and validity of the Last Will and Testament of the deceased dated [date]

AND THE COURT PRONOUNCES AGAINST the force and validity of the alleged Last Will and Testament of the deceased dated [date]

AND IT IS ORDERED that

(1) the Probate / Letters of Administration be [revoked] [handed to the [party] or [his] Solicitors]

(2) this Claim and Counterclaim be dismissed

(3) there be a detailed assessment if not agreed of

(a) the costs of this Claim and Counterclaim of the Claimant / Defendant / Executor named in the Will dated [date]

(b) the costs of this Claim and Counterclaim of the Claimant / Defendant

that the costs specified in (a) and (b) shall above be paid out of the estate of the deceased in the due course of administration

that the Claimant / Defendant do pay to the Claimant / Defendant [his] costs of this Claim and Counterclaim such costs to be subject to detailed assessment if not agreed [delete as required]

A6.223A Appendix VI – Forms

(4) this order shall be served by the Claimant on the Defendant

Service of the order

The court has provided a sealed copy of this order to the serving party:

ABC Solicitors LLP at [address] [reference]

A6.223B

CP13B. Order pronouncing for some words, against others (Form CH29)

(*Heading:* A6.210)

UPON the application of the [*party*] by application notice dated [*date*]

AND UPON HEARING [*names of the advocates and/or those given permission to address the court*] for the Claimant / the Defendant

AND it appearing from a Witness Statement / an Affidavit of the Claimants that the testamentary documents of which they had knowledge and which they produce in this Claim included [three] paper writings now remaining in Court each bearing the date [*date*]

One ("Testamentary document A") beginning with the words " ", another ("Testamentary document B") beginning with the words " " and a third ("Testamentary document C") beginning with the words " " [*amend as appropriate*]

THE COURT PRONOUNCES FOR the force and validity of the last Will and Testament of the deceased late of [*address*] dated [*date*] and of the Codicil of the last Will and Testament being so much of Testamentary document A and Testamentary document B as is mentioned below that is to say the whole of Testamentary document A except the following:

the words beginning with " " down to and including the words " " [*as appropriate*]

AND THE COURT PRONOUNCES AGAINST the force and validity of [*as appropriate*]

(1)　the words beginning with " " down to and including " "

(2)　the whole of Testamentary document B except the words " " and the signature of the deceased and its attestation and

(3)　the whole of Testamentary document C

AND IT IS ORDERED that this order shall be served by the Claimant on the Defendant

Service of the order

The court has provided a sealed copy of this order to the serving party:

ABC Solicitors LLP at [address] [reference]

Index

A

Action, grant limited to an
introduction, 11.376
practice, 11.379
Ad colligenda bona, grant
applications without notice, and, 25.182
Addition of limitation
amendment of grant, and, 16.14
Administration pendente lite
form of order, 11.365
lodgment of papers, 11.367
practice, 11.371
Administration pending determination of probate claim
generally, 2.05
Adoption and Children Act 2002
generally, A1.508–A1.537
Adoptive parents
grants for use of minors, and, 11.161
Affidavits
rules, 22.08
Alternative business structures
executors, as, 4.49
Amendment of grant
addition of limitation, 16.14
errors
deceased, as to, 16.04
grantee, as to, 16.11
errors as to deceased
date of death, 16.04
surname, 16.04
Appearance to caveats
method of entry, 23.60
Applications
inheritance provision orders, and
introduction, 16.50
Applications by summons
caveats, and, 25.221–25.223
practice
form of order, 25.252
hearing times, 25.245
Applications without notice
ad colligenda bona, for grant, 25.182
joinder of co-administrator, and, 7.19
swear to death, for leave to, 25.20–25.20B

Appointee of court, grants to
for use of persons under disability, 11.292
Attorneys, grants to
filing of power, 11.79
form of oath, 11.82
form of power
generally, 11.44

B

Bundles for trial
generally, 37.26
Burden of proof
want of knowledge and approval, and, 34.64

C

Capital transfer tax (CTT)
rates, A4.10
Case management
bundles, 37.26
directions, 37.07–37.09
pre-trial review, 37.21–37.25
reading lists, 37.27–37.28
skeleton arguments, 37.27–37.28
trial timetable, 37.20
Caveats
appearance to
method of entry, 23.60
definition, 23.01
duration
commencement of claim, 23.17
extension, 23.29
generally, 23.15
entry
duration, 23.17
restriction on further, 23.33
extension, 23.29
form
generally, 23.22
precedent, A6.46

191

Index

Caveats – *cont.*
  restriction on further, 23.33
  searches, and
    generally, 23.36
  warning
    generally, 23.39
Cessate grants
  incapable executor, and, 13.96
Children Act 1989
  definitions, A1.451
  general provisions
    care and supervision orders, A1.445
Citations
  accept grant, to
    generally, 24.04–24.19
  forms, A6.48–A6.53
  propound a will, to
    generally, 24.36
  refuse grant, to
    generally, 24.04–24.19
  types
    accept grant, to, 24.04–24.19
    propound a will, to, 24.36
    refuse grant, to, 24.04–24.19
Claim forms
  statements of interest
    form, 29.11
Claimants
  propounding against will
    person opposed to will, 27.10
Colonial grants, resealing of
  change of status, and, 18.37
  class of grantee, 18.51
  copy of will, 18.60
  grant *de bonis non*, and, 13.47
  New Zealand, 18.81–18.84
Common form business
  Rules, 1.49–1.50
Commorientes
  disasters, and, 14.54
Companies
  executors, as
    generally, 4.39
Contentious business
  affidavits, A6.214A
  associated actions
    inheritance provision, 41.41
    introduction, 27.41
    presumption of death, 41.42–41.47
  bundles, 37.26
  case management
    bundles, 37.26
    directions, 37.07–37.09
    pre-trial review, 37.21–37.25
    reading lists, 37.27–37.28
    skeleton arguments, 37.27–37.28

Contentious business – *cont.*
  case management – *cont.*
    trial timetable, 37.20
  categories of claims
    interest actions, 27.22
    revocation of grants, 27.29
  defendants, 28.07
  directions, 37.07–37.09
  disclosure
    DNA testing, 36.27
  DNA testing, 36.27
  estimate of duration, 39.06
  final speeches, 39.15
  forms
    affidavits, A6.214A
    orders, A6.220–A6.223B
    refusal of grant of probate, A6.223A
    revocation of grant of
      probate, A6.223A
    witness statements, A6.214A
  hearings
    estimate of duration, 39.06
    final speeches, 39.15
    opening speeches, 39.09
    time limits, 39.08
    witness statements, 39.10
  inheritance provision
    introduction, 27.41
  interest actions, 27.22
  jurisdiction of court
    High Court, 26.18
  opening speeches, 39.09
  orders, A6.220–A6.223B
  parties
    defendants, 28.07
    introduction, 28.01–28.03
  pre-action steps, 26.31
  pre-trial review, 37.21–37.25
  procedural rules
    pre-action steps, 26.31
  reading lists, 37.27–37.28
  rectification of wills
    introduction, 27.41
  refusal of grant of probate, A6.223A
  removal of personal representative
    introduction, 27.41
  revocation of grants
    administration with will, 27.26
    form, A6.223A
    lodgment of grant, 27.29
    probates, 27.26
  skeleton arguments, 37.27–37.28
  statements of case
    statement of interest, 32.07
  statements of interest
    form, 29.11

Contentious business – *cont.*
  substitution of personal
      representative, 27.41
  testamentary documents
      inspection, 31.15
  trial
    estimate of duration, 39.06
    final speeches, 39.15
    opening speeches, 39.09
    time limits, 39.08
    witness statements, 39.10
  trial timetable, 37.20
  witness statements
    forms, A6.214A
    generally, 39.10
Copies of wills and grants
  generally, 21.17
Corrective accounts
  pre-owned assets, 8.229
Costs management
  family provision claims, and, 41.41
Costs of contentious business
  beneficiary caused litigation, where, 40.30
  opposition to grant (unsuccessful parties)
    beneficiary caused litigation, where, 40.30
    opposing party gives notice to cross-examine, 40.37
Courts and Legal Services Act 1990
  general provisions, A1.469

Defences – *cont.*
  want of knowledge and approval
    burden of proof, 34.64
Defendants
  contentious business, and, 28.07
Directions
  contentious business, and, 37.07–37.09
Disasters, death in
  commorientes, and, 14.54
Disclaimers
  forms
    interest under intestacy, A6.57A
    interest under will, A6.57B
  letters of administration with will annexed, and, 5.99
Disclosure
  DNA testing, 36.27
District probate registrars
  powers, 2.19
District probate registries
  jurisdiction
    administration pending determination of probate claim, 2.16
  location, 2.09
  powers, 2.19
Divorce
  leave to swear to death, and, 25.37
DNA testing
  disclosure, and, 36.27
Domicile
  choice, of, 12.07

D

Date of death
  amendment of grant, and, 16.04
  executor's oath, in
    seamen, of, 4.160
De bonis non, grant
  practice
    form of oath, 13.64
Deceased died domiciled out of England & Wales, grant where
  domicile, and
    choice, of, 12.07
  law of domicile, and
    generally, 12.31
Defences
  incapacity
    nature of the inquiry by court, 34.32
  undue influence
    exclusions, 34.48
  want of due execution
    notice under CPR 57.7(5), 34.13

E

Enduring powers of attorney
  Regulations 2007, A2.145–A2.153
Entry of caveat
  duration, 23.17
  restriction on further, 23.33
Errors in grant, amendment of
  deceased, as to
    date of death, 16.04
    surname, 16.04
  grantee, as to, 16.11
Estimate of duration
  contentious business, and, 39.06
Ex parte applications
  and see under individual headings
  ad colligenda bona, for grant, 25.182
  joinder of co-administrator, and, 7.19
  swear to death, for leave to, 25.20–25.20B
Execution of will (after 1963)
  duty of practitioners to check, 3.95

Index

Execution of will in accord with law of place of execution
formalities, 3.417

Executors
alternative business structures, 4.49
appointees
  alternative business structures, 4.49
  companies, 4.39
companies, 4.39

Executor's oath
date of death
  seamen, of, 4.160
documents to be proved, 4.119

Expedition of issue of grant
generally, 4.90

F

Family and dependants, orders for provision for
costs management, 41.41
introduction, 16.50, 27.41

Family provision claims
costs management, 41.41
introduction, 16.50, 27.41

Fees
grant of probate, for
  introduction, 4.259A
  remission, 4.264A
non-contentious probate, and
  Order, A3.04–A3.10

Final speeches
contentious business, and, 39.15

Forfeiture Act 1982
general provisions, A1.359

Forms
non-contentious probate
  caveat, A6.46
  citations, A6.48–A6.53
  disclaimer, A6.57A–A6.57B
  oaths, A6.103, A6.136, A6.159–A6.160, A6.164
  subpoenas, A6.206
probate claims
  affidavits, A6.214A
  orders, A6.220–A6.223B
  refusal of grant of probate, A6.223A
  revocation of grant of probate, A6.223A
  witness statements, A6.214A

G

Government stock
production of unproved wills, 1.93

Grant ad colligenda bona
applications without notice, and, 25.182

Grant in common form
government stock
  production of unproved wills, 1.93
issue
  settling documents, 2.28
procedure
  personal applications, 2.81
  settling documents, 2.28
settling documents, 2.28
vesting prior to issue, 1.70

Grant limited as to property
part of estate only
  proof of will, 11.315
  trust property, 11.315
trust property only, 11.315

Grant limited to an action
introduction, 11.376
practice, 11.379

H

Hearings
application by summons, and
  times, 25.245–
contentious business, and
  estimate of duration, 39.06
  final speeches, 39.15
  opening speeches, 39.09
  time limits, 39.08
  witness statements, 39.10

HMRC account
assessment
  generally, 8.202–8.203
completion
  exemptions from tax, 8.138
corrective accounts
  pre-owned assets, 8.229
IHT200, 8.03
IHT400
  introduction, 8.03
inheritance tax
  pension death benefits, 8.44
  rates, 8.50
  scope, 8.20

Index

HMRC account – *cont.*
necessity
personal applications, 8.05
PA1, 8.05
payment of tax
generally, 8.205–8.210
personal applications
necessity for account, and, 8.05
pre-owned assets, 8.229

I

IHT200
generally, 8.03
IHT400
introduction, 8.03
Impounding grant
introduction, 17.67
Incapable executor
cessate grants, and, 13.96
Incapable person
impounding grant, and
introduction, 17.67
Incapacity of grantee(s)
defences, and
generally, 34.32
nature of the inquiry by court, 34.32
Inheritance provision
costs management, 41.41
introduction, 16.50, 27.41
Inheritance tax (IHT)
Act of 1984, A1.727
exemptions, 8.138
payment, 8.205–8.210
pension death benefits, 8.44
rates
amounts, A4.10
generally, 8.50
scope, 8.20
Interest actions
generally, 27.22

J

Joinder
minority interests, and, 7.19
Jurisdiction
district probate registries
administration pending determination of probate claim, 2.16
High Court, 26.18

K

Knowledge and approval
defences, and
burden of proof, 34.64

L

Lasting powers of attorney
Regulations 2007, A2.145–A2.153
Law of Property (Amendment) Act 1925
definitions, A1.138
Leave to swear to death, application for
corroboration, and
divorce decree, 25.37
generally, 25.20–25.20B
rescission of order, 25.50
Legal proceedings, grant limited to
introduction, 11.376
practice, 11.379
Letters of administration, grant of
administrator's oath,
description of applicant, 6.391
adopted persons, to,
requirements on obtaining
grant, 6.285–6.286
amendment
addition of limitation, 16.14
application by attorney administrator, 6.16
assignment of life interest, and, 6.27
distribution of estate
failure of statutory trusts, 6.90
parents of illegitimate child, to, 6.75–6.79
statutory trusts for issue, 6.67
general
personal applications, 2.81
vesting prior to issue, 1.70
impounding
introduction, 17.67
legitimated persons, to
marriage, on, 6.199
parents, and
adopted persons, of, 6.310
representative grants, 6.15
retraction
practice, 15.75
same sex couples, 6.31A
Letters of administration (will annexed), grant of
amendment
addition of limitation, 16.14
clearing off
disclaimer, 5.99
disclaimer, 5.99

195

Index

Letters of administration (will annexed), grant of – *cont.*
general
personal applications, 2.81
vesting prior to issue, 1.70
grantees
assignees, 5.253
death by murder or manslaughter, 5.196
estate not wholly disposed of by will, 5.228
persons entitled to share in undisposed-of estate, 5.205–5.224
preference of persons of full age, 5.130
residuary legatee or devisee, 5.111
Rule 20, Class (c), 5.111
Rule 20, Class (f), 5.235
undisposed of estate vested in spouse who has since died, 5.230
impounding
introduction, 17.67
order of priority, 5.05A
persons entitled to share in undisposed-of estate
deceased left surviving spouse, 5.205
disposition of residue not ascertainable, 5.215
generally, 5.205–5.224
no surveying spouse, 5.209
notice to Treasury Solicitor, 5.217
virtual disposition of residue, 5.219–5.224
persons interested in residuary estate
disclaimer, 5.99
gift to charities, 5.86–5.87
retraction
practice, 15.75
Life interests
grants for use of minors, and nomination of co–ordinator, 11.239
joinder of co-administrator, 7.19
one of several children of full age, and, 7.28
Limited grants
action, to an, 11.376
settling oaths, 11.07

M

Manslaughter
letters of administration with will annexed, and, 5.196
Marriage (Same Sex Couples) Act 2013
text, A1.699

Minority interests
grants for use of minors, and nomination of co-ordinator, 11.239
joinder of co-administrator, 7.19
one of several children of full age, and, 7.28
Minors, grants for use of
adoptive parents, to, 11.161
life interests, and
nomination of co-ordinator, 11.239
minority interests, and
nomination of co-ordinator, 11.239
nomination of co-ordinator, and, 11.239
parental responsibility, to person with
generally, 11.161
nomination of co-ordinator, 11.239
parents, to
generally, 11.161
nomination of co-ordinator, 11.239
residence order, to person with
form of oath, 11.171
Murder
administration with will annexed, and, 5.196

N

Names
amendment of grant, and surname, 16.04
New Zealand
resealing colonial grants, and, 18.81–18.84
Nomination of co-ordinator
grants for use of minors, and, 11.239
Non-contentious business
fees
Order, A3.04–A3.10
forms
caveat, A6.46
Non-Contentious Probate Rules 1987
generally, 1.49–1.50
text, A2.44–A2.44A

P

Parental responsibility
grants for use with minor
generally, 11.161
nomination of co-ordinator, 11.239–
Personal applications
generally, 2.81
procedure, 2.90A–2.94

Index

Persons lacking capacity, grants for use of
  appointees of district judge, to, 11.292
  notice to Court of Protection, 11.262
  residuary legatee, to, 11.284

Pre-owned assets
  corrective accounts, and, 8.229

Presumption of death
  applications, 41.42
  effect of declaration, 41.45
  form of declaration, 41.44
  jurisdiction, 41.43
  procedure, 41.46
  register of presumed deaths, 41.47

Pre-trial review
  contentious business, and, 37.21–37.25

Principal Registry
  administration pending determination of probate claim, and, 2.05
  location, 2.01

Probate
  amendment
    addition of limitation, 16.14
  executor's oath
    documents to be proved, 4.119
  expedition, 4.90
  fees
    introduction, 4.259A
    remission, 4.264A
  general
    personal applications, 2.81
    vesting prior to issue, 1.70
  impounding
    introduction, 17.67
  notice to Treasury Solicitor, 4.229
  proof
    fees, 4.259A
  retraction
    practice, 15.75

Probate claims
  affidavits, A6.214A
  associated actions
    inheritance provision, 41.41
    introduction, 27.41
    presumption of death, 41.42–41.47
  bundles, 37.26
  case management
    bundles, 37.26
    directions, 37.07–37.09
    pre-trial review, 37.21–37.25
    reading lists, 37.27–37.28
    skeleton arguments, 37.27–37.28
    trial timetable, 37.20
  categories of claims
    interest actions, 27.22
    revocation of grants, 27.29
  defendants, 28.07

Probate claims – *cont.*
  directions, 37.07–37.09
  estimate of duration, 39.06
  final speeches, 39.15
  forms
    affidavits, A6.214A
    orders, A6.220– A6.223B
    refusal of grant of probate, A6.223A
    revocation of grant of probate, A6.223A
    witness statements, A6.214A
  hearings
    estimate of duration, 39.06
    final speeches, 39.15
    opening speeches, 39.09
    time limits, 39.08
    witness statements, 39.10
  inheritance provision
    introduction, 27.41
  interest actions, 27.22
  jurisdiction of court
    High Court, 26.18
  opening speeches, 39.09
  orders, A6.220– A6.223B
  parties
    defendants, 28.07
  introduction, 28.01–28.03
  pre-action steps, 26.31
  pre-trial review, 37.21–37.25
  procedural rules
    pre-action steps, 26.31
  reading lists, 37.27–37.28
  rectification of wills
    introduction, 27.41
  refusal of grant of probate, A6.223A
  removal of personal representative
    introduction, 27.41
  revocation of grants
    administration with will, 27.26
    form, A6.223A
    lodgment of grant, 27.29
    probates, 27.26
  skeleton arguments, 37.27–37.28
  statements of case
    statement of interest, 32.07
  statements of interest
    form, 29.11
  substitution of personal representative, 27.41
  testamentary documents
    inspection, 31.15
  trial
    estimate of duration, 39.06
    final speeches, 39.15
    opening speeches, 39.09
    time limits, 39.08

Index

Probate claims – *cont.*
  trial – *cont.*
    witness statements, 39.10
    trial timetable, 37.20
  witness statements
    forms, A6.214A
    generally, 39.10
Probate rules
  generally, 1.49–1.50
Proof of grant
  executor's oath
    documents to be proved, 4.119
  fees
    introduction, 4.259A
    remission, 4.264A
Pronouncing against solemn will, claims for
  claimants
    person opposed to will, 27.10
Property, grant limited as to
  part of estate only
    proof of will, 11.315
    trust property, 11.315
  trust property only, 11.315
Propounding a will
  citations, and
    generally, 24.36
Proved wills, copies of
  copies, 21.17
Provision out of estate, orders for
  introduction, 16.50
Public Guardian
  Regulations 2007, A2.145–A2.153
Public Records Act 1958
  general provisions, A1.165–A1.166

R

Reading lists
  contentious business, and, 37.27–37.28
Rectification of wills
  applications for
    introduction, 27.41
Removal of representatives
  applications for
    introduction, 27.41
Renunciation
  citations, and
    generally, 24.11
Rescission of orders
  leave to swear to death, and, 25.50
Resealing
  colonial grants, of
    change of status, and, 18.37
    class of grantee, 18.51

Resealing – *cont.*
  colonial grants, of – *cont.*
    copy of will, 18.60
    New Zealand, 18.81–18.84
Resealing colonial grants
  change of status, and, 18.37
  class of grantee, 18.51
  copy of will, 18.60
  grant *de bonis non*, and, 13.47
  New Zealand, 18.81–18.84
Residence order, grant to person with
  form of oath, 11.171
Residuary legatees
  grants for use of persons under disability, and, 11.284
Retraction
  practice, 15.75
Revocation of grant
  applications for
    administration with will, 27.26
    lodgment of grant, 27.29
    probates, 27.26
  lodgment of grant, 27.29
  new grant, and
    combined application, 17.57
  procedure
    other documents, 17.52
Revocation of wills
  burning, by, 34.87
  cutting, by, 34.87
  destruction, by
    summary of cases, 34.87
  marriage after execution of the will, by
    wills made after 1982, 3.40A
  subsequent marriage, by
    wills made after 1982, 3.40A
  subsequent marriage (wills made after 1982), by
    generally, 3.40–3.43A
  tearing, by, 34.87

S

Searches
  online, 21.09
  proved wills since 1858, of
    copies, 21.17
    public online searches, 21.09
  public online, 21.09
  unproved wills, of
    standing search, 21.14
Senior Courts Act 1981
  general provisions
    jurisdiction, A1.304–A1.305

Index

Settlements with no beneficial interest in possession
inheritance tax, and, 8.172
Settling documents
limited grants, and, 11.07
Principal Registry, in, 2.28
Skeleton arguments
contentious business, and, 37.27–37.28
Standing search
unproved wills, and, 21.14
Statements of claim
statements of interest
form, 29.11
Statements of interest
form, 29.11
Subpoena
non-contentious business, A6.206
Sub-registries
and see **District probate registries**
location, 2.09
Substitution of representatives
applications for
introduction, 27.41
Swear to death, leave to
corroboration, and
divorce decree, 25.37
generally, 25.20–25.20B
rescission of order, 25.50

T

Testamentary documents
loan, 31.12
transmission to relevant office
RCJ, from, 31.15
verification, 31.14
Trial of claim
estimate of duration, 39.06
final speeches, 39.15
opening speeches, 39.09
time limits, 39.08
timetable, 37.20
witness statements, 39.10

Trust property only
grant limited as to property, and, 11.315

U

Undue influence
exclusions, 34.48
Unproved wills, search of
standing search, 21.14

V

Vesting prior to issue
generally, 1.70

W

Want of due execution
defences, and
notice under CPR 57.7(5), 34.13
Want of knowledge and approval
burden of proof, 34.64
Warning to caveat
generally, 23.39
method, 23.42
Wills
execution (after 1963)
duty of practitioners to check, 3.95
execution in accord with law of place of execution
formalities, 3.417
Wills Act 1963, under
formalities, 3.417
Wills Act 1837
definitions, A1.01
Witness statements
contentious business, and, 39.10
forms, A6.214A
limited grants, and, 11.07